Praise for *The Menendez Murders*

"Robert Rand, having covered this case from the beginning, is the only journalist who attended both trials gavel to gavel. He interviewed Lyle and Erik before they were suspects, after they were arrested, and many times since. He earned the trust of the Menendez and Andersen families, and interviewed hundreds of sources connected with the case, including myself. We sat across the courtroom from one another during the first trial and saw all of the evidence firsthand. We are in agreement that the verdict should have been manslaughter, not murder, and that the second trial was a travesty of justice. Robert has spent the time required to understand this complicated case and has presented it in an unbiased, factual, compelling manner. This book tells the whole truth, and nothing but the truth."

—**HAZEL THORNTON**, author of
Hung Jury: The Diary of a Menendez Juror

"What kind of journalist stays on a single story for thirty years? It better be a helluva story—and this is—and then you need a very special, obsessive journalist, still bothered by a case conclusion he's long thought was wrong. Meet Robert Rand, he's excellent company. Even now he's exposed new, hard-fought, deeply concealed pieces that flip the entire story on its head."

—**ARTHUR JAY HARRIS**, author of *Speed Kills*
and *The Unsolved Murder of Adam Walsh*

THE MENENDEZ
MURDERS

UPDATED EDITION

THE MENENDEZ MURDERS

THE SHOCKING UNTOLD STORY OF THE MENENDEZ FAMILY AND THE KILLINGS THAT STUNNED THE NATION

ROBERT RAND

BenBella Books, Inc.
Dallas, TX

The Menendez Murders copyright © 2018 by Robert Rand
First updated edition 2024

BenBella Books, Inc.
8080 N. Central Expressway, Suite 1700 | Dallas, TX 75206
www.benbellabooks.com | Send feedback to feedback@benbellabooks.com
BenBella is a federally registered trademark.

Printed in the United States of America
10 9 8 7 6 5 4 3 2

Library of Congress Control Number 2018025803
ISBN 9781637745977 (trade paper)
ISBN 9781946885272 (electronic)

Editing by Laurel Leigh
Copyediting by Elizabeth Degenhard
Cover design by Bret Kerr and Sarah Avinger
Cover photo courtesy of the Menendez Family
Proofreading by Lisa Story and Cape Cod Compositors, Inc.
Text design and composition by Silver Feather Design
Printed by Lake Book Manufacturing

For my mother, Irene; my father, Robert;
my son, Justin; and my daughter, Rhiannon

CONTENTS

PART FOUR
CALIFORNIA DREAMING

PART FIVE
JERRY AND JUDALON

PART SIX
CLOSING IN

PART TEN
AFTERMATH

PART ONE

MURDER IN BEVERLY HILLS

CHAPTER 1

NIGHTMARE ON ELM DRIVE

I think that possibly if Lyle and I would have been home, . . . if we would've been able to do something about it, maybe . . . uh, maybe my dad would be alive. Uh, maybe I'd be dead. You know, I mean, I don't know. I-I-I wish . . . I definitely would give my life for my dad's.

—ERIK MENENDEZ speaking to author in October 1989,
two months after the death of Jose and Kitty Menendez

ON THE NIGHT OF AUGUST 20, 1989, THE LAST IN THE LIVES OF Jose and Kitty Menendez, their elegant residential street in Beverly Hills was so still you could hear a leaf drop. That in itself was not unusual or suspicious. People pay a steep price to live in such neighborhoods, and they cherish their peace and quiet.

That particular Sunday was a leisurely, relaxed day around the house for the Menendezes, an affluent couple in their mid-forties. Jose, a powerfully built, handsome Cuban emigre who left Havana at age sixteen, was the chief executive of LIVE Entertainment, a leading Hollywood home video distributor. He sat on the board of LIVE's parent company, Carolco Pictures, producer of the *Rambo* and *Terminator* movies. Mary Louise, who'd been called "Kitty" since she was a child, was a stay-at-home mother.

Their two college-age sons, Erik and Lyle, spent the day swimming and playing tennis behind the family's lushly landscaped 9,000-square-foot, eight-bedroom beige Mediterranean-style mansion at 722 North

Elm Drive in a fashionable neighborhood just below Sunset Boulevard. Eight months earlier, the Menendez family had moved to Beverly Hills from Calabasas, a suburb northwest of Los Angeles. Before that, they'd spent a dozen years living in the Princeton, New Jersey, area.

In June 1989, eighteen-year-old Erik graduated from Beverly Hills High School. He was about to enroll at the University of California–Los Angeles and planned to commute to UCLA's nearby Westwood campus. Twenty-one-year-old Lyle was a student at Princeton University. Both young men were highly ranked amateur tennis players with professional aspirations.

When Perry Berman arrived at his West Hollywood apartment just after 1 PM, on August 20, 1989, there was an answering machine message from Lyle Menendez. Berman, a friend and former tennis coach of the brothers, had frequently met them for movies or dinner since moving to California from New Jersey. When Berman returned the call, Jose Menendez told him Erik and Lyle were out shopping at the Beverly Center, a nearby upscale shopping mall. Lyle called Berman back around 5 PM and suggested they get together that evening. Berman was planning to attend the Taste of L.A., a food festival in Santa Monica. He was leaving within the hour and invited Erik and Lyle to join him and a friend, Todd Hall. The brothers were going to the movies, said Lyle, to see *Batman*. He suggested they all meet about 10 PM at the food festival.

After eating dinner at home, the brothers walked out the back gate to Erik's white Ford Escort parked in an alley behind the property and drove to the AMC multiplex at Century City Shopping Center. Around 10 PM, Jose and Kitty were settled in the family room watching a James Bond movie, *The Spy Who Loved Me*, on a big-screen TV. It was the housekeeper's night off, and they were spending a rare evening alone. People close to the family said the couple's marriage appeared to be improving lately. One relative noticed they were holding hands again, something she hadn't seen since their college days.

As he watched the movie, Jose Menendez put his feet up on the coffee table and started to doze off. Kitty was seated next to him. The house was equipped with an alarm system, but Jose rarely turned it on.

His sons were always setting it off by accident. Besides, he felt safe in Beverly Hills.

The French doors behind the couch were closed. Just after 10 PM, a neighbor, Avrille Krom, heard "popping sounds" like Chinese firecrackers quickly going off in a row. Krom noted the time because she was anxiously waiting for her daughter Jennifer to return at 10:30 from a neighbor's house. Her twelve-year-old son, Josh, was watching a TV movie. He wanted to call 911, but his mother didn't think anything of this noise that barely interrupted the crickets' chirping. The idea of gunshots just didn't fit in this neighborhood. But it wasn't firecrackers.

Two people had burst into the Menendez family room through the double doors located off the foyer and begun firing 12-gauge Mossberg shotguns. One of the intruders walked around the back of the couch, put the barrel of the massive gun to the back of Jose's head, and pulled the trigger. Kitty, terror-stricken, turned to find another gun near her mouth. Instinctively, she jumped up and raised a hand to protect herself, but to no avail; a blast catapulted her onto the floor.

What transpired in that once welcoming family room was a brutal slaughter of a ferocity rarely seen outside the fields of war. There was blood spatter covering the couch, on the wall, on the wood window louvers, on the coffee table, and throughout the room. Wielding pump-action shotguns—as opposed to automatic weapons—the killers chose to stand in place and methodically pump shell after shell into the helpless couple.

Five blasts hit Jose. In addition to the point-blank shot to his head, he was struck in the chest, upper arm, and left elbow. A "through and through" wound of his left thigh left a gash three inches around. In the robotized language of his autopsy, the "brain had been predominantly eviscerated" by the "explosive decapitation" of the gaping gunshot wound.

Kitty tried to escape from her attackers but was found lying on her right side, a few feet away from her husband's feet, her face an unrecognizable, gelatinous mass. Every bone in her face was broken. Most of her teeth were shattered. She was ripped apart by nine, possibly ten shots. One almost severed her right thumb. Her left leg, with a large wound at the knee, was broken and bent at a 45-degree angle. Her right leg was stretched out along the bottom shelf of the coffee table. Kitty's sweat-shirt and pants were soaked with blood.

———————

Across town in Santa Monica, Perry Berman and Todd Hall left the Taste of L.A. at 10:20 PM. Erik and Lyle Menendez never arrived. Perry Berman was already in bed when his phone rang fifteen minutes later. Lyle Menendez wanted to know why he hadn't been at the food festival. Perry explained he'd waited until almost 10:30 PM. "What happened to you guys?" he asked. "We got lost," replied Lyle. "We decided to drive downtown because we thought it was on Fourth Street in downtown Los Angeles." After realizing they were in the wrong place, said Lyle, the brothers turned around and drove west on the Santa Monica Free-way, arriving at the festival much later than expected.

"I feel bad we weren't able to get together, but let's go out during the week," said Perry. Lyle sounded apprehensive. He insisted he had to see Berman right away to discuss his tennis game as well as his plan to return to Princeton in September.

"Fine," said Berman reluctantly. "If it's that important to you, I'll meet you in half an hour at the Cheesecake Factory in Beverly Hills." Berman barely had time to get out of bed before Lyle called back. It would be better, he said, to meet at the Menendez mansion. Erik needed to pick up his fake ID so they could all have some beers. "Absolutely not," said Berman. "I'll give you an extra ten minutes to pick up the ID and meet you at the Cheesecake Factory."

When Erik and Lyle pulled up outside their home just after 11:30 PM, the electric gate on the black wrought iron fence surrounding the property was open. The front door was unlocked. The brothers later told police they thought their parents might be out walking the dogs since their two Mercedes—one of them on loan from a local shop while one of the family's cars was being serviced—were in the courtyard next to Lyle's red Alfa Romeo. The lights in the two-story entry foyer were on. The first thing they noticed inside was a gray cloud of smoke hang-ing lazily in the air.

It was a routine Sunday evening for the two operators monitoring 911 calls at Beverly Hills Police Department headquarters. The phones had been silent for over half an hour when BHPD dispatcher Christine Nye answered a call from a distraught young man at 11:47 PM.

> **DISPATCH:** Beverly Hills emergency.
> **CALLER:** Yes, police, uh . . .
> (Scream in background): No!
> **DISPATCH:** What's the problem?
> **CALLER:** (sobbing) Somebody killed my parents!
> **DISPATCH:** Pardon me?
> **CALLER:** Somebody killed my parents!
> **DISPATCH:** What? Who? Are they still there?
> **CALLER:** Yes.
> **DISPATCH:** The people who . . .
> **CALLER:** No . . . No . . . (sobs) . . .
> **DISPATCH:** Were they shot?
> **CALLER:** Erik . . . man . . . stay . . .
> **DISPATCHER:** Were they shot?
> **CALLER:** Yes!
> **DISPATCHER:** They were shot?
> **CALLER:** Yes . . . (sobbing)
> **DISPATCHER:** (dispatching police units)

Two minutes after the 911 call, Beverly Hills patrol officer Mike Butkus and his partner John Czarnocki received an urgent dispatch: "Reported shooting at a residence. Approach with extreme caution. Shooters may still be present!" Turning north off Santa Monica Boulevard onto Elm Drive, they quietly drove past the Menendez mansion. After parking two doors away, they silently watched the house from outside the open front gate.

Suddenly, the patrolmen heard screaming inside. A moment later, two young men came running out the front door, side by side, directly toward the officers. A startled Butkus ordered the pair to "sit down and get on the ground." The men complied immediately. The only illumination came from the old-fashioned streetlamps that look charming but shed little light. Butkus didn't notice any blood on their clothes.

Erik and Lyle Menendez appeared to be distraught. "Oh, my god, I can't believe it! Oh, my god, I can't believe it!" they screamed repeatedly.

At one point, having stood up, the brothers dropped to their hands and knees and began pounding the ground with their fists. For several minutes, Butkus couldn't get a coherent word out of them. Suddenly, they frantically pointed at the house and made an anguished plea: "Just go see. Go in and see!"

———————

Perry Berman was early when he pulled up to the Cheesecake Factory just past 11:30 PM. He sat in his car waiting. A few minutes later, Berman went inside and saw people vacuuming carpets and cleaning tables. He asked if anyone had seen two young men come in, describing them as about twenty years old, dark hair, six feet tall. "No, not at all in the last hour," a hostess told him. When he walked outside, Berman heard the high-pitched shriek of police sirens and decided to drive over to the Menendez mansion. As he turned onto North Elm Drive, Berman was startled to see police cars with flashing lights up and down the street. He became extremely alarmed when he saw officers with drawn guns crouched behind the trees of the Menendezes' neighbors.

Investigators thought there might still be suspects hiding inside the mansion and decided to send a search party through the house. When the search team entered the marble foyer, they observed athletic bags and clothes dropped haphazardly on the floor. To the left of the front door was a small wood-paneled sitting room.

As one officer watched the front door and stairwell, the rest of the group cautiously made a sweep of the formal living room with their flashlights. Sgt. Kirk West approached the family room at the end of the hallway. Some lights were on, and West thought he heard a TV or radio. He made a quick visual check of the bodies. Both had multiple gunshot wounds to the head and chest. West didn't have to touch them. He knew they were dead. The size of the wounds made it obvious that a shotgun had been used in the attack, although there were no expended shells on the gold Oriental rug or polished parquet floor.

Veteran homicide investigators say that the average person who walks into a house and discovers two brutally murdered bodies will run outside immediately and call police from a neighbor's phone. Most people are afraid the killer might still be there. Still, Erik and Lyle's emotional distress appeared to be genuine. Because of their compassion for the agitated brothers, detectives decided to forego routine chemical tests that would have determined if either of the young men had fired a gun that night. Investigators quickly ruled out a murder/suicide by conducting gunshot residue tests on Jose and Kitty.

Maurice Angel was on patrol with his partner Mike Dillard when a radio call was broadcast shortly before midnight reporting a shooting at 722 North Elm Drive. By the time "Mo" Angel arrived, there were already several other officers on the scene. BHPD Lt. Frank Salcido assigned the soft-spoken, heavyset balding patrolman to watch the brothers. Both were hysterical. Initially they'd been placed on the ground, patted down, and searched with their hands behind their backs. Angel watched curiously as Erik rammed his head into a tree several times before trying to sprint away and run back inside. Lyle, seemingly more in control, restrained his younger brother each time.

Unquestionably in shock, Erik shouted out fragmentary phrases:

"I'm gonna kill 'em!"

"I'm gonna torture them!"

"Who would do this?"

"We're gonna get those guys!"

"Who are you gonna get?" asked Angel. He had the impression Erik seemed to know the identity of the killers. But there were no answers.

Mo Angel didn't want to push it. He thought both brothers were "frightened sheep." Lyle was calm enough to give investigators his parents' names and his father's occupation. He said the driveway gate was open when he and Erik arrived home. Normally, it was always closed. As Lyle anxiously chattered on, Angel felt they were developing a rapport.

Lyle described his father's work associates in the movie business as "seedy." Jose Menendez had been harassed day and night, Lyle said, in person and over the phone, by the people he worked with. Lyle also mentioned his father was "stressed out" after unexpectedly returning home from a "road trip" a few days earlier.

The patrolman avoided discussing what happened in the house, but both brothers kept asking about the condition of their parents. They demanded to know why the paramedics and the police were taking so long. "I told them in a humanistic way they were gone," Angel recalled later.

As the ambulances loaded with the bodies flashed down North Elm Drive just before dawn, dumbfounded neighbors stood helplessly on their magnificent lawns. "Please tell me he's a drug dealer," pleaded a woman who lived nearby. Another kept repeating, "Things like this just don't happen here."

But it had happened here in beautiful, elegant Beverly Hills. The town averages two murders a year. In a few brief moments, 1989's quota had been filled.

CHAPTER 2

NO SUSPECT(S).
NO WEAPON(S).

WHOEVER SHOT JOSE AND KITTY MENENDEZ LEFT BEHIND
few clues. But Mo Angel, the patrolman assigned to watch Erik
and Lyle immediately after the murders, didn't think the brothers were being "totally straight." He thought they might know who the
killers were. At times, the brothers' anguished hysteria seemed a "bit
overboard." While he was obviously watching them they were frantic,
but when he looked away they were calm and talked in hushed whispers.
In Angel's years as a street cop he had seen a lot of grief, but, to him,
this didn't fit.

Angel was curious about inconsistencies in the brothers' story of
where they had been earlier that evening. When Lyle repeated it, he
changed the times and locations and order of events. Lyle said that they
went to a wine tasting near the Santa Monica convention center but
the person they were supposed to meet didn't show. Next, he said they'd
gone to a movie in Century City. Since the gate to their house was open,
Angel asked why they'd parked their car on the street. "We were planning to go out again," they told him.

An hour after the 911 call, Erik and Lyle were asked to speak to
detectives at the Beverly Hills Police station, and Angel offered to drive
them there. The brothers wanted to drive themselves. Angel ended up
taking them in his patrol car. Angel sensed that they were "nervous and

scared." They constantly asked questions like "What is going on? When can we leave?"

Sgt. Tom Edmonds, detective supervisor for the Beverly Hills Police robbery and homicide squad, had been jarred out of a sound sleep by a phone call just after midnight: There was a "shooting with two people down." Edmonds got to police headquarters just after 1 AM. Tall, slim, and graying, in his Western-style jacket and cowboy boots he resembled the actor Dennis Weaver.

Angel introduced the brothers to Edmonds as the "sons of the victims." Edmonds asked for their ID. Lyle was not taking it as badly as Erik, and Edmonds tried to calm the younger brother. Before they agreed to talk to police, the brothers spoke briefly with their tennis coach, Mark Heffernan. Erik had contacted him while Lyle made the 911 call. He wanted Heffernan or Lyle to sit with him during the interview. No, Edmonds said.

At 1:20 AM, Edmonds brought out a small Panasonic audiotape recorder and began by gently asking Erik what time he'd left home earlier in the evening to go out.

"We weren't going to leave home—we decided to leave home and we left home at eight, uh, at eight. We got to the movie, we went to see . . . we ended up seeing *Batman*." That was at the AMC Century 14 Theatres, at the Century City Shopping Center.

"We were going to stop at home quickly, so we pulled in front, we pulled in the driveway. We pulled in the side and—and the gate was open, and we went inside and I was smelling smoke. After that we saw them and immediately I started screaming, and—and so I went upstairs and Lyle called the police, immediately."

The front gate to the black wrought iron fence surrounding the property opened with a clicker. Edmonds asked whether it was closed when they left home. Erik said they'd left out the back alley, near the guesthouse.

"Was it locked?"

"I don't think so."

"Did you use your key to get in?"

"No, I don't think so. I think the door was unlocked."

Edmonds asked Erik if he had any ideas of who might have done the murders.

"Uh, not right now, I don't know . . . We should have just stayed in."

Erik was crying, so the interview ended. Edmonds did manage to get him to admit that he called Heffernan from his bedroom, which was upstairs and had its own telephone line. Erik babbled about his puppy that was missing. Then he asked, "Are they dead?"

"Yes," Edmonds told him. As he came out of the conference room, Erik whispered to his brother, "It's okay, you can talk to him."

At 1:42 AM, the sergeant started by asking Lyle Menendez about earlier Sunday. After Lyle told him a story that resembled Erik's account of the day's events, Edmonds asked Lyle about finding the bodies.

"And I thought it was strange in a way and, you know, I smelled smoke everywhere. I sort of looked around and I—I remember I was only in there for a few minutes and I sort of checked my mother out and left and, uh, the smell was bad and I went—I ran back to my bedside and I didn't see anything, and I ran back in and my brother was standing there. He was downstairs in the room."

He called police "right away. As soon as I got my brother, I went to tell my brother and went upstairs and called 911 and, uh, the police responded pretty quick."

"Why did you go upstairs to call us? Isn't there a phone downstairs?"

"Yeah, my brother ran upstairs so I ran after him, and he was crying, screaming, so I just ran into my mother's room and I called, and then I came into his room and he was on the phone."

Edmonds asked Lyle if he had any ideas that could help the police solve the crime. "We have to get personal, you understand. If there's any problems we've got to solve this . . ."

"Well, one of my concerns is that I don't like any bad press about my father now."

Edmonds assured him that they were policemen, not reporters, "so you've got to help us."

Lyle answered that he'd already considered that it might have been a robbery, as Mark Heffernan had suggested to him, but "it didn't look like that. It looked like they definitely wanted to make a mess and it was really, uh, sad."

But unless police discovered there were items missing, "it would be my father that would be the reason that it would happen." He said that Jose had worked for RCA Records but had since gone to work for a smaller company "with a group of people that, from the stories that he brings home and the people that I've met, these are a real seedy group. And even though he was very aware of that and, you know, I don't know if anyone would ever try to kill my father. My dad is a pretty ruthless businessman, and he . . . he believes in the bottom line."

"Do you know any specific people that your dad has had business problems with, with these smaller companies that are getting squeezed?" Edmonds asked.

"I could see how he could step on a lot of toes. He's very curt; he treats my brother and I, you know, extremely well, but firm. And he was, he's a strong disciplinarian. He holds the family together well and he's—he runs the show. At work it's the same way, you know. He yells at a lot of people and he's running the show and he handles everything."

His father was a great man, said Lyle. "He did all these—he had full control of his life, he did what he wanted and, uh, my mother was a great tragedy in all of this."

"How is that?"

"That's the hardest thing for me. I mean, her death, because, she never really got to do anything with her life, you know. She sort of served it with my father. I don't think he's treated her very well. When things were kind of getting better, he was at home more often and stuff and we just went on a fishing trip and the family seemed more together."

About his mother: "She seemed real worried about things. In fact, she—she recently bought a rifle. And so we had two rifles in the house, and we thought that she was nervous about something 'cause she went out and just bought a rifle and didn't—didn't tell my dad why or anything, and that's the first thing I suspected when I walked in the house." The brothers had said they'd smelled smoke when they came in.

"Only my brother and I know this, but she was on the verge of contemplating suicide. She was very—she was very edgy and suicidal in the last few years, and—but she seemed very stable, uh, recently. My dad's been fine, so we—I'm not—I really don't—I never really got a chance to sit down and talk."

CHAPTER 3

LIVING IN FEAR—
HOLLYWOOD AND THE MOB

L ES ZOELLER WOKE UP TIRED. HE'D SNUCK IN A SHORT NAP Monday afternoon after being up all night Sunday processing the crime scene. The Baltimore native had left the relatively quiet, routine crimes of Gardena, California, fourteen years ago for the big time as a detective in America's richest city. His specialty was homicide, but his talents were unappreciated in Beverly Hills.

The athletic-looking, thirty-seven-year-old detective with thick, neatly trimmed brown hair parted down the middle and a bushy moustache had made the big cases before. Months of good, solid door-to-door detective work had solved the Billionaire Boys Club murders. (The BBC was a Ponzi scheme created to support the lavish lifestyles of its wealthy young members. When money ran short, two people were killed as the club tried to raise money.)

When Zoeller arrived at the Menendez murder scene just after 2 AM, the brothers were already being interviewed at Beverly Hills Police headquarters. Zoeller's first encounter with Erik and Lyle came at 5:30 Monday morning. The brothers pulled up in a taxi and announced they "needed to pick up some tennis equipment." They weren't allowed in the house, which was still swarming with crime scene technicians. Zoeller asked them to come back at 8:30 AM. When they returned, the detective warned them not to go in the den. The bodies of Jose and Kitty had been

14

removed, but the blood-soaked couch and rug, gruesome evidence of the violent attack that ended their lives, was still there.

Zoeller's supervisor, Tom Edmonds, had someone wake Perry Berman at 4:30 AM and order him to come to the Beverly Hills Police station immediately. Edmonds believed Berman might be their primary suspect. It was nothing he said, but the veteran detective simply considered Berman's demeanor suspicious. "He stuck out like a sore thumb," Edmonds would testify later. "He's definitely not an Academy Award–winning actor. He made a lackluster performance of grief." Edmonds thought Perry Berman was a phony. After interviewing Berman, he drove over to Elm Drive to survey the crime scene. Edmonds still "felt a little ill" about the interviews he'd conducted earlier with the traumatized sons of the victims.

Later, he would admit he "screwed up" and probably should have given Erik and Lyle gunshot residue tests. After Les Zoeller told him that a window was broken in the family room where Jose and Kitty died, Edmonds remembered that both brothers mentioned they'd "seen and smelled smoke." From experience, he knew gun smoke wouldn't linger long in a room with a broken window. He didn't find out until twenty-four hours later that the killers had carefully picked up all the shotgun shells from the floor. "If I'd known the shotgun shells were missing that would've been a big key—that plus smelling the smoke. I wish I had known earlier."

The morning after the deaths of Jose and Kitty, a Hollywood insider joked that one hundred people were going over their alibis. If all the people Jose Menendez had crossed in his aggressive business dealings were gathered together, police would have needed to rent the Hollywood Bowl. In a confrontation over millions of dollars in the film budget of one of Carolco's *Rambo* movies, Jose Menendez had even faced down Sylvester Stallone, the film's star. Shortly after the killings, a police investigator told the *Los Angeles Times*, "The murders stink of organized crime. They went there to take care of business and to make a message clear."

In the wake of the brutal murders, and the media's assumption of a Mafia hit, LIVE Entertainment leaped to defend its corporate honor. So eager was the video company to distance itself from allegations of its fallen leader's involvement with organized crime that it hired superstar publicist Warren Cowan to organize Jose Menendez's memorial service for the Hollywood community of which he had never really been an integral part. Four hundred people turned out on Friday, August 25, five days after the killings, for an event that was as much corporate public relations as tribute. It was a solemn affair, staged in one of the luxurious screening theaters at the Directors Guild of America just off the Sunset Strip. Almost an hour after the scheduled start, the brothers arrived in a stretch limousine. For more than sixty minutes, Lyle and Erik served as masters of ceremony, calling relatives and their father's coworkers up to the stage.

For many, the most heartrending moment of the gathering came during a eulogy by Lyle, who discussed his father's values in life. One close family friend found it odd that Lyle could deliver such a lengthy speech and show little emotion. "My daughter told me after the service that if I had been shot, she wouldn't be able to get up on a stage and talk for an hour without breaking up." Stuart Benjamin, a movie producer who did business with LIVE, felt the memorial service was "weird" and that both brothers appeared to be "stone cold." Near the end, the Milli Vanilli song "Girl I'm Gonna Miss You" was played.

On the advice of the public relations firm, most family members avoided the media by entering and exiting through an underground garage. But after the memorial, one of Jose's sisters, Marta Cano, approached the eager TV crews. "We think he made the mistake of buying a business that had been used before by the Mafia, and we think he was trying to run it straight," she declared.

Executives at LIVE Entertainment were furious when they turned on the 6 PM news. The primary purpose for retaining the PR firm Rogers & Cowan had been to keep the press away from Jose and Kitty's family. Most employees at LIVE didn't believe there was any connection between the murders and the Mob. Still, there were serious concerns. "We certainly didn't want anybody trying to say that it was organized crime and have somebody connected to organized crime get upset," said one executive. "That does scare you."

Officials from LIVE's parent company, Carolco Pictures, released a statement. They considered speculation that the killings were a Mob hit "bizarre and offensive." Others who knew the evolution of home video from its inception as an outgrowth of the Mafia-controlled adult film industry weren't so sure. A front-page headline in the August 25 *Wall Street Journal* proclaimed "Hints of a Mob Rub Out."

CHAPTER 4

A FAMILY MOURNS

EARLY MONDAY MORNING, AUGUST 21, 1989, ERIK AND LYLE Menendez called their aunt and uncle, Terry and Carlos Baralt, with the shocking news of their parents' deaths. Both brothers cried during a brief conversation. The Baralts, emotional themselves, asked few questions before immediately leaving their home in New Jersey for California. Jose Menendez's other sister, Marta Cano, flew to Los Angeles from West Palm Beach after receiving a call from Jose's assistant Marzi Eisenberg.

Eisenberg picked up Cano in a limo at LAX. "It was too bad that everything had happened just when they were beginning to get along better," said Marta. No, Marzi confided to her, "it was just a façade." Kitty Menendez had recently made threats about what she would do if Jose tried to divorce her.

Family members were stunned and disoriented as they gathered at the Bel Age Hotel in West Hollywood, but Cano decided somebody had to take an immediate inventory of Jose's finances. She spent Monday going through all of her brother's personal files at his office. She didn't see her nephews until Tuesday morning.

Down the hall, Beverly Hills Police Detectives Les Zoeller and Tom Linehan were meeting with David Campbell, an executive who had worked with Jose Menendez since they met at Hertz in the 1970s. Campbell described Jose as a "brilliant businessman" who brought him along to RCA and LIVE.

The investigators asked who he thought might be responsible for the deaths of Jose and Kitty. Campbell believed that somebody—he didn't know who—was trying to pressure someone in the entertainment industry. The Menendezes were killed as an example. Campbell didn't believe the murders were directly related to LIVE Entertainment.

Marzi Eisenberg described herself to the detectives as Jose's "office wife." She met Menendez when he hired her at Hertz in 1976 and followed him to RCA and LIVE. Eisenberg said her boss was "very honest," a "fair person," and a "tough businessman who liked a good fight in the boardroom." She admitted he could be stern and had a way of revealing people's shortcomings. When the detectives asked for the names of Jose's close personal friends, Eisenberg replied she didn't know of any. His business associates were the people closest to him, she said.

As for his personal life, Eisenberg said Jose "didn't have a gambling or drinking problem." She described the Menendezes as a "close-knit family" and said her boss had "run a tight ship" at home as well as at the office. She mentioned Lyle and Erik had been involved in "some type of criminal activity." Eisenberg said her boss was calmer after moving to California. But Kitty Menendez recently became "insecure" and suffered from "bouts of depression" after she discovered her husband's romantic affair on the East Coast.

On the afternoon of Monday, August 21, the brothers took the small family safe to the home of Randy Wright, an attorney and father of one of Erik's Beverly Hills High tennis teammates. The next day, a locksmith was called in who opened the safe in Wright's garage. Inside were jewelry and personal papers but no will. On Wednesday, Carlos Baralt and Brian Andersen, Kitty's brother, went with Lyle to a nearby bank to check the family safe deposit box. Since they didn't have the key, the box was drilled open with only Lyle present. There was more jewelry and papers but nothing else.

The Tuesday after the murders, Erik was with his cousins Henry and Maria Helena Llanio when he noticed a suspicious truck in the alley behind the Menendez property. "Both Mom and Dad had been really nervous lately," he told them. He mentioned that his parents had recently bought some guns for the house.

Four days after the murders, Beverly Hills Police received a call from Richard Knox, an attorney representing the mother of a teenager who went to Calabasas High School with Erik. According to the lawyer, the mother thought the Menendez brothers had killed their parents. Erik had a "best friend named Craig" whom detectives should talk to, said the attorney. The next afternoon, Craig Cignarelli was disturbed when he returned home and saw a Beverly Hills Police car parked in front of his house. He drove around the neighborhood for several minutes before finally going inside. Cignarelli told the detectives he hadn't seen Erik during the previous six months. They told him nobody had been eliminated as a suspect. That included Cignarelli himself.

Erik met Craig in the fall of 1987 when Erik enrolled as a sophomore at Calabasas High School. As a junior, Craig was captain of the tennis team. "I found out he was a tennis player and knew he was going to be on the team," he said. "I walked up and met him and we became buddies almost instantly." Craig, handsome and arrogant, was ranked first for doubles play. Soon, Erik was ranked number one for singles.

The two became inseparable. "When we're together, we feel like we have an aura of superiority," Cignarelli boasted. "People could see that somehow we were different." They sometimes retreated to a special place just off Mulholland Drive in the hills above Malibu, overlooking the Pacific Ocean, where, Craig said, they could "get away from everything that was happening in society and try to dream of a better ideology for the future." There, they shared their fantasies of making millions.

On Thursday, August 24, the brothers went shopping at the upscale Century City Shopping Center for outfits to wear to the next day's memorial service. Both brothers bought sports coats at Bullocks. Erik didn't own one. Then, they walked into Slavacs Jewelers. Lyle wanted to look at Rolex watches. Within five minutes, he picked out an 18-karat gold Rolex President model for himself that cost $11,250. At Lyle's insistence, Erik bought a stainless steel Submariner model. Then, Lyle purchased another stainless steel Rolex with a diamond dial and a pair of money clips. The total sale came to $16,938.12.

Store clerk Mary Ellen Mahar was used to ringing up big sales, but not to college-age buyers. For payment, Lyle presented his father's American Express platinum card with the initials "J. E. Menendez." Mahar recognized the last name from news coverage of the murders. She went back to the office and called the credit card company. The sale was approved. The brothers were authorized to charge up to the card limit of $250,000.

———

Before dinner the night before the Hollywood memorial, Erik and Lyle met with their Aunt Marta in their suite at the Hotel Bel Air to discuss the estate. The family had switched from the Bel Age in West Hollywood to the equally luxurious Bel Air near Beverly Hills because of security concerns. Privately, Erik and Lyle told anxious relatives they believed the Mafia wanted to kill them. The brothers' suite cost $1,300 a night. Carolco Pictures was picking up the tab for the entire family.

Lyle and Erik were shocked to learn they were the beneficiaries of their parents' estate. Their aunt estimated it was worth between $8 million and $14 million. "I can't believe my father had so much money," declared Erik. The brothers said they thought they weren't supposed to inherit anything. Earlier in the summer, their father announced he had removed them from his will.

In the spring of 1989, Marta Cano had several conversations with her brother about drafting a new will. They agreed to continue their discussion in the fall when the Menendezes planned to visit Florida on their way to Cuba. Six weeks before August 20, Jose and Kitty Menendez asked Carlos and Terry Baralt to become the executors of the family estate. Jose confided to Carlos he was "frustrated and disappointed" with his sons. He planned to remove the brothers from his new will. "He was cool and collected," recalled Baralt. "It was just something he wanted to do." When Baralt asked how he was going to break the news to the brothers, Menendez said he'd already told them.

"Are you sure my father didn't change it?" Lyle asked Marta. She reassured them they were the beneficiaries. "I can't believe this! Can you believe this?" he told his brother. "No. It can't be," replied Erik. "There's some mistake here. You're missing something, Aunt Marta." Throughout the meeting, Erik repeatedly broke down sobbing. Several times, Lyle sternly ordered him to "stop it! Aunt Marta's trying to talk to us." Cano told the brothers they'd each receive $250,000 immediately from a life insurance policy she'd sold their father.

The day after the Hollywood service, Saturday, August 26, Jose's cousin, Carlos Menendez, found a will in a bathroom drawer adjacent to the master bedroom. It was Jose and Kitty's 1980 will, which left everything to the brothers. Carlos Baralt told the rest of the family he suspected there might be an updated will because of his earlier conversation with Jose. He contacted a dozen lawyers around the country who did business with his brother-in-law but found nothing. Carlos Menendez searched the personal computer in Jose and Kitty's bedroom and came across a file titled "WILL." He was unable to access it. Even if there were a draft of a new will on the computer, Carlos Baralt didn't believe it would be a legal document since there would be no signatures. Still, relatives were curious. Carlos Menendez and Marta Cano's daughter, Eileen, who worked for IBM, each made separate appointments for computer experts to come search the hard drive September 1.

When he learned about this on August 30, Lyle rushed back to Beverly Hills from New York. The next afternoon, he flipped through the Yellow Pages in Beverly Hills before calling Leviathan Development, a West Los Angeles computer firm. He told the office he "needed some files erased." Howard Witkin phoned Lyle from his car after his office beeped him at 1:30 PM. As Witkin sat down at the outdated IBM XT model in the master bedroom, Lyle told the computer expert he "needed to recover a series of files marked "ERIK" . . . "LYLE" . . . "WILL." Witkin thought these were the first names of people. Lyle also wanted to see a file titled "MENENDEZ." Witkin discovered somebody had overwritten three of the files. He couldn't determine if it was accidental or deliberate. The fourth file, "WILL," had only fifty-four characters in it.

According to Witkin, Lyle said he wanted to be sure nobody could recover any of those files. Over the next half hour, Witkin tried to pull up the information but was unsuccessful. For the computer expert, it was a failed assignment. Curiously, his customer seemed pleased. Then, Lyle announced he was selling the computer and needed the entire hard drive erased. Lyle then asked if the data, minus the four files, could be reloaded to look as if Witkin had never been there. It was an odd request, but Witkin completed the job.

On Monday, August 28, family members and close friends gathered in Princeton for the funeral. Terry and Carlos Baralt had returned to New Jersey over the weekend. At a viewing the night before the burial, cousin Trudy Coxe and her family were struck by Lyle's "calmness." The brothers arrived late for the viewing. "Erik was a mess, falling apart and crying while Lyle stayed cool," recalled Trudy's brother Dan Coxe. Several relatives thought it was strange when the brothers didn't even show up for a family dinner.

Early the next morning, a Catholic mass for immediate family members was held at St. Paul's Church where the Menendezes had occasionally attended services. It was followed by a brief Protestant ceremony at the Mather-Hodge Funeral Home. Jose was raised Catholic and Kitty was brought up Protestant, so relatives wanted multiple services.

After prayers at the funeral home, more than one hundred people gathered on campus for a service at the magnificent Princeton University chapel with its soaring spire and cavernous, warmly lit interior. Lyle spoke eloquently for twenty minutes about his father's "extraordinary life" and "his complete loyalty to the family success and the generations, and how he wanted that to carry on." Lyle said the brothers would "try to live up to what he wanted" for them. He also told the mourners his parents would've wanted everybody to "put their best face forward and put this behind them and not grieve."

Family members were touched by the depth of the eulogy. "People normally speak from the heart at funerals, but this was a unique speech and people were quite moved by it," recalled Trudy Coxe. Inside, Lyle was churning with anxiety. "I felt that my dad would want me to do that and he would've been proud of me to get up there and do it, even though I didn't want to," he said later.

The morning after the funeral, Lyle contacted D. B. Kelly Associates, a private Princeton security firm. He had decided to hire bodyguards on the theory—his theory—that the Mafia was after him. Richard Wenskoski, a former police officer with eighteen years of law enforcement experience, and John Aquaro teamed up to guard Lyle. Each was armed with a Browning 9mm handgun.

Wenskoski later said Lyle told him he was "in fear of his life" and that "his parents were murdered by either the South American drug cartel or the [Italian] Mob." After hearing this, the two bodyguards bought bulletproof vests. One evening, the limo driver told Wenskoski his office learned the FBI was following Lyle.

But a few days later, the veteran cop noticed something odd. Lyle no longer appeared to be afraid of anything. The bodyguards had to remind him several times to let them walk out of buildings first. During lunch one afternoon, Lyle told Wenskoski he reminded him of his dad. "I want to thank you, Rich," he said. "You've stood by me and helped me out a lot." In stores, Lyle would line up shoes or jackets and ask if they "looked good on him." The bodyguard was becoming a father figure.

Lyle's roommate at Princeton, Glenn Stevens, became very upset after hearing about the murders from a friend who worked at RCA. He attended the Princeton memorial service and saw Lyle wearing a gold Rolex. Lyle told him the watch belonged to his father. Stevens was worried about his friend. "Lyle was a doer, and I was afraid that he might try to go out and find out who did it and maybe do something stupid," he recounted. "I knew he idolized his father, so after the funeral when he seemed to disassociate himself from the incident completely, I couldn't understand it."

As they shopped around Princeton, Lyle and Stevens frequently laughed and joked. Wenskoski wondered why Lyle wasn't more upset over his parents' deaths. After a week, Lyle told Wenskoski he no longer needed any protection. His uncle, he said, had spoken with a "Mob figure" in New York. The brothers were no longer in any danger.

To onlookers, Erik seemed more deeply affected by his parents' death. He never stayed with Terry and Carlos Baralt for more than twenty-four hours. His pediatrician from Princeton diagnosed his complaints of severe stomach pains as stress related. At one point, Erik became overwhelmed and turned to a family member for help. All the police questioning, all the media badgering, all the friends who meant well—it had all grown to be too much. He needed some privacy and a refuge.

He found it at the home of a cousin in the San Fernando Valley, only a few miles north but light years away from Beverly Hills. Maria Menendez's nephew, Henry Llanio, was twenty years older than Erik. He had never been close to Jose, Kitty, and the brothers. In fact, he'd only seen them two or three times since their arrival in California three years earlier. Henry's wife, Maria Helena, and his own teenage son, Kiko, were away in Texas, so the two cousins spent time together and developed a close bond. One evening, they took a two-hour walk in spite of Llanio's slow recovery from an injured foot. As they passed by seemingly endless rows of tract homes, Erik suddenly blurted out, "If Lyle did it, I'll kill him!"

Erik told Henry his account of the night of the killings wasn't entirely true. When Henry asked if the brothers had been together the entire evening of August 20, Erik admitted "they'd been apart for about ten minutes." Henry speculated Erik was telling a half-truth—he thought they'd been separated, but probably for longer than ten minutes.

Over the next week, a clearly terrified Erik was too frightened to sleep in a bed by himself. Frequently, he'd walk into Henry's bedroom. Some nights, he'd lie down on the floor, but on other occasions, he'd crawl into Llanio's bed like a small child after a bad dream. One night, Erik fell asleep on the living room couch while watching television. When Henry got up to go to bed, Erik bolted upright and asked him where he was going.

A few weeks later, Erik made his first trip back to the house since the night his parents died. As he entered the grand, two-story entrance foyer, he froze. His eyes locked in on the family room at the end of the hallway. The bloody carnage of August 20 was gone. The walls and floors were scrubbed clean. The beige sectional sofa and the ornate oriental rug had been destroyed. The history books his father loved to read and quote were still on the shelves. The tennis trophies he and Lyle won still lined the length of one wall.

He was drawn to the family room as if a huge magnet were pulling him closer, but as he approached the double doors, he stopped and started to tip-toe as if trying to avoid disturbing something. Relatives watched curiously as he craned his neck around the wide doorway to see if anyone was there. After he was inside, he kept walking on tiptoes as he slowly moved around the room before crouching down behind the large wooden wet bar in the corner. He was quivering.

CHAPTER 5

THE INVESTIGATION BEGINS

O N AUGUST 30, 1989, AFTER NINE DAYS OF INTENSE, AROUND-the-clock detective work, Erik and Lyle Menendez were deemed potential suspects in the search for their parents' killers. The BHPD received approval for two sealed search warrants requesting phone records for the Menendez mansion. Investigators were trying to trace the calls Lyle said he had made to Perry Berman from the Santa Monica Civic Center.

In New York City, Lyle's former close friend Donovan Goodreau read about the murders and immediately tried to call him. But there was no answer. After that, he left several messages on the brothers' answering machine and with the Beverly Hills Police.

Les Zoeller phoned him where he worked at Boxers restaurant in Manhattan. Goodreau told the detective he hadn't spoken to Lyle since being kicked out of his Princeton dorm the previous May. A few days later, Zoeller called and said he was coming to New York with Tom Linehan. They wanted to meet him. Goodreau was extremely nervous.

On Saturday, September 16, the two detectives drove directly to Boxers from JFK airport. Goodreau told the visitors he wished Lyle would call. He couldn't understand why he hadn't heard from him. The detectives asked about the dispute that ended with Goodreau being kicked out of Lyle's dorm. "They knew a lot, and I spilled my guts," said Goodreau when I interviewed him in July 1990.

Over the next three hours their talk covered many topics, including the relationship between Jose and Lyle Menendez. Goodreau was scared. Was he a suspect? "This is all routine," the detectives reassured him.

The next afternoon, September 17, Zoeller and Linehan drove to Cranbury, New Jersey, outside of Princeton, to interview Jose's sister Terry and her husband, Carlos. They had met the Baralts briefly in Beverly Hills just after the murders. When the detectives arrived at the Baralts' split-level house at the end of a cul-de-sac, they had no idea that the brothers were staying there.

Later, Zoeller would testify he was suspicious of the brothers as of that September visit but didn't consider them his primary suspects. He wanted to learn more about this family everyone kept describing as "close-knit." In the family room, they sat down with Lyle on a semicircular black leather couch lined with pictures of the Baralts' four daughters and a snapshot of Jose, smiling, with his arm around Kitty. In front of them, on a coffee table, the detectives placed a tape recorder. Like many interviews, this one began with small talk.

Linehan brought up the movie that the brothers had said they'd gone to see and asked what time they'd left the house.

"By the time I got to the movie, it was approximately eight o'clock," answered Lyle.

"Had you ever seen *Batman* before that night?" Zoeller asked.

"Yeah. We saw it one time before. Uh, we originally went to see *Licence to Kill*. They were sold out. So we saw *Batman*, which was ten minutes later." Lyle said the movie ended at about 10:15 PM.

"You went from there to Santa Monica?"

"Straight over there. Yeah. We went straight over there."

Zoeller asked if he still had the movie theater ticket stubs.

"I don't know, unless they're in the car. They'd probably be in the car, you know. I wouldn't know."

After the brothers called Perry Berman to meet them at the Cheesecake Factory and left Santa Monica, "then you went back to the house?" Zoeller asked.

"Yeah, we went back to the house to pick something up."

"What were you gonna pick up at the house?"

"Uh, my brother's ID, so he could drink."

"Know what name that ID was in?"

"Erik would know that."

Lyle said that Erik saw the bodies first, and Lyle heard him scream-ing and crying. When Lyle entered the den, "I couldn't check 'em out too good. I was just trying to take care of my brother, but I was won-dering whether the people were still there. We went back to check if someone—"

Zoeller interrupted. "Your aunt mentioned you felt bad that you didn't go and check your mother—that you might have been able to save her."

"Yeah, definitely," said Lyle.

"Your mother was gone at that time. So if you have any concerns that you could've gone over and saved her by being there just five min-utes earlier, don't worry about it," said Zoeller. "They both died instan-taneously."

Zoeller asked if there had been any recent problems between Lyle and his parents.

"Uh, not really. My mom and I are, had a, some sort of fight the night before."

"[You] don't remember what it was?"

"'Cause she'd lock the door. And I . . . forgot a key and had to wake her up to open the door. I got upset at her because she makes you wake her up to unlock the door. She knows I forget my keys."

Linehan asked if Lyle's mom was paranoid.

"In my opinion she was always edgy all the time. You know, I mean, real, kind of, you know, just nervous, unfortunately. She never slept well. I don't think she really enjoyed the area too much, though. They got in fights."

Lyle complained about the press coverage focusing on organized crime. "'Cause the rumors would cause some serious damage," he said.

"It's serious damage for you, obviously, because they were your par-ents," answered Linehan. "But even Carolco, I mean, you know, face it. They're in sort of damage control for their stockholders. We get calls from them, too, wanting to find out if this thing or that thing is true or not."

"I don't believe the organized crime thing until I see something. You know?" said Lyle.

"That makes two of us. And I haven't seen anything," replied Zoeller.

"Makes three of us," added Linehan.

Then Zoeller asked about the bodyguards he'd hired.

"Oh, we were being followed."

"By whom? Do you know?"

"Uh, we don't know."

To end the hour-long interview, the detectives asked, "Is there anything you've been involved in that would've led to this?"

"No. Absolutely nothing. Nothing that I was involved in . . . I mean, Erik's gang-related things I don't know too much about."

"That appeared to be long over," said Zoeller.

"It's a dead issue," added Linehan.

Terry Baralt went upstairs and woke Erik.

"Let's just run through this real quick. We'll be done with it," said Linehan. "You both entered the house that night through the front door."

"Yeah," said Erik. "It was open."

"And you went directly into the family room?"

"Well, yeah, I usually do. I was actually heading to the kitchen. I believe my brother ran upstairs and came down ahead of me. There was a lot of smoke in the room, and I guess it was . . . there was basically just a lot of blood everywhere."

"Did the smoke that you smelled when you came in, what'd it smell like to you, like your dad's pipe smoke?"

"No, no. I have this thing where I smell the smoke every day. Actually, when I smell the burning of the car engine that's been overheated— reminds me of the smoke. Every day I remember the smoke. And, uh, probably will for a long time. It was just a slow haze. The room was like dark yellow. It was like a full, slick haze and sitting there from what I remember and it smelled like, I remember, like it immediately smelled to me like it was gun smoke, obviously, when I saw them."

"You know what gun smoke smells like?" Linehan asked.

"Well, I had never really smelled it before but, you know, I-I never really . . . I imagine, uh, you know, it would've . . ."

Erik said he stayed in the room for what "seemed like a long while before Lyle got there. So I had a chance to look over there. I didn't throw up. I was just, I guess, in such shock that I wasn't crying at first. I was calling for my brother."

After Lyle came down, they both went upstairs, Lyle to their parents' room, Erik to his.

"I called my coach in my room . . . he was the closest person I've been to besides my brother. He had been like my best friend because he was with us every day." After that, Lyle told him they had to go outside—the police were there.

Later, Erik said there was something else he'd been thinking about: "The gate was open. The alarm was off. The door was unlocked. You think it could have been someone they knew?"

Zoeller answered that the indications were that "it's somebody they knew, because it doesn't appear that either one of your parents, one, struggled with them, seemed to be disturbed."

"There was no struggle?"

"Right."

"My mom was really nervous lately. And I know she bought a gun."

"She already had the two other guns," said Linehan.

"Yeah, exactly, and which that didn't make any sense. And when I questioned her about it, she was like, she didn't say anything. She did write a note, which we found before."

"What was the note about?"

"About—it indicated that—that she was—might be expected to die, that's what it indicated." He said that Lyle showed the note to Kitty's brother, Brian. It was "basically saying we love you a lot."

"Did you have any recent problems with your parents at all?"

"We spent the whole summer together playing tennis. I spent every second of the day with him. And, we're usually pretty close, right up until the day they died." One argument he and his father had had was in April or May when Jose "thought that I wasn't opening up—opening up in tennis."

"Sounds like he was being a typical father," said Zoeller.

"Yeah, exactly. We wanted to go to college, really bad. We were getting away from him, you know."

Erik asked the detectives if they had spoken with Jerry Oziel.

"Who?" asked Zoeller.

"Jerry Oziel—he's a psychiatrist."

Zoeller and Linehan had never heard the name before.

"Probably kept out on purpose—slipped through the papers," said Erik.

"Nothing slips through the papers from us," replied Zoeller.

"Oziel. O-Z-I-E-L . . . a Beverly Hills psychiatrist. My parents made us get one after the Calabasas thing. He's a very good friend of mine. He spent a lot of time with us basically after this. We had many meetings with my parents together. I don't know what he's gonna tell you about, but I'm sure he may be able to help you out. I'm probably still gonna see him."

"I think it'd be a good idea," remarked Linehan.

Les Zoeller explained that they wouldn't be able to talk with the therapist because of "doctor confidentiality." But if Erik were willing to call him, he could waive the privilege. Erik promised he'd make the call.

Several days later, attorney Gerald Chaleff called the BHPD and asked that any future interviews with Lyle and Erik be arranged through his office.

CHAPTER 6

MILLIONAIRE ORPHANS

AS THE WEEKS PASSED, POLICE INVESTIGATORS WERE DIS-
inclined to blame the Mob. They noted that Mafia hit men usually
perform their executions with a single, relatively surgical shot to
the head. They rarely, if ever, kill innocent wives, let alone invade their
victims' homes. The cops were much more interested in the behavior of
Lyle and Erik Menendez, and how they chose to express their grief. Les
Zoeller and Tom Linehan were annoyed the brothers didn't return their
phone calls. During a typical murder investigation, relatives are anxious
to stay in close contact with police, hungry for any shred of information connected to the hunt for the killers. The Menendez brothers didn't
seem to care.

What fascinated detectives the most were the spending habits of
the millionaire orphans. Lyle began staying at expensive hotels, shuttled
between the East and West Coasts on MGM Grand Air, and made sure
that he didn't leave home without his dead father's American Express
card, with which he quickly ran up a $90,000 tab. Both brothers were
always free spenders. As part of the control over his sons' lives, Jose
Menendez gave Erik and Lyle very little cash but allowed them access
to charge accounts that he could monitor. But now the controls were
gone. Police tabulated that Lyle and Erik spent a cool $1,000,000 in
the first three months after the killings. Even for Beverly Hills, this was
living large. Jose and Kitty's will was months away from being settled,
but the brothers had received the $500,000 life insurance payout. Lyle's
purchases included a $64,000 silver Porsche 911 Carrera complete with

a computer alarm system that warned you in a *RoboCop* voice to "move away from the vehicle." There was also the gold Rolex and $24,000 worth of merchandise bought in one afternoon at a stereo/TV store. Erik's dreams initially seemed more modest. He bought a $17,000 tan Jeep Wrangler but also took refuge in fancy hotels and condos.

None of the relatives ever thought to ask the brothers for their parents' wallets. Carlos Baralt sat down with Lyle and asked him to "slow down on the spending." Family members rationalized Lyle's extravagance as his way of dealing with grief. Kitty's friend Karen Weire thought Lyle bought the Porsche to simply show off. Weire's son Steve also played competitive tennis. The two families had met at a tournament in Texas, and Kitty told Karen that the Menendezes might someday move to California. When they got there, she called Weire first. "As far as I know, I was Kitty's only friend," Weire said. "We used to pal around a lot. She wasn't real social."

"We talked several times about how the money wasn't doing it for him, as far as cushioning the blow," reflected Glenn Stevens. "I think it's quite possible the spending was an escape for him."

The epic scale of the brothers' buying spree, together with their seeming indifference to the search for the killers, suggested to the cops and the district attorney that a case might more plausibly be made against the Menendez brothers than against some shadowy family with tenuous roots in Palermo or Medellín. The only problem was the absence of any evidence connecting Lyle and Erik to their parents' death.

CHAPTER 7

WHO KILLED THE NEXT SENATOR FROM FLORIDA?

MY ASSIGNMENT FOR THE *MIAMI HERALD* IN SEPTEMBER 1989 was not to cover the Menendez murder investigation; it was to write a 5,000-word biography about a Cuban American success story that ended in tragedy. My piece was slated to appear in *Tropic*, the newspaper's Sunday magazine. My in with the family was Jose's sister Marta Cano, who lived in West Palm Beach, Florida. When we met, about two weeks after the murders, I sat in her living room for four hours as she shared the Menendez family history going back a hundred years. In each generation from Spain to Cuba to the United States, there was a pattern of struggle followed by great achievement. For Jose, the largest part of that was still on the drawing board; he had a five-year plan in which he would retire from the entertainment business, move to Miami, and run for the U.S. Senate.

Marta insisted that to really understand how close and loving her family was I had to meet Erik and Lyle. They were supposed to come to a memorial service in Miami in about a week. But the brothers skipped Miami and never made it to Aunt Marta's house. Instead they'd gone to Daytona Beach with their girlfriends, telling Marta they couldn't emotionally handle what by then was a third memorial service.

On the expectation that I would meet them in California, I went there. I set up a time to speak with them, but the night before they called to cancel. That happened four or five more times. Meanwhile, I talked with people who knew Jose Menendez in business: employees at LIVE Entertainment and others in the home-video industry who'd negotiated against him. Nobody had mushy opinions; people either loved or hated his rough-and-tumble, take-no-prisoners professional style. At LIVE, everyone insisted that the murders had absolutely no connection to their company.

At Ed's Coffee Shop in West Hollywood—a hangout of the Beverly Hills Police—on a chilly, gray morning in early October, I met with Les Zoeller and Tom Linehan, the detectives in charge of the Menendez investigation. During an hour-long meeting, we discussed the difference between Mob hits by Italians and Colombians. The detectives played down media speculation about a possible Menendez drug connection, saying it was probably fueled only by Jose's Latino heritage. They thought he was a straight arrow whose public life was beyond reproach, which agreed with what I knew so far.

After two weeks of failing to get an interview with Lyle and Erik, my editor at the *Herald* ordered me home. From Florida, Marta Cano called her nephews on my behalf, insisting that they had to meet with me. We made another appointment for 3 PM on Friday, October 20, at the mansion at 722 North Elm Drive. This time they didn't cancel. The door was opened, not by either of the brothers but by Kelly Kolankiewicz, who told me she was Erik's girlfriend. The brothers "were delayed," she said. She was in her early twenties with blonde hair and a cheery smile. She invited me inside. We made small talk before she offered to show me around the mansion.

I felt a chill as we walked by the open double doors leading to The Room. It was empty of furniture and had a bare hardwood floor. The floor-to-ceiling bookshelves were filled and above them on a narrow ledge were dozens of tennis trophies. If I lived in the mansion, I decided I would close those doors. After passing by a second time, I thought, if my parents had been murdered in that house, I wouldn't even be living there.

Erik and Lyle showed up, at 3:45 PM, wearing tennis whites, in sharp contrast to their dark tans. We sat down just off the kitchen in a breakfast nook, around a circular glass-topped wicker table. Within five minutes, Lyle told me the brothers were thinking of writing a book about their father's "extraordinary life." Would I be interested in working with them? I agreed that Jose Menendez's backstory was fascinating.

But when I brought out a tape recorder, Lyle stopped me. "We can only meet for a short time today," he said. "Let's just talk and get to know each other—no tape recorders and no notes."

Over the next hour, Lyle did 90 percent of the talking. He compared his father to John F. Kennedy and Martin Luther King Jr. and described his death as a "tragic loss for the Cuban people" who "didn't even know who he was or what he was going to do for them." Erik told of the books his father read, his suffering in Cuba, and that Jose was a regular contributor to Radio Martí, the Spanish-language equivalent of Radio Free Europe broadcast to the island from transmitters in Florida.

The few times Erik spoke when Lyle was in the room, he looked to his older brother as if seeking his approval. He was low-key and measured. Lyle was much more outgoing and confident, and maintained eye contact. We agreed to meet the next afternoon, Saturday. But late Friday night, Lyle called to cancel; something came up. We rescheduled for Sunday at noon.

In a light drizzle, I arrived at the mansion on Sunday, and this time the brothers' grandmother, Maria Menendez, answered the door. She said that Lyle unexpectedly had to leave for Princeton on a red-eye Saturday night. Erik was upstairs, asleep. I explained to her that I was returning to Miami on Monday, and this was my last chance to speak with them. After serving me a *café cubano*, she went upstairs and woke Erik.

Minutes later he came down, looking sleepy, his hair wet from a shower. He wore a light-blue Ralph Lauren polo shirt and well-worn blue jeans with holes at the knees, and was barefoot. In a corner of the living room we sat down at a card table. He was warm, outgoing, animated, and with a quick wit—a striking contrast from two days before.

This time the tape recorder was on. Erik started by talking about his colorful family history and their migration from Spain to Cuba. His grandmother Maria's father was the "greatest baseball player in Cuba, ever" and was in the Cuban Hall of Fame. Maria herself was a swimmer, and "ten years after she had stopped swimming, she could just up and dive in the pool and was faster than any person." As for his dad, he was the number one swimmer in Cuba, and they were the first family to be in the Hall of Fame in Cuba. "And so they belonged to the top club in Cuba. And, uh, it was important to belong to that club." And his father "was just—girls wanted him—and he was very good-looking, and he was just like everything [Erik] wanted to be."

But at age sixteen, "after being expected throughout the world as, um, breaking the world records, the Olympic time—and he was expected to win the gold medal," Castro took over Cuba and Jose had to leave the country for the United States. "And my mom, too," he added, was an athlete, a "phenomenal skier."

Erik spoke of his father in the present tense. He said his dad "loves practical jokes. Loves corny jokes, tells the stupidest jokes over and over and over again, and just laughs at them . . . but he's not an idiot, he just enjoys the silly humor."

Regarding his and Lyle's intensive sports training, he said that Jose "would just teach us in the right ways." Erik admitted that it frustrated his father when, as a child, Erik had complained that he didn't want to swim competitively. "It was a big deal when I had to tell my dad that I didn't want to go on swimming—it was hard for him. And he used to go to the pool, just for an hour, and dive. He used to be the only—no one else there. He would just be teaching me dives, teaching me dives, teaching me to dive perfectly . . . He just wanted, you know—it didn't matter because he was with his son at least."

It was impossible to win an argument with Jose, he said, because his father was a master of debate. "Even if the man didn't know what he was talking about, he would not let you know that he didn't know what he was talking about. And knew enough that he would win the argument, and unless you were a professor and an expert in that subject, you would not win. And he would convince you that you were wrong. Just amazing convincing power."

Jose "was not a social man . . . He had a lot of friends who were men who admired him, but usually—see, the problem with my dad is that he moved up from one space to another so fast, that there were no times for him to get real close friendships, and people became jealous of him. And so the only people that he was friends with were people that he admired. I mean, people that admired him.

"On the weekend, he wouldn't want to socialize. He—he'd want—I would always stay home . . . Instead of going to the movies with my friends, I would just—I would stay home with him. And, uh, in fact it was weird. We'd even take showers together. With Lyle, my—he got this big bathtub and Lyle, me, and my dad would just—we would take showers together, we would do everything together. We would watch football, we'd, you know, and play tennis. I mean, very, very, uh, wanting to be with us. Amazingly so."

When Jose got a job offer in Los Angeles, Kitty hadn't wanted to leave New Jersey and her friends there. There'd been a debate, but the "debate was over just, my dad, you could not debate . . . I don't know how their marriage was going at that time either. I think they had a little rough spot right there, um, in their marriage, and so it was a real big thing . . . he said, yeah, well, you can stay here with Lyle, and I'm gonna take Erik and we'll go to Los Angeles. And Mom's like, you're not taking Erik, no. And she finally agreed to move out . . . [she] was pretty depressed.

"People were afraid of him, because they would walk in the room and know that this man was more powerful. This man was more intelligent. This man would get his deal. And, uh, if he did not like you—I would not like for my dad not to like me. I mean, that is—if I was a person, I'd wanna be on my dad's good side."

Erik talked about the plans Jose had had for the near future. He was going to move the family to Miami and launch his political career.

"He was going to become senator of Florida, which I don't think he would have had much problem doing. People say he would've been incompetent, but I doubt it . . . And then he was gonna spend his life making Cuba a territory of the United States. He was gonna spend his life getting Castro out of Cuba."

Erik and Lyle's personal plans were to complete their father's dreams.

If he made it on the tennis tour, Erik planned to stop playing at age thirty and then finish his education, if he hadn't already, and then go into politics, "you know, basically do the same thing my dad was gonna do at his age. You know, forty-five years old or younger, hopefully, and, my brother wants to become President of the United States. I think that's great.

"But I basically just want to become senator of Florida . . . be with the people of Cuba my father loved so much, and make Cuba a territory of the United States. It was a goal of my father's, an incredible goal . . . and he had to give this much and he went this far and I'm gonna finish it and my brother's gonna help out, of course."

An hour in, I told Erik that although my assignment was to write a profile about Jose Menendez, I needed to ask a few questions about the murder investigation. When I mentioned I'd met with the Beverly Hills Police, he quickly asked me for details. The detectives had tried to reach him but he hadn't called them back, he admitted.

As for the latest in the investigation, "Uh, I wish I knew. For a long time they were looking for a possibility that had something to do with—that—with something that Lyle and I were involved in. I mean, not Lyle and I did it but something that we were involved in and that may have been—had the result." That something, he said, was a gang fight he'd gotten into, which had started on a high school tennis court and ended for him with a broken nose and cheekbone.

I asked him to tell me about the night of the murders.

"I've never seen anything like it. My grandmother died, and her dog, and I saw that, but . . . they weren't real. They didn't . . . wax . . . they looked like wax. I've never seen my dad helpless, and we were sad to think that he would ever be. And, uh, I don't think there was any torture. I hope it was sudden . . . It was a rough evening, and I'll never forget it."

Soon after, the cassette in my tape recorder ran out. As I replaced it, he asked, with mist in his eyes, if we could stop talking about the murders. He then suggested people I should interview who knew the brothers and the family well.

"If you talk to them, you'll see the respect that we have for our father, and see that things we did are very similar to—for my father. If you look at—and you can see the marks of my father in Lyle and I. We are basically—Lyle and I—I consider us prototypes of my father. My father wanted Lyle and I to be exactly like him."

Back in Miami, I had follow-up questions, of course, and over the next few weeks left several messages on the brothers' answering machine. They never called back. Finally, a family member told me that all press inquiries were now being answered by their criminal defense attorney, Gerald Chaleff. The brothers themselves were no longer available for interviews.

Shortly before my final deadline in early December 1989, their aunt, Marta Cano, called and asked me not to use a family portrait she'd given me. She warned me the brothers were in danger. "We can't have their picture published because they have been getting death threats," she said. After we hung up, I contacted Detective Zoeller to find out more about the threats.

"What death threats?" said Zoeller. It didn't make sense. If your parents were brutally murdered and you were receiving death threats, it seemed logical you'd share that information with investigators.

I asked Zoeller directly if the police had eliminated the brothers as suspects. He was circumspect and polite without revealing anything but left the door wide open to speculation. "The boys never call me—why, I don't know," he told me.

As we finished the article, my editor, Tom Shroder, turned to me and said, "The brothers did it." I told him I disagreed. That moment began my decades-long quest to resolve that disagreement and determine what really happened at 722 North Elm Drive on the night of August 20, 1989.

PART TWO

THE PARENTS: JOSE AND KITTY

CHAPTER 8

THE MENENDEZES OF HAVANA

I N 1938, TWENTY-SEVEN-YEAR-OLD JOSE MENENDEZ PAVON married his next-door neighbor, Maria Carlota Llanio, who turned twenty-one on their wedding day in Havana. She was the youngest of Enrique and Carlota Llanio's two girls and three boys.

As a teenager, Maria won five gold medals for swimming at the 1935 Central American and Caribbean Olympic Games. She was the first woman inducted into the Cuban Hall of Fame. "Pepin," as Jose was called, became a pro soccer player and owned a small accounting practice.

Their marriage produced two daughters, Teresita, born in 1940, and Marta, two years later. Pepin and Maria's third child, Jose Enrique Menendez, was born on May 6, 1944. He was bright, terrifically energetic, precociously self-possessed, and disarmingly arrogant. "When he was three, four, and five, my brother was totally unbearable," remembered Marta. "He was my mother's baby—she loved him dearly. She would discipline Terry and me, but not him. He was her 'cute boy.' If he did something wrong, it was always 'cute.'"

The Menendezes lived in Vedado, a quiet neighborhood about fifteen minutes from downtown Havana. Growing up, Jose ran track and played American football. Maria and Pepin sent their kids to a Jesuit boarding school in Kentucky. But in 1959, Cuba's by then prime minister Fidel Castro cut off sending money out of the country. Cuba began teaching revolutionary propaganda in its schools. Fifteen-year-old Jose became an outspoken critic of Fidel Castro. His parents worried that their son would be arrested or indoctrinated.

Maria Menendez was hysterical about getting all of her children out of Cuba. When last-minute seats became available for a flight to Miami in October 1960, she asked Terry's fiancé, Carlos Baralt, to take Jose with him.

They moved in with distant relatives—Travis and Gergie Coxe, who lived outside of Hazleton, a rural community in northeastern Pennsylvania. Overnight, Jose was uprooted from his comfortable life in Havana. He wouldn't talk and rarely left his room, overwhelmed with home-sickness and depression. When he finally spoke, it was only in Spanish. Jose directed his anger at Fidel Castro and announced he'd be returning to Havana soon to fight against the revolution. Sometimes, he locked himself in his tiny attic room for hours, listening on a small shortwave radio to hear news from Cuba. Although he was broke, Jose Menendez had cachet as someone from a faraway island. He picked up English but was taunted for his Ricky Ricardo accent. Soon, any lack of belonging was overshadowed by his swimming talent. He became the star of the school team. He boasted that he'd become successful and famous some-day. Everyone would know his name.

CHAPTER 9

TRUE LOVE

*The marriage of my parents was probably a union that should
have never happened, and that's where the parallels lie.*
—JOAN VANDERMOLEN, Kitty Menendez's sister, to author

J OSE'S FATHER REFUSED TO FLEE WITH THE MASSES HEADING
for Miami, but Maria Menendez made up her mind. With both
her daughters pregnant in the states and Jose homesick, she was
going, too. Pepin gave up and joined her in 1962 after Castro seized all
his properties.

Jose won a swimming scholarship to Southern Illinois University.
During his sophomore year, he took a philosophy course where he met
Mary Louise Andersen, a senior majoring in communications. She was
attractive and athletic, and everyone called her Kitty. Their friendship
started with playful arguments. No one had ever challenged him like
Kitty Andersen. The couple began meeting at night, talking about books
and the future. She was as arrogant and confident as the man she would
marry.

Mary Louise Andersen was born October 23, 1941 in Oak Lawn, Illinois, a working-class Chicago suburb. Kitty was the youngest of Andy
and Lula Mae Andersen's four children. She had two brothers, Brian
and Milton, and a sister, Joan, who was ten years older. Andy owned

a commercial refrigeration and air-conditioning business. Mae had dreamed of becoming a concert pianist, but Andy Andersen wanted a traditional stay-at-home wife.

Kitty was a "little entertainer," said her sister Joan VanderMolen. "She loved to make a flap and prance around in front of us." In July 1944, Andy walked out on Mae, ending their fifteen-year marriage. According to Joan, his departure was a relief for her brothers, whom Andy frequently slapped and punched. Kitty told friends that after her father left she used to cry herself to sleep.

Andy insisted that Mae always agree with him because it was important to present a united front to their children. "That usually didn't happen, and that would irritate my dad," remembered Joan. "Mom tried to interfere and ended up getting hit herself. Then dad left her. I think years later, Kitty saw that in her subconscious. Maybe she wasn't even aware why she was doing it, but standing up for [her] kids caused [our] mother to lose her husband and led to a divorce . . . I think Kitty grew up with a distorted value system."

Kitty Andersen became a pretty teenager, a popular girl with light brown hair and a radiant smile. She hung out with girls who called themselves the "Party Dolls." In September 1962, a month before her twenty-first birthday, she was named queen of the Oak Lawn Round-Up beauty pageant. The local newspaper said that Kitty "hopes to work in broadcasting as a producer-director as well as appearing in dramatic parts."

Kitty broke gender barriers by working behind the camera at SIU's campus TV station and doing play-by-play for sports events. But in the spring of 1963, she began to spend all her time with the exotic foreigner her friends called "Hosey." Jo McCord, her roommate, said that "Jose and Kitty had a beautiful relationship. They had found their one and only, and that was it."

On July 8, 1963, the couple were married. By the end of the summer, the financially strapped newlyweds moved in with Pepin and Maria in New York City before renting their own tiny apartment in Queens.

Jose had been a lackadaisical student at SIU but after enrolling at Queens College, he became diligent, studying accounting at night school. His day jobs included washing dishes at New York's 21 Club and keeping the books for a chicken wholesaler who encouraged him to finish school. Kitty became a teacher and supported the couple by teaching at a high school in the Bronx. Jose never wanted his wife to work in radio or television; broadcasting was for men.

Jose and Kitty sometimes bought a salty ham and ate from it all week. For extra heat, they opened their oven. A professor at Queens College remembered when Jose couldn't cover a $3 class fee; he said he'd have it on payday the following week.

Two months after his mother's death, Erik Menendez told me that she always spoke fondly about the early days of her marriage. "My mom says that's the closest they've ever been. The happiest days they ever had were during that time because it brought them so close together. Money kind of brings you apart. It loosens the ties because you no longer need to be as close."

CHAPTER 10

THE AMERICAN DREAM

WITH MAJORS IN ECONOMICS AND ACCOUNTING AT QUEENS College, Jose Menendez graduated in 1967 in the top 10 percent of his class. He was hired at the first place he applied—the Big Eight accounting firm of Coopers & Lybrand. The pay was $25,000 a year, substantial money in the late 1960s.

When Coopers & Lybrand sent Jose to Chicago to audit Lyons Container Services, he discovered that the company was near bankruptcy. Menendez presented them a restructuring plan that included firing their comptroller. They offered Jose the job for $75,000 a year. Kitty quit her teaching job, and the family moved to Hinsdale, Illinois, near Chicago. In Menendez's first year at Lyons, revenue rose from $2.8 to $5.2 million. In the third year, it was up to $12 million. In spite of the success, Jose was forced out by new owners in the summer of 1972.

Out of work with a $725-a-month mortgage, a wife, and two young sons, Jose asked Pepin for a loan and got a lecture about the importance of saving money. Jose turned that back on his father: "You saved a lot of money, and now Fidel has it. You lost it. You never enjoyed it. I'm going to enjoy life." Pepin paid his son's mortgage while Jose searched for work.

Jose landed a $75,000-a-year job as director of operations for Hertz Rent-a-Car. Within two years he was vice president of the car and commercial leasing divisions. When Menendez presented Hertz his first blueprint for change, CEO Bob Stone told him, "You're either brilliant or an idiot."

"Fire me if I'm an idiot," replied Menendez. His analysis was accepted, and many people were reassigned or fired, and budgets were cut.

Menendez traveled to field offices all over the country constantly looking for ways to save money. Within two years, he was in charge of all U.S. operations.

Many coworkers disliked how Menendez would berate people and wear down their opposition. "When you walked into a meeting that he was running, there were no holds barred," recalled Kevin McDonald, a former colleague at Hertz. "You could go into a meeting and he'd keep you in there all day, and he'd just go on and on and on. You'd walk out of there—I mean you'd just say to yourself, 'My god, I never want to go through that again.'"

Carlos Baralt said his brother-in-law was "brutal" and "alarmingly lacking in compassion and respect for his colleagues and subordinates." He said Jose would ridicule his staff in a cold, sarcastic manner. If some-one said anything Jose didn't like, he'd "begin asking confrontational questions in a controlled tone of voice." If the person answered defensively, Jose would relentlessly mock him. One of his favorite phrases? "Well, then, you haven't really done your job, so what are we paying you for?"

"Jose had this remarkable ability to make people feel very, very small," said Baralt. "He considered himself superior to others."

PART THREE

"THE BOYS": ERIK AND LYLE

CHAPTER 11

A CLOSE-KNIT FAMILY?

A S THEIR FINANCES IMPROVED, JOSE AND KITTY STARTED A family. Jose was twenty-three years old when their first son, Joseph Lyle Menendez, was born on January 10, 1968, at Flatbush Hospital in Brooklyn. Almost four years later, Erik Galen Menendez was born on November 27, 1970, at St. Barnabas Hospital in Livingston, New Jersey, about forty miles from their home in Monsey, New York.

When Carlos and Terry Baralt moved to Princeton, Terry invited her sister-in-law to visit. After touring the area, Kitty Menendez proclaimed, "Terry—this is my town!" In 1977, Jose and Kitty rented a house near the Baralts and their four daughters. Two years later, they built a four-bedroom, split-level home that overlooked a man-made lake. Then, Marta Cano moved her three girls and two boys from Puerto Rico to Princeton.

"As young boys, Erik and Lyle were two earthquakes," said Marta. "Our kids were very disciplined, but when Jose's kids arrived the house trembled and things broke." The Baralts were concerned because Jose didn't believe in disciplining his sons. When Carlos brought up the boys' lack of manners, Jose replied it wasn't necessary to teach them how to behave: When they were old enough, they'd figure it out.

The Baralts and Menendezes spent many weekends cooking big meals and watching sports on TV. Lyle would hug his Aunt Terry and tell her that he loved being there because she had such a "happy family." For Erik and Lyle, it was a rare opportunity for them to play with other kids. Jose Menendez didn't want his sons to have close friends. He told relatives it would be "too distracting" for his boys.

Marta's husband, Peter Cano, bonded with Kitty, who confided to him that she had a drinking problem. Peter had seen her get drunk, vulgar, and lose control. He thought she didn't particularly care for her children.

One morning, he saw five-year-old Lyle race around the living room, unable to sit still. Jose shouted "Stop!" but Lyle didn't listen. Jose jumped up and grabbed Lyle, and then glared into the child's eyes and whispered in his ear. Suddenly pale and trembling, Lyle wet his pants. Then Jose punched him hard in the chest with a closed fist, knocking the wind out of him before rushing him down the hall to his room. Outraged, Peter followed close behind, screaming at his brother-in-law: "That's no way to raise a child!"

"If you don't like it, leave," Jose told him. "This is my house, and I'll raise my children any way I see fit!" The Canos immediately packed up their five children and left.

There were other troubling incidents. Once, at a local mall, five-year-old Lyle and two-year-old Erik ran wildly, knocking over store displays, and then disappeared. "Don't worry," Kitty told Marta Cano. "They'll be fine. They know what to do." Moments later, a voice on the public address system said, "Mrs. Menendez, come pick up your children at the security office."

"Oh, great!" Kitty told Marta. "We know where they are, so we can keep on shopping." Forty-five minutes later, she retrieved her sons.

Marta couldn't understand why Kitty didn't seem to show much affection for her sons. Little things would set her off. "She would suddenly get very violent and throw things and bang things and scream at the kids," said Marta. "She would pick them up by the arm just like Jose used to do and shake them and throw them and send them to their room. Frequently, she called them 'idiot,' 'stupid,' or 'clumsy' after becoming frustrated over seemingly inconsequential things."

One afternoon at an amusement park, six-year-old Erik was scared to go inside a tent full of tire tubes. His cousin Anamaria, who was the same age, happily jumped in, but Erik refused. Kitty was furious. "You're a coward! I don't see what you have to be afraid of!" Erik began crying uncontrollably and wouldn't budge.

At the end of the school year, seven-year-old Lyle brought home a rabbit from school. Two days later, Kitty told him, "Dad wants you to get rid of it or give it away." Lyle hoped his father would have a change of heart, and kept the bunny in an empty aquarium. He became upset when it was missing a few days later. "You were supposed to get rid of it," said Kitty. "Go talk to your dad." Jose told him to look in the garbage. Horrified, Lyle found the rabbit beaten to death and covered with flies.

Lyle would regularly bully Erik. Rather than stop him, Jose encouraged Erik to fight back or sneak up from behind and hit him. Jose knew that an angry Lyle would beat up his younger brother. Erik kept coming back for more even though he knew he'd be attacked. "Erik has to learn to fight back," replied Jose when Carlos Baralt complained. "He has to learn how to defend himself." Kitty would tell Lyle to stop it, but Jose would demand she leave the boys alone.

As they grew older, Jose let his sons be extremely disrespectful to Kitty. When the Baralts asked Jose why he didn't insist that the boys show more respect for their mother, his reply was nonchalant: It was good for the boys to know they were the "man of the house." Jose frequently humiliated Kitty in front of the brothers, sometimes sternly ordering her to "shut up."

Both Jose and Kitty were determined their sons would become star athletes like their dad. "I never saw parents like the Menendezes," said Meredith Geisler, the boys' swimming coach. While Erik was "hard-working and polite," on weekends his father would embarrass him by running alongside the pool shouting, "Harder! Harder!" every time he came up to breathe. Soccer coach Steve Mosner thought that the brothers were never able to do enough to please their father.

CHAPTER 12
GROWING UP MENENDEZ

W HEN ERIK AND LYLE WERE AGES NINE AND TWELVE, JOSE told them they had to choose between tennis and soccer because they couldn't excel at both. Jose's preference was tennis because it was an individual sport, and perhaps because it was considered more upper-class. As always, the boys followed Jose's choice; he mixed the traditional authority of a Latin parent with the drive of a modern corporate executive. Suddenly, tennis was not just a sport for them to play but part of a family destiny to fulfill, and private coaches were hired to transform their game. Jose built a court next to the house and even took lessons himself so he could help coach his sons, who decided they wanted to be tennis stars. Kitty was disturbed by her husband's preoccupation with the brothers, who always came first. Marta Cano tried to cheer her up.

"Oh, Kitty, don't feel bad. It's just that Jose is so obsessed with the boys, that's all he thinks about."

"I don't think so," Kitty replied. "Sometimes I feel like garbage."

Success was so important to the Menendezes that Kitty told a friend she was thinking of holding Erik back in school for a year because he wasn't at the top of his class. Later, Kitty's friend Faith Goldsmith mentioned that her daughter was a year behind Erik. "No, they're in the same class," Kitty insisted. "They've always been in the same class." And, as with other Menendez family secrets, Kitty didn't want to discuss it.

Jose wasn't extravagant, but Kitty and the boys spent freely. They could go through 500 tennis balls a month. When their ball-serving machine broke, they bought a new one. Kitty gave Lyle's old clothes to Marta's kids because she didn't want Erik to have hand-me-downs. Kitty thought it was easier to buy new clothes than do laundry.

On a typical day, Jose called home four or five times to check on the progress of a tennis lesson or the grade of a test at school. When the brothers played in a tournament, he insisted they phone him immediately with the results. At five in the morning he'd wake them so the three could hit tennis balls for several hours before leaving home. He conveyed a simple plan: You will become national tennis champions, you will attend an Ivy League school, and you will become a success in business, just like me.

The brothers' tennis coaches were mixed on just how overbearing Jose and Kitty were. Lawrence Tabak said that Jose would "quietly but forcefully signal his sons during matches, like a bidder at an art auction." Tennis rules forbid coaching during a match, but Jose would still pace the sidelines flashing subtle gestures. On close calls, both he and Kitty would appeal to officials. Lyle became known for on-court tantrums, and Erik had a reputation as a "bad actor" on the court.

Jose lectured Lyle that other kids weren't trained the same as he was. They didn't come "from the same bloodline," and they had a "disease of mediocrity" that was "contagious."

"It was very trance-like," Lyle testified. "I usually had my eyes closed . . . I was a weak person and I seemed to be tempted to hang out with other kids. And I needed to remind myself. So we worked on it."

Jose would have Lyle memorize and repeat lines from *The Greatest Salesman in the World*, a self-help book by Og Mandino.

Today I will be master of my emotions . . . From this moment I am prepared to control whatever personality awakes in me each day. I will master my moods through positive action and when I master my moods I will control my destiny.

Once when Lyle was playing a match with an injured ankle, Jose began ridiculing him. "What a baby. Look, he can't run. Oh, poor baby. Can't play tennis." Finally, losing control, Lyle shouted, "Why don't you just shut up?" Jose turned red, grabbed a tennis ball, and threw it hard at him. Then he ordered Lyle to get in the back of the waiting limousine. Inside, he took hold of Lyle by the neck and punched him in the face.

"Don't ever embarrass me like that again, or I'll kill you," Jose warned.

The boy was shocked and speechless as blood dripped from his chin onto his shirt.

"Is that perfectly clear?"

Lyle meekly nodded yes.

When the boys lost a match, Jose would stay quiet until they were away from other people; then he'd berate and humiliate them. When they won, he gave no congratulations or encouragement. He'd analyze their play and often took them right back onto the court for more practice. Nothing was ever quite good enough.

CHAPTER 13

HERTZ MAN

B Y JUNE 1980, JOSE MENENDEZ WAS IN CHARGE OF HERTZ'S rental car division and responsible for all North American and Latin American operations, with revenues exceeding $1 billion. Menendez was hoping to be named company president, but a man in his midthirties was considered too young for the job. RCA Records "borrowed" him to investigate its problematic Latin music division. After his recommendations improved business, Menendez was made RCA's vice president of finance.

At RCA Records, people called Jose the "Hertz man" and questioned his chops for the music business. "Menendez was not a nice man," said one executive. "He would scream and shout. He became extremely manipulative. He took maximum advantage of everyone around him."

Menendez liked meeting pop stars. Big names regularly came to his office: Barry Manilow, Kenny Rogers, John Denver, James Brown, the Jefferson Starship, and the Eurythmics.

"The industry was riddled with strange corruption," musician Dave Stewart told the BBC. "It was gangsterland." He and Eurythmics costar Annie Lennox had a strange encounter with Menendez in 1985 after finishing their fourth studio album, *Be Yourself Tonight*.

"I remember thinking, blimey, that's weird. What does he know about music?" said Stewart. "He shook my hand when I delivered the album and said, 'Stewart, I love it. It's just like *Ghostbusters*.'"

"What are you talking about?" Stewart replied. He said Menendez wanted to market the album as if it was a blockbuster film and part of his plan was "to put our picture on top of Coca-Cola vending machines."

RCA had previously farmed out its Spanish-language business through licensees in South America, Puerto Rico, and Spain. Menendez opened an RCA office in Miami. Within months, the label signed prominent Latin acts, including José Feliciano, Emmanuel, and high-energy salsa and merengue artists. One risky deal was Menendez's signing of the bubblegum pop group Menudo. The boy band's background was outlined in a fanzine titled *All About Menudo*:

> Menudo began as the dream of a man named Edgardo Díaz. Back in 1977, Edgardo had a dream of creating a new and exciting musical group that would capture the spirit of Puerto Rico's young people—a group that would stay young forever.
>
> Edgardo called the group Menudo. That's Spanish for "small change." Diaz set rules for Menudo when he first formed the group. Menudo members were to be chosen for their singing and dancing talent, not just because they were cute. Menudos had to be at least twelve years old and of course speak Spanish . . . And they had to leave the group when they turned sixteen or when their voices changed. Edgardo wanted to make sure that Menudo would always have a youthful image . . .

Menudo's initial success in Puerto Rico had exploded into record sales throughout South America. Within two years, group members, who received a modest weekly salary, made millions for Edgardo Díaz. Since its membership was fluid, any performer who caused problems or challenged Díaz's accounting practices easily could be replaced. When American record labels noticed this money-making machine, fierce competition developed to sign them. Jose Menendez won with a bid of $30 million. For a group that had never recorded a song in English, the deal was considered a ridiculous gamble.

Menendez took an obsessive personal interest in the group, which was unusual for the head of a record label. He spent weeks on tour with Menudo in Brazil and Italy. He hired a tutor to teach the group English. When they came to New York in 1984, Menudo's shows at

Radio City Music Hall quickly sold out. The group later returned and sold out Madison Square Garden. But Menudomania and sold-out concerts didn't translate to big record sales for RCA.

Music executives were in the office at 8 AM, but the creative people didn't show up until around 4 PM. It made for long days. When he went to concerts or dinners, Jose stayed overnight in an RCA suite at the Waldorf Astoria. Kitty accused him of having affairs. She left the house and checked into a motel.

Jose told Carlos Baralt that he wasn't having any affairs but admitted that he didn't love his wife. The only reason he was keeping the family together was because she was "running the house and his children the way he wanted." Baralt thought Erik's close relationship with his mother was one reason Kitty didn't file for divorce. Possibly even more important, from her point of view, was that if she left Jose, she would lose her social status—something she'd experienced when her own parents split up when she was three years old.

Menendez rose to RCA Records's executive vice president and chief operating officer with a $500,000 salary. He set his sights on the top job, but a year later, in 1985, General Electric bought RCA. Menendez didn't get the job but walked away with a golden parachute of one million dollars.

Over the next six months, Jose Menendez looked for a new position. He had two offers to run record companies, but he wanted to own a piece of whatever company he worked for. John Mason, a Beverly Hills entertainment attorney, contacted him about a new executive opening running the home video division of Carolco Pictures, in Los Angeles.

PART FOUR

CALIFORNIA DREAMING

CHAPTER 14
INCONVENIENT WOMEN

Throughout my life, I lived with a tormented mother who bared
her soul to me and I could always feel her hurt but was powerless
to help her except by a show of strength. I lived in a broken home
and knew of no other like mine. I swore this would never happen
to me.

—Letter from Kitty to Jose Menendez

To Kitty, the idea of moving was devastating. She'd built a world of friends, lunches, and charity work in Princeton. One evening, Jose suggested that she stay in New Jersey with Lyle, who was about to enroll at Princeton University. He'd go to California with Erik, who was still in high school, and commute on weekends. Kitty quickly said no. Menendez went back to Carolco Pictures, the owners of LIVE Entertainment, and asked for a "ridiculous amount" of money. When his offer was accepted, he was sorry he hadn't asked for more. Kitty and the boys dutifully moved with him to Los Angeles. Initially, the family leased a house in Calabasas, a tranquil Los Angeles suburb just north of Malibu. A few months later, they bought a beautiful 8,000-square-foot home on fourteen acres of woods in the same suburb to make Kitty feel better about being uprooted. Their real estate broker was cousin Henry Llanio.

Before they moved into their new home, Kitty began a project to remodel it. To create space for an entertainment area, she wanted to move the swimming pool a few feet. As the work dragged on, Jose joked with friends that they would never get to live in the house.

———————

Jose's first meeting with Megan, an attractive booking agent, had been a four-hour lunch at a cozy Italian restaurant in Hollywood three years earlier when they were both in the music business. They'd spend hours on the phone, with Jose soaking up everything he could about show business. Megan thought Jose was funny, extraordinary, and charming—someone she wanted to spend more time with.

Within a year, it was a romance.

A Nebraska-born blonde with a remainder of a Midwestern twang, Megan believed that neither of them planned the affair—it just happened. "I was always attracted to Jose. There's something that's very sexy about a man who's powerful, full of himself, and as charming as he was. He absolutely gave off this sexual thing." Since they attended the same business dinners and conventions, it was easy to arrange assignations. Jose could play committed husband and family man while he and Megan had secret holidays all over the world.

"Why do men look for anything outside their marriage? It's what they're not getting at home. He was exciting, and he wanted excitement. He didn't get excitement at home," Megan told me over dinner in the spring of 1990. When they met, she said, Jose was "sexually uptight." It was an accomplishment to get him to loosen up.

Megan assumed that Jose's marriage was over, that he'd outgrown the woman he married at age nineteen. He said that Kitty was devoted to their sons, and his only criticism was her indulgence of them.

Still, Lyle and Erik got in the way. Megan complained that Jose often shortened or canceled their intricately organized trysts because he had to go to one of the boys' tennis matches. When she met the brothers at a music business awards show, she thought that they were "arrogant little snots in their little tuxedos."

One night, Jose told Megan he had a second extramarital relationship with a woman named Charlotte, a corporate executive in her forties who lived in New York City. "In your girlish dreams, I suppose you want to think that you are something extraordinary, special, and singular. The relationship existed when I met him, however, and it was not my business to suggest that it end."

Jose spoke daily with his sister Marta, and one of their topics was divorce. Marta had left her husband, and she agreed with Jose that for the children it could be better to end a bad marriage than stay together in constant tension. But Maria Menendez insisted her son stay married because of Erik and Lyle.

Going through Jose's credit card bills, Kitty discovered her husband's eight-year-long affair with Charlotte and their "business trips" that he'd lied about. Cornered, Jose confessed and assured his wife that the affair was over. Despondent, Kitty began dropping in unannounced at his new office at LIVE to search his phone logs and Rolodex. Marzi Eisenberg created a system to deceive her.

Following the Menendezes' move to California, Megan ended her affair with Jose. "I didn't want to drive down Rodeo Drive and see my lover and his wife and their children," she said. She invited Jose to lunch and told him it was over. Jose became angry and didn't understand. But Megan had been smothering in the relationship. Jose would put everything in his life into boxes, she said. There was a box for her, a box for Kitty, a box for the boys, and a box for work. "He always wanted to control me like he controlled everyone else in his life. We had a big fight, and it was the last time we talked. I was in love with him, but I couldn't stand the control anymore."

Back in New Jersey, Kitty had told Marta, "Jose never gives me a minute." But in California, he started leaving the office at five and their marriage showed improvement. Nonetheless, Kitty's psychologist, Dr. Edwin Cox, feared that beneath her façade a lonely, depressed Kitty was suicidal. Kitty told Cox that it was "too painful to be alive," and she had no "support system" in Los Angeles. In therapy sessions from October 1986 to February 1987, Cox concluded that Kitty was dependent on prescription drugs and alcohol. She drank daily and was proud that her favorite, cognac, was a "high-class drink." Her depression made sleeping difficult and caused her to withdraw. Relatively routine situations triggered emotional outbursts.

As therapy continued, it was hard for Kitty to talk about anything other than Jose's affairs. She became so consumed with Charlotte that she hired a private detective to find her, and then flew to New York to stalk her. One morning, she stood for hours outside Charlotte's apartment building, waiting for her to leave. After snapping some pictures from a distance, she approached to get a closer look at the competition.

She told the therapist that divorce was out of the question. "I love my husband very much. I'm very angry, but why should I divorce him? I have no place to go." In a letter to Jose, Kitty wrote:

> For 24 years, I lived in a dream. I tried so hard to keep my marriage complete but didn't know how . . . I thought if I concentrated on the house and our boys—their grades and sports—that you would feel fulfilled . . . My fantasy about you and I and our family was my own destruction.
>
> I locked myself in a dream that began in my childhood . . . I married a man just like my father in disguise—the very man I tried to run away from.

Erik and Lyle became frightened by the dramatic changes in their parents' relationship and the transformation of their mother since the family had moved to California. The new assertive and sarcastic Kitty thought nothing of publicly embarrassing Jose. "She would attack him verbally, and he would just take it," recalled Lyle in his trial testimony. "He seemed very tense, and he just continually took it and tried to placate her." Lyle believed that his father decided to "do whatever it took to keep the marriage together." It seemed obvious Kitty knew that.

CHAPTER 15

TROUBLED SONS

At Calabasas High School, Erik Menendez was a star on the tennis team. While he was practicing on a court behind the school one afternoon, the spectators included some local gang members. One of them yelled out, "Nice body, faggot!" Erik answered, "Nice face, ugly!" He knew that wasn't smart, but he thought it was something his dad would've said.

"They started hitting my car and spit on my friend, Craig Cignarelli," he recalled. "I demanded they apologize, and somebody hit me. I hit back, and a fight started." It left Erik with a fractured nose and cheekbone, and bruises all over his body. "The police thought I was in a gang, but that's ridiculous. I was warned not to press charges, or the next time I would bleed."

Detective Imon Mills, who investigated the incident, reported that the same gang members had made death threats against another student. Erik wanted to file charges, but his father wouldn't allow it. Instead, Jose Menendez hired twenty-four-hour bodyguards to protect the family and even discussed sending one to school with Erik.

In the weeks after the incident, the Menendezes got several threatening phone calls. Erik struggled in class, and Jose hired Norman Puls to tutor him in math. Puls said Erik had trouble concentrating. "There were times when his attention span was nonexistent, times when he was spaced out. He would look at me and look right through me, and I would look at him and I'd realize there's nobody there behind the eyes. He was just not there."

During tennis lessons Erik had similar difficulty staying focused, realized his coach, Doug Doss. "Erik was a very hard worker on the court. He basically did everything he was asked to do. But there were times he would just disappear mentally. He just spaced out."

———————

Jose wanted Lyle to enroll at Princeton University, but his initial application was rejected. When the rest of the family moved to California in the summer of 1986, Lyle had stayed behind, living alone in the boathouse on the New Jersey estate. That fall he attended nearby Trenton State University. A year later, he was admitted to Princeton.

Jose imagined Lyle as a tennis star and a scholar. He made the tennis team as a starter but was ranked last. Teammates said he was often late for practice and rarely apologetic.

In his first semester at Princeton, Lyle racked up so many tickets in his red Alfa Romeo Spider convertible that his driver's license was suspended twice. To get around he hired a limousine. "He just wasn't cut out for the Ivy League," said one of his pals. "He really didn't have the desire to work hard. He would go to class, but there was no point."

Lyle was accused of plagiarizing a paper for his psychology class. He denied it to the Baralts, claiming it wasn't "that big a deal." The Baralts insisted he call his parents. Jose immediately rushed to Princeton.

Lyle was brought before the school's disciplinary committee for a hearing that lasted four hours. They ruled that Lyle could voluntarily leave Princeton for a year or be expelled. He chose to leave. Humiliated and heartbroken, Jose appealed his son's case, without success. Jose wasn't angry with Lyle. "Jose blamed the university for it," said Terry Baralt. "He was there to make sure he stayed at Princeton. I think the main issue of cheating was forgotten."

Both Jose and Kitty lied to friends about Lyle's suspension. Marta Cano found out when Erik called her son Andy. Terry and Carlos weren't comfortable about being drafted into the cover-up. They knew that Jose and Kitty had often done their sons' homework during high school and even college; Jose wrote some of Lyle's papers and sent them by overnight mail to the Baralts in New Jersey. "They didn't think there was anything wrong with that," Terry said.

Unbowed, Lyle came home to Los Angeles. He played tennis, delivered Domino's pizza for pocket change, and for a while worked at LIVE Entertainment. Jose told him, "If you don't study, you will work. You're going to learn the business." He put Lyle in the sell-through division of LIVE, assigned to find discrepancies in expense reports. Lyle worried that if he found anything wrong, people would be demoted or fired. The executive assigned to supervise the boss's son remembered that Lyle walked in with an attitude of "I don't want to be here, but I'm forced to, so here I am."

The first day, he stayed twenty minutes. People were uncomfortable that he never looked anyone in the eye. One called him an "iceberg," and another "nasty—I just felt uncomfortable around him, and I don't feel that way around many people." He arrived late, left early, and struck the staff as arrogant and groundlessly self-satisfied. The job, as it was, lasted a month. "I failed that job pretty miserably," Lyle admitted later. "I was basically getting in the way."

Both brothers fell in with crowds of privileged young men cut from the same synthetic cloth: glib within the vocabulary of Valley Speak; indifferent to the world around them; wary of any commitment or compassion; and perpetually, poisonously bored. All of the brothers' tennis companions were solid players but some came to matches stoned. One morning, Kitty found empty beer cans, poker chips, money, and marijuana roaches on the family property. She accused the construction workers but later discovered they were left by Erik and his pals.

Some of their friends burglarized homes—apparently for kicks. They called them "hot prowls." In the summer of 1988, Erik was implicated in two of them. The first burglary was in Hidden Hills, an upscale Calabasas neighborhood. While the List family vacationed in Europe from June to August, their teenage son was home alone. Neighbors told police they'd seen several parties as well as a parade of teenagers visiting the house, including the son's friends Erik Menendez and Craig Cignarelli. The homeowner told police that jewelry valued at $100,000 as well as $2,400 cash was missing from the family's bedroom safe. Nothing else in the room was disturbed.

The second house hit belonged to Michael Ginsberg, whose children were also friendly with Erik and Craig. The Ginsbergs had only been out for the evening. The burglars cut the screen of a rear window and entered the living room. They left with a hundred-pound safe from a closet in the den, jewelry from the master bedroom, china, silverware, and a computer.

Kitty found out about the burglaries when her friend Karen Weire told her that L.A. County Sheriff's deputies had interviewed her son, Steve. Then one afternoon police knocked on the Menendezes' door, looking for Lyle and Erik. Kitty couldn't understand why. "Erik was running around with a bad bunch of guys," said Weire. "They were spoiled rich kids. I didn't like a lot of my kids' friends."

An informant, who many believed was Craig Cignarelli, told detectives that some of the loot was seen in the trunk of Erik's car. Other teens questioned by detectives told their parents that Craig and Erik had accidentally found the combination to the Lists' safe and opened it. In a later statement to police, Cignarelli admitted that he'd been present when the safe was opened.

Then, Erik confessed. He was arrested, charged with burglary, and released to his father. Days later, September 16, 1988, a van arrived at the Malibu sheriff's station with most of the loot, which had been hidden in a storage locker. Inside the van were Jose Menendez and Gerald Chaleff, the Santa Monica criminal defense attorney who'd represented Angelo Buono Jr. in the high-profile Hillside Strangler murder case. In a statement to police, Erik admitted that he'd spent some of the money from the Hidden Hills burglary. As compensation for the value of the property that was never recovered, Jose wrote a check for $11,000.

Here's what Lyle later told me: The first burglary was carried out by the son of the Hidden Hills family along with Erik and Craig. Lyle didn't even know about it until Erik showed him some of the stolen money and jewels. Lyle claimed Erik and Craig had discussed committing other burglaries. Lyle talked his brother into returning the stolen property, but some of the loot was returned to the wrong house. Lyle admitted he was with Erik during the second burglary.

Chaleff made a deal with the district attorney's office: As a minor without prior arrests, Erik was put on probation and ordered to do community service for the homeless. The agreement had one more stipulation: Erik had to undergo counseling. Kitty's psychiatrist, Lester

Summerfield, recommended Dr. Jerome Oziel, a Beverly Hills psychologist who had a handful of celebrity patients. He was an odd choice; his primary practice was sexual therapy and phobias.

According to Lyle, Dr. Oziel was hired to provide an evaluation for the court. Erik signed a document allowing the therapist to reveal everything Erik told him to Jose and Kitty. "It wasn't like Erik was seeing him for therapy," said Lyle. "My dad wanted to bring this to court and put it all behind us. My dad would never risk putting Erik in therapy—that would never happen at all. Erik was well aware that Oziel was somebody hired by Dad to resolve this burglary issue—not to be discussing life issues or anything else." The entire family met with Oziel as part of the evaluation.

Lyle said morality hadn't been his father's reason for voluntarily surrendering Erik. Jose Menendez was used to not following the rules. "My father told me that he did not want anything to come up from this ten years from now," said Lyle. "He was worried this would be very bad for his reputation and his future plans to run for the U.S. Senate." The case was settled in chambers in juvenile court. No charges were filed against Lyle.

Dr. Oziel told Jose and Kitty that Erik's involvement was a bid for attention. Unfortunately, that attention had extended throughout Calabasas. Embarrassed if not disgraced, Jose Menendez decided to move the family again, this time to Beverly Hills.

CHAPTER 16
KITTY'S WORLD

BEFORE THE MENENDEZES MOVED FROM CALABASAS, KITTY was admitted to the intensive care unit of Westlake Community Hospital. The diagnosis was "acute Xanax and alcohol ingestion along with depression." Dr. Warden Emory noted:

> 43-year-old female has one year history of moderate depression and panic attacks . . . She is not self-harmful and there is no reason to keep her in the hospital. She is having breakthrough anxiety . . . Suspect personality disorder.

On the ER admittance form was a nurse's note that read: "Do not give patient her own medications—attempted to put more pills in mouth when I was not looking."

Emory was concerned that Kitty was trivializing her overdose, although at times she seemed frightened. He recommended that she spend several days in the hospital's psychiatric unit until she stabilized. Both Jose and Kitty insisted everything was all right. Kitty signed out against medical advice.

Over the next year, other doctors prescribed Kitty higher than average medication dosages, including Xanax three times daily and the antidepressant Tofranil. Kitty saw Dr. Emory twice a month, but he felt that she was secretive and unwilling to discuss her issues with him.

"What struck me about this person was that she seemed inordinately more distressed than many people I usually see with these diagnoses," he recounted in his notes. "It was my opinion that here was a woman who apparently had some kind of marital problem but was unable to extricate herself from it."

One afternoon, Kitty threatened to poison herself and the rest of the family. Lyle said there was "screaming and threatening and my dad saying that he didn't trust her." After that, Jose sometimes refused to eat at home and would take Erik and Lyle out to a restaurant for dinner. That infuriated Kitty. The brothers looked to their father for cues on when it was all right to eat the food at home.

Kitty began frequently shouting at Lyle in front of Jose. She called Lyle a "major problem in her life." Jose didn't respond, and Lyle didn't know why. After Erik found a suicide letter that Kitty wrote, Lyle told his mom she should leave Jose and come live with him in Princeton.

"I wanted her to know that it wasn't that I loved my dad more. That I loved her and my brother loved her," said Lyle. "And if she seemed like she wanted to stay in Princeton . . . we would side with her in a divorce and stay in Princeton. Because that seemed to be what was causing her to want to kill herself, was the divorce. And I wanted her to know that her family would be with her. I tried to let her know that we loved her, but she didn't ever acknowledge that."

Marta Cano was shocked one day when Kitty said "she wished her children had never been born." According to Kitty, ever since Erik and Lyle arrived, her relationship with Jose had been destroyed. She kept writing anguished letters to Jose:

> You are a brilliant, aggressive, soft-hearted man and I am truly in love with you even as I write this. Please find someone you can truly fall in love with and start again, build a new family. I know our boys will always be most special to you—they are special—my gift to you . . .

CHAPTER 17

FRIENDS

AFTER JOSE MENENDEZ BOUGHT THE SPANISH-STYLE MANSION at 722 North Elm Drive in the flats of Beverly Hills, the real estate agent phoned and declared, "Kitty, you've got your zip code."

Weeks later, an airline wouldn't let the Menendezes' dog Rudy on board for a Christmas vacation trip because they hadn't crated him properly. Jose volunteered to wait with the dog and take the next flight out. Kitty became enraged, and a major fight ensued. "Oh, so you can meet your girlfriend Charlotte in the bar?" she shouted. "I'm not that stupid," snapped Jose. When tempers cooled, Jose announced, "Okay, Kitty. We'll wait. We'll all wait for the next flight." And they did.

Kitty began to diet frequently, seeming to live on coffee and cigarettes. She had always wanted to be a size six or eight. In February 1987, Terry Baralt saw Kitty at Pepin's funeral and noticed that she had lost twenty pounds. A few months later, she had a facelift. It was supposed to be another Menendez family secret.

Erik enrolled at Beverly Hills High School for his senior year. He was on the tennis team and had a solid B average. In drama class he memorized and performed a soliloquy from Shakespeare's *Richard II*, impressing his teacher, who offered him placement in a special program. But Jose nixed that. Suddenly, Erik's drama grades plummeted, and then he began failing chemistry. Jose gave him a stern lecture, demanding improvement. Erik was upset that his father never listened to his problems. As usual, Kitty sided with Jose.

During an hour-long parent-teacher meeting with Erik's English literature teacher, Dr. Barbara Zussman, Jose Menendez did all of the talking. "I thought he was very condescending," she remembered. Erik's performance in Zussman's class lagged behind the quality of his homework.

Late in the second semester, she realized he had a reading problem. The class did a lot of sight reading while studying Shakespeare. Erik liked to take part because he enjoyed acting. After seeing him invent words with the right beginning sound in place of difficult words in the text, Zussman realized, as had his previous teachers, that Erik had dyslexia.

At another conference alone with Kitty, Zussman asked about Erik's reading disability. Kitty didn't deny it. "Oh, yes, we know that. We had him tested when he was younger, and we were told that Erik was dyslexic."

"I wish you had said something when enrolling Erik in the school," said Zussman. "We might have been able to help him. If it isn't handled early, by the twelfth grade, there's not much a school can do."

One of Erik's few escapes from the pressure at home was his relationship with Kirstin Smith, a tall, slim, blonde tennis player. They met the previous year at Calabasas High after Kitty had delivered an odd ultimatum: Erik had to find a girlfriend within six months. Erik wrote her affectionate love letters and lavished her with gifts. Their first kiss was awkward, "sort of a hit or miss thing," she said. Their relationship cooled off after he moved to Beverly Hills.

A closer friend of Erik's was Craig Cignarelli, whose father was an executive at MGM Television. One night, Erik took Cignarelli and another friend for an evening drive in his father's Mercedes-Benz 560SL. Jose called on the car phone and ordered Erik home immediately. When they pulled in the courtyard, Jose stormed out of the house and shouted at Cignarelli, "If I ever see you on my property again, I'll fucking kill you." Erik jumped in front of Craig's car and shouted, "You're not leaving!" Later, the friend claimed he'd seen Jose holding a gun.

Jose was angry at Cignarelli because he thought the young man had been the police informant against Erik during the Calabasas burglary investigation. Erik insisted it was Craig who'd found the combination to the Lists' home safe, but Craig was never charged.

During several days at a cabin in Central California owned by Cignarelli's family, Erik and Craig had written a screenplay about committing the perfect burglary. Police thought that the second Calabasas burglary might have been an attempt to live that out. The pair also wrote two more screenplays. In the opening of their third and most ambitious script, titled *Friends*, a character named Hamilton Cromwell finds his parents' will and realizes he's in line to inherit $157 million. Young Hamilton "smiles sadistically," and in the next scene the script reads:

A gloved hand is seen gripping the doorknob and turning it gently. The door opens, exposing the luxurious suite of Mr. and Mrs. Cromwell lying in bed. Their faces are of questioning horror as Hamilton closes the door behind him gently saying . . . "Good evening Mother. Good evening Father." (His voice is of attempted compassion, but the hatred overwhelms it.) All light is extinguished, and the camera slides down the stairs as screams are heard behind.

After murdering his parents, Hamilton kills three other people before getting arrested.

The five murder victims are found frozen in a basement vault before Hamilton's friend shoots and kills him. "The evil genius dies smiling." Later in court, Hamilton's voice is heard in a tape-recorded message: "You must understand, that the price a player pays for failure in the game of life is death."

Kitty helped type the script, and Erik fantasized about impressing his father and getting a lucrative screenplay deal. According to a family friend, Kitty "picked the script apart and laughed over it." Nothing suggested that she sensed its significance or that Jose ever read it, let alone pondered an anguishing passage in which young Hamilton says of his father:

Sometimes he would tell me that I was not worthy to be his son. When he did that, it would make me strive harder . . . just so I could hear the words "I love you son." . . . And I never heard those words.

CHAPTER 18

PRINCETON

I N 1986, LYLE MET A PRETTY BLONDE TENNIS PLAYER FROM Pittsburgh while playing in a tournament in Alabama. Jamie Lee Pisarcik was five years older and trying to make it as a pro. Her maturity and independence were a change from the sweet high school girls he'd dated in Princeton. Jose and Kitty weren't sure if they approved of this older woman. They were concerned that she controlled him, but her nurturing was appealing. A few months later, Lyle surprised her with a diamond ring and the couple announced their engagement, much to the chagrin of Jose and Kitty.

After Lyle returned to college in 1989 following his suspension, Jamie got a job as a cocktail waitress at the local TGI Fridays, where she met twenty-two-year-old Donovan Goodreau, an exuberant, elaborately mannered young man who was also newly hired. Pisarcik helped him as he struggled to learn the Fridays system. Goodreau had left Los Gatos, California, where he'd been a student at nearby San Jose State University. His original destination was New York City, where he had cousins. Donovan told Jamie that he moved to New Jersey after he was accepted at Princeton University. It wasn't true.

When he arrived in New Jersey, Goodreau was broke. It was winter, and he slept in his 1964 International truck camper shell. The nights were so cold, his water bottle froze. Jamie suggested that he might be able to stay on her boyfriend's couch until he found an apartment. He had to meet Lyle, she told Goodreau, because he reminded her so much of him. She predicted that the two would be best friends.

Donovan was guarded. "Whenever someone says that to you, you're defensive," he said. "I thought I would hate this guy." On their first night together, the three had dinner and Goodreau repeated his lie about planning to enroll at Princeton. Lyle asked him about his family background and plans for the future.

The conversation moved to their hard-driving fathers and the pressure they imposed on their sons. The two young men quickly became close. Meanwhile, in March 1989, Donovan and Jamie decided to share an apartment, but there were problems from the beginning. One morning, she found a woman's driver's license that Donovan had brought home from work. After discovering a pile of unpaid parking tickets, she began calling her new roommate "the criminal."

Little things started disappearing from their apartment, she said. Then Donovan began stalling on paying his share of the bills. The final straw came when money she'd hidden in a shoebox disappeared. Jamie told friends that Donovan confessed he'd stolen the cash. But Donovan insisted Lyle took it. The young men were constantly broke and needed money for golfing and gas.

When she broke up with Lyle at the end of April 1989, Jamie blamed Donovan. Lyle felt sorry for his once again homeless friend and invited him to move into his dorm room suite with his three other roommates. Within a week, an expensive green leather jacket, a gift to Lyle from Jamie, had disappeared.

Late one evening in May 1989, four months before the killing of Jose and Kitty, Lyle and Donovan had a candid conversation at a Chinese restaurant near Palmer Square. "You're my best friend. I know everything about you, and I love you," Lyle told his confidant. "From now on, we're family. My two greatest concerns are my mother and my brother. I try to help them as much as I can."

Lyle made Donovan pledge that if anything ever happened to him, he would help Erik. In return, if anything happened to Donovan, Lyle promised to look after his friend's mother and brother. "I always want us to be together," Lyle said. "Is there anything I don't know about you?"

Donovan believed he was being tested. With hesitation, he admitted that as a child, while spending the weekend at the home of a family friend, he'd been molested. "I remember the pictures on the wall, the color of the carpet, what time it was, everything," he said. He'd never told anyone before. Donovan cried as he described the memory. Then Lyle shared a secret of his own.

"He told me his father had been sexually abusing both Erik and him since they were little," Goodreau said. "Erik was the most affected because he was younger. He said Jose would take baths with them, and that they were both scared because the new house [under renovation] in Calabasas had a huge bathtub, which was supposed to be for sex scenes." Lyle told Donovan that he didn't like his father's dream house at all.

CHAPTER 19
EXPOSED SECRETS

IN LATE SPRING 1989, DONOVAN GOODREAU'S LIFE AT PRINCETON unraveled. From reading papers that Donovan had helped Lyle write, their roommate Glenn Stevens saw that Donovan had problems with spelling and grammar. "There's no way he's getting into Princeton," thought Stevens. Then, Stevens saw a T. S. Eliot poem on a plaque and recognized lines that Donovan had put his own name on. After a neighbor couldn't find money he'd hidden in his room, Stevens warned everyone on the hall that Donovan was a "con artist" who was going to rip them off and disappear.

The next afternoon, Lyle confronted Donovan: "I don't want to come home and find my computer missing." Donovan was shocked. Later, Jose Menendez called Lyle, furious and shouting. "This kid lied to me about being enrolled at Princeton. You move that fucking kid's stuff out of your room."

"Maybe he has an explanation," said Lyle. "I'll talk to him."

"I'll fly out there and move the shit out myself," screamed Jose. Lyle promised he'd handle everything.

The next morning, while Donovan was asleep, Lyle, Glenn, and Hayden Rogers, another of their suitemates, packed everything Donovan had into milk crates. There wasn't much. Then, all of them burst into his room. "You're outta here! We want you out right now!" yelled Glenn. Off to the side, Lyle began to cry softly.

As Lyle went to get Donovan's truck, the ousted roommate sat with Glenn and Hayden. "You hurt my friend. He really liked you," said an emotional Glenn. Donovan was choked up himself. "I really care about him," he said. The truck was backed up to the dorm window and loaded. Inside, Lyle asked Donovan if he'd been honest about his feelings. Lyle wanted to know if their friendship was genuine. As Donovan drove off, he looked in the rearview mirror and saw Lyle crying. His head was down, and his hands were stuffed in his pockets. He looked crushed.

"It was the last time I saw him," Donovan said. "It was a huge emotional thing. I had a great friendship with all of them, under false pretense, but yet still a great friendship."

"Donovan's leaving broke my heart," Lyle recalled later. "He wanted to explain everything, but Glenn Stevens was rushing us and wouldn't give him a chance to talk."

Goodreau left in such a hurry that he forgot his wallet, which he'd kept on Lyle's desk. He realized it when he stopped at a gas station on the way to New York. "There wasn't any money in it, just ID cards, but I was worried about being pulled over because of my weird truck. I ended up with a sweater of his. They had packed me because they wanted to go through my stuff and make sure I didn't steal anything."

Later, Lyle showed the wallet to his friends. To learn more about their mysterious ex-roommate, Lyle and Glenn went through it. Inside were pictures, a Wells Fargo bank ATM card, and a California driver's license issued to Donovan Jay Goodreau.

In New York, Goodreau got a job as a bicycle messenger before being hired to manage Boxers, a neighborhood bar in the West Village. He didn't replace his lost driver's license but got a New York State identification card. He tried to reach Lyle in Beverly Hills but always got an answering machine and never a call back. Donovan fantasized that Lyle and the gang from Princeton would find him and come walking into the restaurant.

Donovan told me that shortly before their falling out, Lyle startled him late one evening by saying that he was extremely upset about something. "My dad had an affair that really hurt my mom. She's becoming a basket case."

When Lyle said that he could kill his father for what he was doing, Donovan didn't take the remark literally. "People say that all the time."

CHAPTER 20
CHOICES AND FEARS

SIX WEEKS BEFORE SHE DIED KITTY MENENDEZ TOLD HER psychiatrist, Lester Summerfield, she was hiding "sick and embarrassing secrets about her family." She was concerned that her sons might be sociopaths. Kitty had been acting erratically for a while. In the first week of August, a former Princeton neighbor of the family, Alicia Hercz, visited California and had an odd encounter with her. She wanted Kitty to join her family for dinner. Kitty wasn't sure she could make it but said she wanted to see Hercz and asked her to stop by the mansion for a drink.

A half-hour later, Hercz knocked on the front door but no one answered. Fifteen minutes later, Kitty finally appeared. She invited Hercz and her son to come in, but three of Hercz's friends stayed in the car. On this bright, sunny afternoon, the house was closed up and dark. Kitty's behavior was disturbing. She stared blankly at Hercz. "I have to call Lyle because now you're living close to Lyle," she said. She approached the phone several times but didn't make a call. She complained about his "gold-digger girlfriend," and said she wished that Jose had "taught Lyle the facts of life better."

She couldn't go out for dinner, she said, because she was frying fish. She also said she was going to visit relatives in "Quito, Peru." Everything in her conversation seemed disjointed. As they were leaving, Hercz and her son had to hold Kitty's waist to help her walk.

Kitty had a lot of travel booked, but no one in the family knew of any plans that included South America. She was planning to go to

Princeton on September 9 to help Lyle move into the new two-bedroom condo that Jose had bought for him. One of the bedrooms was to be for Jose and Kitty when they visited. Kitty wanted Terry Baralt to have a spare key so she could spy on Lyle and see if Jamie Pisarcik was staying with him. "You're putting me in a very difficult position," Terry told her sister-in-law. But it was hard to say no to Kitty, who was supposed to be back in California by September 24 to help Erik get started at UCLA.

On August 9, the family was supposed to go to Canada after Erik played in a tournament in Kalamazoo, Michigan. They were going to see Kitty's father, who was dying of cancer. But after Erik lost, Jose became angry and told Kitty she could go alone. He and Erik were going home. Kitty accused him of rushing back to be with a girlfriend. She refused to go anywhere without him. The trip to visit her father was canceled, and all three flew home together.

––––––––––––

From here on, there are no other living witnesses except the brothers— this narrative of the days leading up to August 20, 1989, is based on their testimony and interviews with Lyle and Erik Menendez.

On the evening of Tuesday, August 15, at home in the den, Kitty and Lyle had an argument. Kitty suddenly exploded, screaming and flailing at him with clenched fists.

"Your tennis is going to cause my dad's death!"

Lyle raised his arms to defend himself.

Then his mother ripped the hair off the top of his head.

It was his toupee, and it came off like a savage scalping. To be fitted for the hairpiece, the crown of Lyle's head was shaved, and then the wig was attached with high-strength glue. Removing it, carefully, took a special solvent. When Kitty tore it off, Lyle felt intense pain. While he cried, she raged on about the $1,500 it had cost. He thought she would take it away permanently, but instead, she threw it at him.

"You don't need your fucking hairpiece!" she shouted.

He'd had it for two years. Jose had told Lyle that his future was in politics, and to be successful, he'd need a thick head of hair. By high school, he was already starting to thin on top. Before he met the important new contacts he'd make at an Ivy League school, Jose had insisted he get a full hairpiece.

Then, to his even greater horror, Lyle turned around and saw Erik at the door. His shocked brother had seen everything.

"Erik didn't know I wore a piece. There were so many things we didn't talk about," Lyle said, later. Erik was trembling and said he needed to speak with his brother. But Lyle ran out to the guesthouse and reattached his hair. When he came out of the bathroom, Erik was sitting in a corner of Lyle's bedroom, whimpering. Something else was bothering him.

Erik had been anxious for his freshman year at UCLA to begin so he could live on campus in a dorm and be on his own. That was the dream that had kept him going, that someday he'd leave for college and escape the nightmare his life had become.

But two days earlier, Jose announced he'd changed his mind: Erik would sleep at home three or four nights a week so Jose and Kitty could supervise his schoolwork. Erik was devastated.

"I'm sad we're not a family," Erik told his brother. "I never knew about your hair. We have so many secrets." He began to shake and sob.

"Those things with Dad are still going on."

"What things?"

"You know what things."

It was Lyle's turn to be stunned. Erik confessed their father was sexually molesting him.

"How come you didn't tell me before?" Lyle demanded. "Do you like it? Why didn't you fight back?"

Erik began to wail. He hated it. He'd been forced to do everything.

His brother's crying was unbearable, and Lyle believed him. As they sat in the sunny guesthouse on a bright yellow and green couch, Lyle blamed himself. When they were ages ten and thirteen, Lyle had been suspicious that their father was molesting Erik. He had confronted Jose, who assured him it was over. Why hadn't he followed up? thought Lyle. Somehow, he had to help his brother. Erik was despondent. Lyle worried that Erik might kill himself, so he decided he would confront his father again.

"We're holding all the cards," he told his brother. "We can threaten to tell people."

Lyle came up with a simple solution, a deal: Jose would let Erik move with him to Princeton. They simply wanted the sex with Erik to end, he'd explain. There'd be no need for retaliation. Clearly his father would realize that he had no choice.

That night, on the king-size bed on the second floor of the guest-house, Erik and Lyle lay next to each other. Erik slept but Lyle couldn't. He wondered how the molestation could have continued for so long.

Jose had done the same things to Lyle when he was age six, although the behavior had tapered off within a couple of years. He'd dismissed his own experience as something that happens to little boys. Jose was so loving when he explained that this was how fathers and sons bonded, and that Roman and Greek soldiers had done the same before battle. Later the family rules had always been strict: No one ever went near Erik's bedroom when Dad was in there with him. Now Lyle continued to ponder why his younger brother had never fought back. As dawn broke over the tennis court, Lyle decided that after he had a serious talk with his dad, who was due back Thursday night, the world was going to be different.

———————

The next day, Wednesday, August 16, the brothers had lunch at the Olive Garden in Westwood near UCLA. Lyle assured Erik that everything would work out with their dad. He urged him to keep up his spirits. Previously, Jose wouldn't let Erik apply to Princeton. Now, their plan was to be together at the same school. Erik would be free.

In the early evening, Lyle decided to rehearse his talk with his mother and try to enlist her support. In spite of her recent tantrums, it seemed that now she was wielding the power in the family. In the past weeks, Jose had been willing to do anything to avoid upsetting her. Maybe she'd help convince him to let Erik go. Lyle was sure she'd be thrilled to get rid of both of them.

As he and his mother spoke in the sparsely furnished master bed-room, Lyle began by saying that there were going to be some changes. He wanted to be independent and handle his own problems. Erik would be coming with him to Princeton, he told Kitty. If school wasn't an option, the brothers might move to Europe.

"Dad is doing things to Erik again," he blurted.

"What kinds of things?" Kitty demanded.

"Sexual things."

Once again, Kitty became angry and immediately ordered Lyle out of the bedroom. Back in the guesthouse, he told Erik that his talk with Mom hadn't gone well. He didn't tell Erik that he'd disclosed his secret.

That same evening in Manhattan, Jose's dinner appointment canceled. He called his mother in northern New Jersey and hired a limo to drive him so he could spend the evening with her. It would be the last time they saw each other.

───────────

The next day, Thursday, August 17, Lyle spent anxious hours awaiting his father's return. He scrawled notes and read aloud to himself, carefully deciding what he wanted to say. The shorter, the better, he thought. He edited his speech over and over again. Late in the afternoon, Kitty told him that Jose's flight was delayed. Lyle didn't believe her; he thought she wanted to talk with Jose first. Over the next few hours, his anxiety soared even higher. When Erik called from Westwood, Lyle told him about the delayed flight. Erik didn't want to be home when his brother confronted their father.

Finally, just after 11 PM, Jose Menendez arrived like a hurricane, as usual, dropping his travel bags in the marble foyer. Lyle immediately approached him. "I need to talk to you," he said.

Jose told Lyle to wait in the wood-paneled library, where they always had their serious talks. Jose said he wanted to change clothes, and then disappeared upstairs with Kitty.

Lyle took a seat. He didn't want to take out his script, for fear of his father seeing it. When Jose entered, he sat down facing his son. He lit a cigarette. Lyle expected his father to speak first, as he always did, but Jose didn't say anything. For Lyle, the beat of silence was unnerving.

His heart pounding, he started by blurting, "I know everything going on with Erik. We'll leave the house if you want, but this all must stop!" As he continued, he tried to carefully choose his words.

Jose played with his right ear. "Are you finished?" he asked quietly. He uncrossed his legs, leaned forward and put out his cigarette. Then he shouted: "You listen to me! What I do with my son is none of your business!"

Lyle knew he'd failed.

"Don't throw your life away," Jose told him. "You're going back to Princeton, and your brother is going to UCLA. We're going to forget we ever had this conversation."

Lyle screamed back something he immediately regretted. "You're a fucking sick person! I'll tell everybody about you, including the family and the police!"

He thought his father was going to hit him. But instead, Jose was once again calm. He sat back and spoke quietly:

"We all make choices in life, son. Erik made his. You've made yours."

"I'll only tell if it doesn't stop," Lyle replied, nervously.

"You'll tell anyway," said Jose.

Lyle's mind raced: Now, he believed, he and Erik were in serious danger. His father would have no choice but to act. His sons were going to ruin him. To stop them, Lyle expected that his mother would go along with whatever Jose said was necessary. Their public image was their entire life.

Lyle went back to the guesthouse. Erik quietly walked in the front door, went upstairs to his room, and locked the door. Minutes later, he heard footsteps coming down the hall. He hoped it was Lyle.

It was his father. "Open the goddamn door!" Jose screamed.

Erik was scared, realizing that Lyle must have confronted their father. After a moment, he unlocked the door and retreated to a far corner of the room.

In a low voice Jose said, "I warned you never to say anything to Lyle. Now, he'll go tell everyone. I'm not going to let that happen!"

Erik had never seen his father so furious. He was like a bull about to charge.

And then he did, violently throwing Erik onto the bed. Erik scrambled away. In the scuffle, a typewriter was knocked to the floor. Erik ran from the room. Curiously, to Erik, his father didn't follow.

Downstairs, Erik burst into the family room, where Kitty was watching TV.

"What's the matter with you?"

"You wouldn't understand," Erik said.

There was a smirk on her face. She seemed heavily medicated, and her voice had an off quality.

"I understand a lot more than you think," she said, sarcastically.

Erik was stunned.

"I know . . . I've always known. What do you think, I'm stupid?"

A wave of revulsion washed over him.

"I hate you!" he told his mother.

Crying, he ran out the back door. Kitty chased after him. At the guesthouse, he screamed to Lyle, "Mom knows! Mom knows!"

Kitty rushed in right behind him. "Nobody ever helped me!" she said.

"How could you have known and never done anything to help Erik?" Lyle asked her.

"You bastards!" she said. As quickly as she'd come, she spun around and left.

Erik was hysterical.

They should leave home right now, Lyle urged. No, that was crazy, Erik said. Their father would track them down and kill them. Where would they hide?

Sitting in the guesthouse, they considered their options. Earlier that year, their mother had purchased two rifles; Erik suggested they take the guns and buy ammunition. Lyle didn't like that plan; Jose and Kitty might realize the rifles were missing. Also, the brothers were concerned that their parents might have handguns.

Erik came up with another idea. They could tell everything to the rest of the family, beginning with Aunt Terry, with whom Lyle was close. She was the only one who'd ever stood up to Jose. But after some thought, they decided that wouldn't work. While Lyle was at Princeton, he was sure their aunt had reported his actions to his parents. They considered going to the police, but if they did that, the brothers thought, they'd be killed for sure.

They decided to buy handguns for protection.

At a sporting goods store in West Los Angeles, just west of the San Diego Freeway, they were told that the state had a two-week waiting period for handgun sales. As they drove south on Interstate 405, Erik divulged more details. Lyle got sick to his stomach. He hadn't imagined his father was capable of the level of sexual violence his brother described. "It was very different from what happened to me," Lyle said, later. "These were forceful, sick things." Erik explained that he'd never spoken up before because Jose had threatened to kill him if he told anyone.

At a small store north of San Diego, an elderly salesman showed them various shotguns. When they said that they were ready to buy, he asked for a California driver's license, which posed an awkward dilemma. Lyle's license had been suspended three months earlier; Erik didn't have his license with him. They drove on.

In San Diego, just after 8 PM on a busy Friday night, a young man at the counter in a Big 5 Sporting Goods store said he wanted to buy two shotguns. He knew which ones: 12-gauge Mossbergs, which hold six rounds. One was mounted on the wall behind the counter. Assistant Manager Amanda Adams brought it down and showed him how to load the shells.

As identification, the customer presented a California driver's license. The price for each gun was $213.99, paid in cash. Across the store, a second young man bought a box of birdshot shells from a display of ammunition stacked in a pyramid.

As the shotgun buyer left, he noticed video surveillance cameras at both ends of the long counter. He didn't know it then, but they were dummy cameras to scare off shoplifters.

The federal form No. 4473 required for any gun purchase listed the Mossbergs' buyer as Donovan Goodreau. The address on the license was 10646 Rosewood, Apartment A, Cupertino, California. The buyer told the clerk that he'd moved recently, and on the form he gave a local address: 63 August Street in San Diego. In the license photo, Goodreau had a thin moustache. To cash a check, Big 5 needed two forms of identification, but only one was required to buy a gun.

In New York at Boxers restaurant at 6:07 Eastern time that evening—about five hours before the gun purchase across the country—Donovan Goodreau logged in on the basement time clock. One of the hosts had called in sick, so Donovan was stuck with the additional duty of seating people.

CHAPTER 21

KILL OR BE KILLED

D URING THE RIDE BACK FROM SAN DIEGO, ERIK AND LYLE practiced loading their guns. When they got home they didn't see Jose, but Kitty told them that the family fishing trip scheduled for noon Saturday would be later in the day. Jose had told a business associate that he was an experienced deep-sea fisherman, so before going shark fishing with an important client, he needed to learn the basics.

Erik and Lyle thought: We're going fishing? In the middle of a grave family crisis? What did it mean? In their spiraling paranoia, they decided that the change in time indicated the fishing trip might be part of a plot to kill them. What the brothers didn't know was that the charter boat captain had told Jose that evenings were better for shark fishing.

Erik and Lyle decided they should leave the house early Saturday and get home late. Jose and Kitty would be gone fishing. Both boys hid their loaded guns under their beds. That night, Lyle felt less and less in control. He worried that Erik might do something impulsive. Maybe, thought Lyle, Jose was wavering on any plan to kill them?

The brothers woke up early Saturday, hid their guns in a closet, and left before Jose and Kitty came out of their bedroom. Then, they drove to a gun store in Van Nuys, fifteen miles away. Lyle told a salesman they'd bought pump shotguns for protection and wanted to make sure that their birdshot ammunition would work. The man suggested buckshot instead.

Saturday afternoon, Karen Weire called Kitty from Santa Barbara to cancel their Sunday evening bridge date. "Even if you get in late, call me from the valley and see if it's not too late," said Kitty, disappointed. She'd probably be too tired then was Weire's reply.

After leaving the gun shop, Erik and Lyle's plan was to drive around all afternoon. Jose and Kitty said they were going to leave at 3 PM, so the boys stayed away until 4 PM, but when they got home their parents hadn't left yet. Now they were trapped. Lyle thought he and Erik might be safer if they took their own car, but Jose decided they'd all drive together.

Dockside in Marina del Rey, Captain Bob Anderson explained the basics of shark fishing and gave the Menendezes a tour of the boat, named *Motion Picture Marine*. Also on board were Anderson's girlfriend, Leslie Gaskill, and a deckhand, Richard Campbell. The cabin cruiser wasn't the kind of boat their father typically would rent, the brothers thought—it was too small.

As they motored onto the water, Kitty became seasick and disappeared below to the cabin. Jose stayed near the stern, and Lyle and Erik went to the bow, as far away as they could get from him. Anderson thought the whole family seemed "snooty."

The seas were choppy, and the boat constantly bobbed. It was breezy and chilly. The boys were wearing shorts and T-shirts. Erik and Lyle huddled together for the whole trip; they thought if anything happened, they could jump off. Then a wave soaked them, leaving them shivering. Anderson didn't understand why they stayed up front.

The only time Jose and the boys gathered together was when they started fishing on a reef near a sunken ship just south of Redondo Beach. Erik and Jose each caught a small brown shark. On the way back, Jose vomited over the side of the boat. When they docked, just before midnight, the Menendezes were exhausted and glad to be on land.

Back at home, Jose and Kitty said goodnight before locking their bedroom door. Relieved but still apprehensive, the brothers drove to the UCLA campus and anxiously talked. When they came home, all the doors were locked. Normally, everything was left open, so the brothers were sure that they'd been locked out on purpose. They rang the doorbell. When Kitty came downstairs, she yelled at them for waking her up.

Lyle was sarcastic. "If you trusted us to have a key, we wouldn't have to bother you."

Kitty went nuclear. "I hate you! You're nothing but a problem! I wish you'd never been born!"

Lyle was stunned. Erik tried to defend him.

She turned to Erik and glared. "If you had kept your mouth shut, things might have worked out in this family."

Upstairs, a little later, Erik heard footsteps coming down the hall. Jose pounded on the door. "Open up!"

Terrified, Erik retrieved his loaded shotgun and pointed it at the door.

"You'll have to come out in the morning, and I'll be there!" Jose promised before stomping away.

Cradling his shotgun, Erik trembled the rest of the night.

Early the next morning, Sunday, August 20, 1989, the brothers decided they should stay apart all day. If their parents were plotting to kill them, it would probably happen when they were together. Erik drove to the Church of the Good Shepherd, a few blocks away on Santa Monica Boulevard, but when he arrived he couldn't go inside: He was afraid that God would tell him he had to endure more suffering. Instead he drove aimlessly around Beverly Hills and Westwood, his anxiety compounding as the day went on.

Lyle called Perry Berman to make plans for that evening. If they were with friends, he thought, his parents would have less of a chance to strike. Berman didn't pick up, so Lyle left a message on his answering machine.

In the midafternoon, Lyle walked into the family room to check his parents' mood. Jose and Kitty were watching a tennis match on TV. He tried to make conversation, but they ignored him. Jittery, he retreated to the kitchen. On a second try, he asked about a tennis camp his father had wanted him to attend.

"It doesn't matter anymore," sighed Jose.

Outside, Lyle sat near the pool. He felt like a ghost.

Perry called back, but Jose told him that both brothers were out shopping. Lyle hadn't gone anywhere. When Perry told him about the call later in the day, Lyle decided, that was it. Something was going to happen that night. Now he was sure of it.

Erik got home around 9:30 PM, and Lyle told him about the nonconversation, about the tennis camp, and the lie to Perry Berman. The brothers panicked. They had to leave the house right away, but Kitty stopped them by the front door. Lyle said they were going to the movies. She was tense and cold. No, they couldn't leave.

"I'm meeting someone, and we're leaving," Lyle said. Kitty stammered, without a reply.

Then, suddenly, Jose was at the entrance to the family room. No one was leaving. He told Erik to go upstairs to his bedroom and wait for him. It was a code that Erik knew well.

Lyle screamed, "You're not going to touch Erik anymore!"

"You've ruined the family!" Kitty shrieked.

Jose grabbed his wife's arm, took her into the family room, and closed the doors.

Lyle's mind raced. Erik was already at the top of the stairs. Lyle caught up to him and shook him hard by the shoulders.

"It's happening now!" he said.

Erik was terrified, certain the closing of the doors to the family room was a signal the brothers were about to die. Lyle told him they had to get their guns immediately.

As he ran to the guesthouse, Lyle felt like his life was slipping away.

———

The brothers met at Erik's Ford Escort parked on the street and loaded the shotguns with the buckshot they'd bought the day before. Then they sprinted back inside the main house and burst through the family room doors. Erik entered first and began firing. Lyle was close behind.

Jose jumped up and shouted, "No! No! No!"

A shot blew away his left thigh. He fell back onto the couch.

They kept firing. All over the room, glass and wood shattered. The noise they were creating was deafening. Swirling smoke blurred their vision. The only light was from the TV. Lyle thought he saw movement by the side of the coffee table. It was Kitty, on all fours.

Lyle had emptied his gun. He panicked. He had more shells in his pocket, but he ran out to the Ford Escort. Erik, already outside, handed him a single birdshot shell. Lyle reloaded and ran back inside.

Reaching over the coffee table, his gun muzzle brushed his mother's cheek. He fired.

It was over.

CHAPTER 22

WHAT HAVE WE DONE?

AFTER THE LAST SHOT, LYLE DROPPED HIS GUN AND RAN INTO the foyer. Erik was on the floor, crying and shaking.

Why weren't the police there yet? Surely, somebody heard the noise and phoned 911.

"When the police come, don't tell them anything about what happened with Dad," Lyle told Erik. They had to protect the family image. It was what their parents would have wanted.

But nobody came.

Lyle decided they should leave. But first, they had to pick up all the shotgun shells; he knew that from the plenty of movie murder mysteries he'd seen. Back in the family room, they turned on the lights and tried not to look at their dead parents. They stuffed the stray shells into their pockets, picked up their guns, and ran out to Erik's car. Lyle drove.

"What are we going to say?" Erik asked.

Lyle had an answer: "We'll say we were at the movies together." They should buy tickets because the police would probably ask for the stubs.

They also had to get rid of the shotguns.

At 10:30 PM, they arrived at the AMC theaters in the Century City Shopping Center, a short distance west of Beverly Hills. Few people were in line. Their idea was to buy tickets for a screening that began before they fired the shots, and of a movie they'd already seen. There was an 8:15 PM screening of *Licence to Kill*, but it had sold out. The only other film they'd already seen was *Batman*, but it was almost over. The woman behind the counter told them that the theater didn't sell tickets twenty minutes after a start time. Lyle pleaded to no avail. They bought tickets for the next show, hoping there wouldn't be a show time printed on them. There was. Erik threw the tickets away, and they left.

Next, they drove up Coldwater Canyon, a steep, sharply curved road that connects Beverly Hills to the San Fernando Valley. Lyle had trouble handling Erik's stick shift. He thought they could dump the guns somewhere near the top. Lyle drove west along Mulholland Drive for about a mile and then stopped. On the north side facing the lights of the valley, Erik scampered down and threw the guns into the brush. They tumbled several hundred feet.

Adrenaline wildly pumping, Lyle turned the car around. Next, they had to meet Perry Berman at the Taste of L.A. festival in Santa Monica. At some point, Erik realized that he had blood on his pants, plus their pockets were full of shotgun shells. In the back of his car, Erik kept tennis equipment and spare clothes. They changed behind a gas station in Santa Monica, where they tossed the bloody clothes and spent shells into a dumpster.

"I didn't really think about what we had done at that point," Lyle said, later. "I was just lost and numb and thinking about what we were doing." Erik was in worse shape—trembling, crying uncontrollably, and repeatedly shouting, "Oh, my god!"

Erik couldn't understand why it was so important to find Perry Berman. Lyle told him that it would be better to go back to the house with a friend. He didn't want to have to call the police himself. Besides, Erik wasn't in any shape to help out.

The food festival was minutes from closing, and they couldn't find Perry. When Lyle called his apartment, Berman said that he'd waited but the brothers never showed up. Lyle insisted they get together that evening. Berman wanted to postpone but finally agreed to meet them at the Cheesecake Factory in Beverly Hills.

But on the way to the restaurant, Lyle began to lose control, too. They couldn't carry off a nonchalant meeting with Berman. Lyle fell apart even more as they drove around. He decided he'd call the police himself.

When they walked in the front door, Erik ran into the family room and began to scream. Lyle pulled him away before going upstairs to call 911. His parents were dead, and Lyle had trouble believing that it was real. The stress of the past few days had left him exhausted. "I felt really raw," Lyle said, later. "I was just crying for crying's sake. I don't know. Crumbling."

While Lyle was on the phone, Erik went back in the family room and started screaming again. Lyle yelled for him to get out. Within minutes, police cautiously pulled up to the mansion gate. A dispatcher called back and told the brothers to come out the front door. Erik was hysterical and rolling on the ground. He couldn't stop crying.

On the way to Beverly Hills Police headquarters, Lyle whispered to Erik, "What do you want to do?" He wasn't going to "give a stupid story" and then have Erik tell the truth. Erik answered, "It's okay. We'll just say what we were going to say." Lyle told him, "You try and go in and talk first, and you let me know if it's okay."

The brothers agreed they'd say that Erik's car had been parked in the alley behind the mansion, in case any neighbors had seen anyone running out the front door carrying shotguns. After his fifteen-minute interview ended, Erik whispered in Lyle's ear, "It's okay. You can talk to him. Stay with the plan."

At 5:30 AM, when the brothers returned home by taxi, they asked to go inside to get some tennis equipment. Detective Les Zoeller said no, but they could come back in three hours. Lyle was frantic. The brothers aimlessly wandered around Beverly Hills on foot until it was time to return to the house.

Parked on the street just outside the yellow crime scene tape, 30 feet from the front door where a uniformed Beverly Hills officer stood watch, was Erik's Ford Escort. Asking to get their sports equipment from inside the house was a diversion. Inside the car were the items the brothers really needed: their unused shotgun shells and the receipts from the San Diego and Van Nuys stores where they'd bought the guns and ammunition.

When the brothers were able to check the car, the items were still there. Lyle put everything in a tennis bag. No one noticed.

PART FIVE

JERRY AND
JUDALON

CHAPTER 23

A FATEFUL MEETING

TWO MONTHS BEFORE THE DEATHS OF JOSE AND KITTY Menendez, Leon Jerome Oziel, a gregarious, articulate forty-two-year-old psychotherapist with a round face and sandy hair, was contacted by Judalon Smyth, the owner of a small business that combined audiotape duplicating with the sale of crystals. Petite and attractive with auburn hair, the thirty-six-year-old divorcée called Oziel trying to find the man behind a series of quick-fix, self-help audiotapes.

Smyth was interested in therapy but couldn't afford Oziel's rate of $160 per session. A series of phone calls between the pair followed. Jerry Oziel listened for hours as his new friend told her life story. Smyth began selling Oziel on the idea of his own tape line; the phone calls fast-forwarded into a torrid affair, despite the fact that Jerry Oziel was married with two daughters.

"Over time, our business relationship evolved to include a social relationship," said Oziel, later. "She seduced me and insisted on sexual interaction. The reality is she was forcing herself on me, and I didn't want her."

Oziel described the development of their relationship as an "emotional entanglement" that he tried to escape from over the next few months. He never stopped loving his wife, but Judalon Smyth, he said, wanted to "go legitimate" with him. He realized the affair with Smyth had become a problem when, he claimed, she started camping out in his waiting room. In passionate letters she wrote: "I function when we're apart but I live when we're together." In another: "What I want is forever and I don't want to let you go. I want to love you to the fullest each day. I'm trying not to drive you crazy." She may have been trying, but she wasn't succeeding. In fact, one could argue that they drove each other crazy—or crazier.

In the awful, enthralling drama of the Menendez murders, Judalon and Jerry would become, strictly speaking, plot devices. A minor character, though an exotic one, Judalon would appear briefly but with significant effect. Jerry's role was essentially passive, that of a professional listener to whom dangerous secrets would be confided. Like Shakespeare's Rosencrantz and Guildenstern, these bit players would keep popping up on center stage to greatly change the course of events.

CHAPTER 24

THE CONFESSION

JERRY OZIEL AND JUDALON HOTLY DISPUTED WHO WAS PURSUED and who was the pursuer, but they do agree that their lives, already in turmoil, were about to be further complicated by an astonishing twist of fate: They would be drawn together into the vortex of one of the most celebrated murder cases in U.S. history.

On Monday, October 30, 1989, Oziel, who had been staying at Smyth's house, called home to pick up his messages—including one from Erik Menendez.

Erik made the call at the urging of his cousin Henry, who had witnessed the younger brother's distraught state of mind. Based on what he knew of the family from previous counseling sessions, Oziel had an uncomfortable suspicion that Lyle and Erik might not be telling the truth. Erik, sounding agitated, said he wanted to see Oziel the next day and insisted that it be the last appointment of the afternoon. Oziel agreed to see Erik at 4 PM. Beneath his calm demeanor, the therapist knew he was facing a crisis. He was all but certain Erik Menendez intended to confess to the murder of his parents.

The events of the next forty-eight hours would be hotly debated and litigated for years to come as the four participants—Oziel, Smyth, and the Menendez brothers—gave conflicting accounts of what actually took place during two therapy sessions.

On Tuesday, October 31, Erik arrived at Oziel's office on North Bedford Drive just before the appointed time. Erik appeared anxious and depressed. He had lost weight. When the session began, Erik talked about feeling "very isolated and alienated." He told the therapist he was having nightmares with vivid images of his dead parents. Erik said he didn't know if he wanted to live or die and thought perhaps he should be on some type of medication.

After an hour, Erik said he wanted to take a walk. After crossing Bedford Drive, the pair stopped at a park along Santa Monica Boulevard. After a long discussion about what a great man his father was, they headed back to the office. Just before entering the front door, Oziel said Erik leaned back against a parking meter, let out a deep sigh, and announced, "We did it."

"You mean you killed your parents?" Oziel asked.

Erik said yes.

Oziel's fear had come to pass. Suddenly, he was more than a therapist talking to his patient.

"I was having trouble telling him about why I was suicidal since I hadn't told him that I killed my parents, and so he wasn't really getting it," recalled Erik. "And so I just decided that I needed to tell somebody, and I decided to tell him right then . . . I really wanted him at that point to tell me that I wasn't a bad person. And he couldn't do that unless he knew that I killed my parents."

Back in the therapist's fourth-floor office, Oziel said Erik Menendez discussed the night of August 20 in detail. According to the doctor's version of the conversation, Erik told him that the idea arose a few weeks before the murders. Erik was watching a BBC program about someone who had killed his father. Erik called Lyle into the room and they had a conversation, at first casual, about how it would feel if the person dominating and controlling your life just weren't there anymore. They began to discuss their own father, how impossible to please he was, how damaging he had been to them and their mother, whom they viewed as an abused spouse, and, as Oziel put it, "a pathetic shell of a human being." The brothers agreed Jose Menendez was not possible to live with. The only solution was to kill him.

At some point, Oziel claimed, the brothers began to plan in earnest. After some debate, they agreed that there was no way to get away with killing their father without killing their mother as well. She would know what they had done, and turn them in. Besides, they reasoned, although miserable in the marriage, she would not be able to survive on her own.

The brothers went back and forth on this point, Oziel said Erik told him, but ultimately they agreed that both would have to die. Erik said his mother had stopped taking her medication and had become a "scary person." They debated timing. Lyle wanted to delay, to give them longer to plan. But Erik wanted to do it quickly, before he lost his resolve. Lyle conceded.

Erik couldn't understand Oziel's apparent exhilaration. The therapist kept interrupting with questions, asking for more details about the evening of August 20. "He cut me off when I was talking about depression and suicide."

Erik explained that they drove to San Diego to buy the shotguns with a phony ID, then set up an alibi by agreeing to go with a friend to the food festival. Shortly before they were to meet their friend, they waited outside the door of the TV room where their parents were sitting on the couch watching television. Lyle didn't trust Erik to go through with it, so he made Erik go in first.

Erik rushed in, his shotgun leveled at his father. Jose turned away shouting, "No, no, no!" as he was shot. Lyle "finished off the job." Kitty half stood before falling to the floor from the barrage of shotgun blasts. But their mother wasn't dead. She was moaning, attempting to crawl through her own blood. The brothers, their shotguns now empty, went outside to the cache of ammunition in their car to reload. When they returned, Lyle administered the coup de grâce—a point-blank shot that struck Kitty in the face. Erik said the room was a bloody mess.

Oziel said the brothers called it the "perfect crime."

Only Erik was having a hard time living with it. He kept dreaming about the gory scene in the TV room. His guilt was overwhelming him.

He had to confess to someone. Naturally, he had picked his therapist. Nobody had witnessed the crime. Nobody had found the weapons. Nobody had challenged their alibi. Nobody could point a finger at them.

Except now, of course, Oziel could.

"Does Lyle know you're telling me this?" Oziel asked.

"No," Erik said, adding that his brother might kill him when he found out. He said he planned to tell him during an upcoming vacation. Or maybe not at all.

"No. You definitely should," said the therapist.

The last thing Oziel wanted was for Erik to leave his office and tell Lyle what he had done. He persuaded him that it would be much better, for all of them, if they called Lyle right then and asked him to come to Oziel's office immediately to work through this together.

A few blocks away at the Menendez mansion, Lyle was passing out Halloween candy with his girlfriend Jamie Pisarcik. When Lyle answered the phone, Oziel stated Erik had told him "everything."

"What do you mean?" asked Lyle.

"Come over," the therapist pleaded. "I don't want to talk about this on the phone."

With his heart pounding, Lyle drove to Oziel's office. He had a strong feeling Erik had confessed the brothers' involvement in the killings. Besides not trusting Oziel, Lyle worried that Erik and the therapist had discussed the brothers turning themselves into the police.

While waiting for Lyle to arrive, Judalon Smyth claimed Oziel took her into an outer hall and told her that, as he'd suspected, both boys were responsible for the killings of their parents. "I'm really afraid for you and my kids and myself," he declared.

————————

Lyle arrived sometime after 6:30 PM. Judalon Smyth said she was sitting in the waiting room when Lyle walked in. She saw him push the call button marked "Oziel" and then sit down, pick up a magazine, and flip through it. "Been waiting long?" Smyth said he asked her. She shrugged, lamely. "You know doctors," she said. Then Oziel opened the door to his office and invited Lyle in.

When Lyle walked in, Oziel seemed nervous. Erik was even more tense, anxious about how Lyle would react. In Oziel's recall, Lyle was menacing from the moment he arrived. He said he'd have to think about how to handle this, now that Oziel knew. As Lyle sat down in a straight-back chair facing the doctor's pale purple recliner, Oziel said he wanted to explain what he'd already discussed with Erik.

"I don't want to hear it," said Lyle. "I just want to talk with Erik alone."

"Your brother told me everything," declared Oziel.

"What do you mean by everything?" Lyle asked.

When the answer became clear, Oziel said Lyle began to rant at Erik. "I can't believe you did this!" he yelled at his brother. "I can't believe you told him! I don't even have a brother now. I could get rid of you for this."

Lyle couldn't understand why Erik had gone to Oziel first instead of coming to him. He said the confession had been "stupid."

Erik tried to defend himself. If he had approached Lyle, his brother would have said, "No, absolutely not," and then they would have had a huge fight and Erik would have confessed anyway.

Both Oziel and Judalon Smyth would testify under oath (although Smyth later said she was only repeating what Oziel had told her) that Lyle then announced to Erik, "Now I hope you know what we're going to have to do. We've got to kill him and anyone associated with him."

Smyth claimed she overheard a sobbing Erik reply, "I can't stop you [Lyle] from what you have to do, but . . . I can't kill anymore." Both brothers categorically denied they ever threatened Oziel or discussed committing the "perfect crime." Lyle admitted he did say he "didn't believe there was any way for [the brothers] to be safe now" since Oziel had heard Erik's confession. He was "extremely upset."

Oziel's notes from the session reflect that Lyle was "very unhappy," and he was getting the message that "Lyle was considering killing me . . . and Erik had the same feeling."

"It was a very intense meeting with me yelling at my brother, Oziel telling me that I seemed menacing to him, and me sort of feeling— actually feeling cornered more than my own fault because I didn't want to go talk to them about what they wanted to talk about, yet I really couldn't leave," Lyle would later recall.

Oziel tried to tell Lyle that the patient–therapist relationship was confidential in most situations, but Lyle wasn't buying it. "I can understand Erik, but he shouldn't have done this," he said. Oziel said that Lyle glared at him and said he didn't want to have anyone looking over his shoulder. That was why he killed his parents to begin with. He couldn't feel safe now that Oziel knew.

As they talked, Erik, racked with guilt and sobbing, jumped up and ran out of the office. Lyle and Oziel followed him out into the hall. This was not a good way to leave the session, Oziel was saying. They really needed to go back in and talk about this.

"He told me that he felt threatened by my demeanor, and . . . he just felt very uncomfortable and wanted me to stay, at least since my brother was clearly not going to stay." But Lyle wanted to find Erik and talk to him before deciding anything.

Oziel pleaded with Lyle at the elevator, still trying to persuade him to continue their conversation. Lyle said he wasn't sure he had anything more to say to him. He shook Oziel's hand and, looking him in the eye, said, "Good luck, Dr. Oziel."

Dr. L. Jerome Oziel went back upstairs and locked the door to the waiting room, then he locked the door to the hall, and then the door to his office. He got on the phone. The first call was to his wife. He explained the situation and told her she was in danger. He advised her to leave the house and find somewhere else to stay for a few days, making up a story for the kids about a gas leak in the kitchen. Then he called Dr. Jeff Lulow, his supervising psychologist, to think aloud about his dilemma.

Lulow listened to the scenario Oziel described with growing dismay. Lulow told Oziel he had an obligation to warn everyone he reasonably believed was in danger, revealing as much as they needed to know to appreciate the gravity of the threat and to take measures to protect themselves. He said that Oziel should make a record of the confession and put it in a safe-deposit box, giving the key to his attorney or someone he trusted with instructions that if anything suspicious happened to him, the notes should be turned over to police. He should then make sure his patients knew about that arrangement. Finally, Lulow suggested Oziel hire someone to protect him and send his family out of town on vacation.

While Smyth phoned a detective agency to inquire about hiring a bodyguard, Oziel made several other calls, to lawyers, to other psychologists, and at least one, anonymously, to a small-town police station where he laid out a hypothetical situation. He told his attorney, Brad Brunon, that he had clients who had committed a serious offense.

Oziel would later maintain that he believed reporting the brothers to police without succeeding in having them arrested would have been a fatal mistake. While Oziel was on the phone, Smyth said she was there, rubbing the back of his neck and shoulders as he talked. Oziel claimed she was never in his office that night—he went to Smyth's house after he'd finished his calls, to warn her that her association with him put her in danger, and to avoid leading the brothers to his own home. But Smyth said they went together to Oziel's house to pick up a suitcase his wife had left for him by the door.

That night, Smyth said, Oziel obsessed about the need to get the brothers to come see him one more time. The therapist expressed his fear and told her more details about the confession. If he could only have them in one more session, she said he kept repeating, he could get them under control.

CHAPTER 25

NOVEMBER 2, 1989

THE FIRST THING DR. OZIEL TOLD LYLE AND ERIK WHEN THEY arrived at his office on November 2 was that he had placed notes detailing their confession in three separate safe-deposit boxes with instructions for documents to be revealed in case of any "suspicious accident." According to Oziel's version of the events, Lyle laughed and said, "You were right to feel threatened." When Lyle had followed Erik down to the street two days earlier, the first thing he said when he got into Erik's Jeep was, "Now, how do we kill Oziel?" Erik told him he wasn't up to killing anybody else right then and if Lyle wanted to kill the psychologist, he should go ahead and do it. In the car, they sat discussing Oziel's fate, looking up at the office window, until it occurred to them that Oziel was probably looking down at them, terrified because he knew what they were talking about. (Both brothers insist that conversation never took place.)

Lyle asked Oziel if he was frightened. "I really don't choose to live in fear," Oziel responded.

"Neither did my father," Lyle said.

Oziel didn't want to get in a staring match with Lyle. He conceded that anybody could be killed. "I get the message," he said. "But the point is that what we're trying to do here is . . . work to resolve whatever issues you had emotionally that led you to kill your parents to begin with."

According to Oziel, Lyle said he had nothing to work on anymore, because the problems that had made him commit the murders were both dead.

The therapist tried another tack. Not only could he help them with their own feelings, Oziel told the boys, but if they ever were arrested, his record of their therapy sessions and understanding of the "family constellation" and the underlying emotional causes of their crime might aid in their defense.

Erik and Lyle must have accepted that argument, or been thinking of those three safe-deposit boxes, because they began to talk.

According to his own account of the therapy session, Oziel moved the conversation away from himself. He wondered if Lyle had any of the remorse Erik was feeling. He asked the older brother if he felt guilty having millions of dollars from their parents' inheritance. Lyle laughed and said, "No, but this wasn't done for the money."

The boys said their lives had been a lie. To the world, they appeared to be the perfect family. In fact, they were a disaster. Their mother and father had almost no relationship, except that the father was emotionally abusing her and treating them with rejection, criticism, and humiliation.

"The two boys acknowledged that they didn't think they would ever commit anymore crimes, but that they had always known that they had hated their father and that they had felt they had to kill him due to the fact that he totally controlled them, made them feel inadequate and inferior, dominated them," Oziel recalled.

After a lengthy discussion of guilt, motive, and a question of whether the brothers were able to commit the perfect crime, Oziel used the word "sociopath" to label them. Lyle asked him to define the term. Oziel described first a murder committed in passion, then a sociopathic murder. "Each of the boys looked at each other and looked at me and said matter-of-factly, 'We're sociopaths. We just got turned on by planning the murder.'"

In audio notes he recorded later, Oziel said, "It struck me throughout the session that Lyle was almost a complete sociopath with no evidence of remorse whatsoever that I could detect, and that he had even considered killing Erik after Erik had confessed the murder to me. Erik seemed to be much less capable of committing such an act without Lyle and was clearly overwrought by the scope of what he had done to his own parents." Oziel dictated that Lyle was very protective of Erik and wanted to be involved in Erik's therapy with him, "I believe as a way of making certain that his brother did not disclose any further events to me or details to me that Lyle didn't want him to disclose. I believe that it never occurred to Lyle that Erik would ever disclose to anyone the fact of the murder . . . The magnitude of what they had done in murdering their own parents seemed to have entirely escaped these two boys."

Oziel felt that had he not told them about the safe-deposit boxes, "these boys would absolutely have killed me." The other factor working in Oziel's favor was that if their therapist had been murdered about two months after their parents, police would have made a connection.

After the session ended, Oziel dictated, "I did not remain convinced that I was in anything but danger with respect to these two boys in terms of their plans for me. I only ended the session feeling that they weren't necessarily going to kill me at any time in the near future. Although I did not trust this conclusion very strongly."

The brothers had a much different recollection of the November 2 session. Lyle and Erik contend they said very little. Dr. Oziel did most of the talking, offering his opinion of the Menendezes and speculating about what he thought might have happened.

CHAPTER 26
"DON'T GO TO THE COPS!"

FOR THE NEXT THREE DAYS, THE OZIELS HID OUT WITH THEIR
daughters at a hotel near their home in Sherman Oaks. On November 6, Jerry Oziel bought shotguns for himself; his wife, Laurel; and Judalon Smyth, and he had his home security system repaired. Smyth said that Oziel told her his life was still "in mortal danger."

"This is more serious than I can imagine, and maybe I really can't work this out," he said.

He warned her that her life was in danger as well, she told friends. "He told me he was the only one I could trust. I'm your only friend in the world. Don't go to the cops. We have to work together," she later explained to *Vanity Fair*.

Oziel decided his best strategy was to become an ally of the Menendez brothers. He reiterated that he could be "potentially helpful in the event that they were arrested and tried for their parents' murder." According to Judalon Smyth, Oziel advised Erik and Lyle that it was important any prospective defense show they had continuing therapy sessions after the confession. Smyth said Lyle originally refused, but Oziel told them, "We'll set up the appointments and you pay as though you have just been coming, and if you need to come in, you can, and if you don't, don't. But it has to look like you have remorse and know you did wrong and are getting help." Smyth repeated this claim of alleged extortion in a lawsuit she filed later against Oziel.

Oziel insisted he was trying to end his affair with Smyth, but it continued. On November 25, 1989, she gave him a paper designed to look like a legal contract pledging her devotion. The "Most Official Sex I.O.U." was signed Judalon Rose Smyth. The two "witnesses" to the contract were her black and white cats—Shanti Oz and Ishi Kitty—who "signed" with their paw prints.

In a phone conversation recorded by Smyth that evening, Oziel spoke of how his daughters would eventually be "positive" about Judalon because he was positive about her. "I told them all these things [about you] that I know will impress them . . . [that you're] the biggest crystal seller in the world."

In two other phone calls recorded by Smyth over the next week, it was clear their romantic relationship was not over as Oziel would later claim. He gave Smyth the impression his marriage was breaking up. "We're talking about what to do," he told her. "We're trying to figure out what to do in terms of house and money and splitting up attorneys and all of that."

In another call, it sounded like Oziel was conducting therapy with Smyth, an allegation she would later pursue in a malpractice lawsuit against the psychologist. Then, the conversation turned to the Menendez brothers.

OZIEL: She feels these guys are not a danger anymore at all.

SMYTH: Well, I don't agree with that.

OZIEL: I think you should call her up, and you should use one of your disguise voices [and say], "Hello, Laurel, this is Erik. You're in trouble. I'm going to kill you."

SMYTH: I don't necessarily agree with that . . . I think, I mean I don't think that you're . . . I mean . . . they're nuts!

OZIEL: Gee, it took you a long time to get to that.

SMYTH : (laughter)

OZIEL: I thought it was pretty straightforward.

SMYTH: They're crazy.

OZIEL: It's true.

PART SIX

CLOSING IN

CHAPTER 27

ONE NIGHT IN MALIBU

C RAIG CIGNARELLI WAS TELLING FRIENDS AROUND CALABASAS that Erik confessed to him that he killed his parents. Cignarelli bragged that he was writing a screenplay about the murders and was going to make millions from the deal. "I know the facts," he told classmates.

On November 17, Les Zoeller and Tom Linehan met Cignarelli near the University of California–Santa Barbara, where he was a student. Cignarelli told the detectives that Erik had discussed killing his parents when he spent a weekend with Cignarelli in late August.

But at the end of the revelation, Erik had qualified everything with, "It could have happened." Did Cignarelli really think Erik was involved in the murders? No, he told the detectives.

But Cignarelli agreed to wear a body wire for the police. On the evening of November 29, he met Erik at Gladstone's 4 Fish, a famous seafood restaurant on Pacific Coast Highway. As Cignarelli waited for Erik in the parking lot, the detectives were hidden in a nearby van.

As dinner started, Erik bragged about his latest girlfriend and about going skiing in Utah, and said he'd ordered a $6,800 pool table for his new apartment in Marina del Rey. The tone turned serious when Erik said his Aunt Marta had sent a priest to the Menendez mansion for a "healing mass."

"He heals the soul, heals you, makes you feel better . . . This fucking healing man . . . starts doing this thing in Latin . . . fuckin' A . . . I could not open my eyes, and I went through a trance for at least nine, ten minutes.

I go, 'What the hell happened?' But I went, I saw the swirling circle like this . . . and I'm, going through this black hole with this . . . around me. I'm going through the center of it. Then, all of the sudden, I saw my parents. I saw the souls being lifted up to heaven. I saw my parents in heaven . . . they were standing, I was praying in front of them on my knees."

Much of their conversation was Erik telling Craig about his latest draft of their screenplay. Cignarelli offered to help with the rewrite.

"Well, we'll dramatize it, and we won't use real names, and we won't make it exactly real, but just a script like that . . . basically, the same as *Friends*, as the original *Friends*. Kid kills the parents, or somebody kills the parents—"

Erik stopped him.

> ERIK: Don't even fuck with that.
>
> CRAIG: I know, but . . . You already told me you did it.
>
> ERIK: No, don't, don't even fuck with that anymore.
>
> CRAIG: Well, but . . .
>
> ERIK: Don't fuck with that anymore. You know I didn't kill my parents.
>
> CRAIG: I know.
>
> ERIK: You know there's no way I could have . . .
>
> CRAIG: I wanna find out who did it.
>
> ERIK: . . . especially in the way that it happened.
>
> CRAIG: You still scared of Lyle?
>
> ERIK: No, Lyle didn't do it. He was with me.
>
> CRAIG: Could he have had someone did it? I hate to press the issue, but, man, I wanna know.
>
> ERIK: I don't know. He wasn't involved with any drugs or anything like that, you know?
>
> CRAIG: Are you still checking it out?
>
> ERIK: There's not much I can do, man, but I carry a gun around with me.
>
> CRAIG: I know. You told me.
>
> ERIK: And general shit. I don't know what the detectives are asking. They fuckin' think it could have been us.
>
> CRAIG: I'm still a suspect, as far as I know.

Erik asked whether the police had spoken to him. Craig admitted that they had.

> **ERIK:** Surely you would never have told them anything that
> I told you. Like that, 'cause, I mean, that's . . .
> **CRAIG:** Yeah, that's what I'll tell them. Hi. Erik killed his
> parents, yeah.

Erik speculated that the Mafia or Fidel Castro might have murdered his parents, and that he'd pay a million dollars to anyone who could find their killer.

> **ERIK:** I'm almost afraid to know who it was. I find out who it
> was, I'm gonna kill him . . . If I don't find out who it is, I'll
> be paranoid for the rest of my life.

The rest of the dinner was spitballing ideas for getting rich. Erik said he might also make it big as an actor. His parting words were, "I'm telling you. We should be senators. All right?"

As Erik drove off after dinner, Cignarelli leaned over, spoke into the microphone on his chest, and apologized to the detectives. "Well, I guess that didn't help much, huh?"

A few weeks later, Cignarelli told Zoeller that he'd written a "journalistic recollection" in a school notebook of Erik's confession, the Calabasas burglaries, and another killing. To find it, police executed a search warrant at the home of Craig's mother in Calabasas on January 25, 1990. Police found two notebooks, but there was nothing in them about a confession or a murder. Craig was furious about the search warrant.

Zoeller and Linehan asked Cignarelli if he wanted to see some of the gruesome photographs of the crime scene. Craig responded with a fax to the BHPD hand-printed in large block letters:

ATTN: HOMICIDE
FATE AND CIRCUMSTANCE
SOMETIMES FORGE UNEXPECTED ALLIES
As I walk through the valley of the shadow of death I shall fear
NO EVIL

Betrayal signifies evil
Living Is An Art necessitating tact not fueled by greed!
This you shall suffer from ignorance.
YOU are NOT to be
TRUSTED !
And as they looked out over their empire,
they were saddened for there were no more lands left to conquer.

It was signed Hamilton Cromwell.

CHAPTER 28

THE OZIELS— SHE HELD US HOSTAGE

I N THE EARLY AFTERNOON OF DECEMBER 9, 1989, JUDALON SMYTH fainted and became incoherent. Smyth had recently begun taking a new medication for depression. Her father was with her and immediately phoned Jerry Oziel, who rushed over to Smyth's apartment, worried she might have taken an overdose. When he arrived, Smyth seemed confused. Oziel and Jim Smyth drove her to a doctor's office. Judalon's vital signs were stable but something was obviously wrong. Then, Oziel drove her fifteen miles across Los Angeles to the emergency room at a hospital near his home in Sherman Oaks.

"I took Judalon there not as a psychologist but as a friend helping someone who could've been medically ill," Oziel recalled later. "While she was there, she talked about depression, which a doctor determined made her possibly suicidal . . . She felt insecure after the hospital thing and couldn't stay with a friend—she wanted to be close to me," recounted Oziel. "She was dysfunctional and begged to come over."

Jerry and Laurel Oziel felt sorry for the frightened, nervous woman. They invited Smyth to move into their housekeeper's room for two days.

Initially, Smyth happily made herself at home. But sometime during the next forty-eight hours, the Oziels said Judalon became dark and moody. Then came what the Oziels described as intimidation. Judalon began repeating her threat to commit suicide. At times, she rambled with other subtle warnings. The one threat not taken lightly was to tell the police what she knew about the murder of Jose and Kitty Menendez. "It was the first time she made the double threat," said Oziel. "It was dual manipulation—threatening to commit suicide or go to the police."

Later, Smyth claimed in a lawsuit that Oziel continually reminded her she was depressed and suicidal and told her she would be committed to a state mental hospital if she moved out of his house. The Oziels vigorously denied that. Oziel insisted he referred Smyth to other psychologists for treatment, but she refused to make an appointment. The Oziels believed that Smyth "liked their family life and threatened us so she could stay."

In the fall of 1990, Jerry Oziel told me that he and his wife had never had an open marriage, been separated, or planned to divorce. In fact, Laurel Oziel remained steadfastly by his side. Although Oziel denied it, Smyth claimed their love affair continued after she moved in with the Oziels and that she and the doctor shared romantic encounters in the housekeeper's room. According to one of Smyth's attorneys, one of Oziel's daughters walked by the room one morning and saw her father in bed with Judalon.

In mid-January 1990, Oziel loaned Smyth $5,000. Judalon signed a promissory note to repay him. When asked if Smyth was extorting money from him, Oziel replied, "It's hard to know. She told me she needed the money. She never specifically said blackmail, but that was probably part of my thinking and decision." Smyth made only one payment on the loan. She claimed she was in a "drugged state" when she signed the note.

Oziel described Smyth as being "seductively aggressive." In an early February 1990 letter, Smyth wrote: "As strong and as well as you're handling all this, I can see that you need some taking care of as well. Thank you for loving me and protecting me and sharing your home and family."

Smyth later said she wrote those impassioned letters because Oziel "demanded I write him a love letter every day. If I didn't write enough to please him, he would hit me." She claimed in a lawsuit that Dr. Oziel "threatened her with closed fists . . . striking her twice on the legs and arms." A month after that, in early March, she said that he pulled her hair and choked her, and then raped her.

One evening, the Oziels came home from work and Smyth had rearranged their furniture. During an explosive argument, Oziel said "she demanded Laurel and the kids should leave and I should stay. It was at the point where our lives were going to be destroyed if we let her stay in the house." Oziel asked Judalon to leave. He explained that he loved his wife and was not going to be with Smyth. At this point, Oziel claimed Smyth became hysterical and made "major threats" that she was going to murder him and his family.

The next morning, Jerry Oziel was panicked. He had Smyth sign a document he drafted declaring she wouldn't carry out her threats. Handwritten by Oziel on stationery from the Beverly Hills Psychiatric and Psychological Center, the letter dated February 17, 1990, is titled "Reaffirmed Confidentiality Agreement" and echoed a previous agreement Smyth signed to protect the confidentiality of Oziel's patients— including Erik and Lyle's confession.

Smyth scrawled her signature at the bottom of the letter. She would later claim Oziel woke her out of a deep sleep, thrust the paper in front of her, and forced her to sign without reading it. "She intentionally scribbled her signature. I demanded she sign the document or I was going to call the police," said Oziel. Smyth promised to move out of the house within two weeks.

The Oziels believed Smyth spent that time going through everything in their home, including personal papers and professional files. When asked if she could have obtained patient information during this period, Oziel simply said "she was in the house for long periods of time alone."

In the end, Smyth said, it was she who escaped him, after three months of living in his house. She told a friend that he'd kept her on drugs and forced her to have sex with him. She'd survived like a "prisoner of war" and believed that her life was in "extreme danger."

Two former nannies of the Oziel family obliquely lent credibility to some of what Judalon claimed. The nannies told ABC *Primetime*

Live they had romantic relationships with Jerry Oziel in the 1980s. In interviews with ABC, both women claimed that Oziel was abusive, gave them prescription drugs, and was psychologically manipulative. The women told ABC they used to affectionately call the therapist "Dr. Daddy."

Oziel rebuffed the nannies' stories. About Smyth, he said that her allegations "were completely untrue," and denied that she had been his girlfriend. Their relationship was as therapist and patient, and as such was "legally confidential."

CHAPTER 29

THE INFORMANT— JUDALON SMYTH

N THE MONTHS SINCE THE MURDER OF JOSE AND KITTY Menendez, Lyle's friends had become increasingly suspicious that he was involved in their deaths. Now they felt certain.

On Friday, March 2, 1990, Lyle, Glenn Stevens, and Hayden Rogers flew from Newark to Los Angeles to scout a site near the UCLA campus where Lyle could open a branch of the chicken wing restaurant he'd bought in Princeton with a $300,000 loan from the estate. During the flight, as Hayden slept, Glenn said Lyle described Dr. Jerry Oziel as the best psychologist in Beverly Hills. He said that the therapist and Gerry Chaleff, the brothers' attorney, were the only ones who knew the "whole story" of what happened to his parents.

He said that Oziel had taped some of the brothers' therapy sessions, which was okay because the police would never be able to hear them. Surprised, Stevens said he'd heard of cases where the doctor-patient privilege had been legally circumvented. Lyle looked shocked. "If the police get their hands on those tapes, I'm fucked!"

Halfway through the flight, Lyle phoned Gus Tangalos, the manager of his restaurant in Princeton. Gus told Lyle that shortly after he'd left for the airport, Les Zoeller and Tom Linehan walked into Mr. Buffalo's. After a meal of spicy wings, the detectives asked Gus if Lyle owned any guns. Lyle was extremely disturbed to hear that. He took out a roll of cash, peeled off $1,800, and divided it between Rogers and Stevens. If he was arrested, they should call Chaleff and use the money to bail him out.

Shortly before they left New Jersey, Lyle and Glenn had met in New York with a man Stevens knew who allegedly had Mafia connections. Stevens went to the bathroom for five minutes. After they left, Lyle told him the man had revealed who killed Jose and Kitty. Unknown to Stevens, Lyle and Hayden made a second trip to New York to meet with the same man. The visit included a discussion of getting a gun permit for Stevens so he could become Lyle's bodyguard.

In California, Glenn thought Lyle was "acting weird." Lyle left the house every morning by eight; in Princeton, he never got up that early. Stevens didn't understand why Lyle wasn't making more of an effort to find out who killed his parents. Lyle explained that his father had told him if anything ever happened to him, Lyle should get on with his life.

On Monday, March 5, Lyle called his former bodyguard, Richard Wenskoski, in New Jersey to ask if he knew why the detectives had stopped by Mr. Buffalo's. Days earlier, Zoeller had told Wenskoski that the brothers were now "strong suspects" in the murder of their parents. Wenskoski taped the call from Lyle and suggested he call the police. "No, no, I don't think so," Lyle replied, adding that there was something else he wanted to talk about that he couldn't say over the phone.

Later that day, the Beverly Hills Police got a call from L.A. County Commissioner Murray Gross, who said a friend wanted to tell police what she knew about the Menendez murders. They arranged a meeting at the police department for the next day.

On Tuesday, March 6, Les Zoeller, Tom Linehan, and L.A. Deputy District Attorney Elliot Alhadeff met Judalon Smyth. She told them she'd been living for months at the home of the psychotherapist Dr. L. Jerome Oziel, who had just kicked her out on Sunday (contradicting her later story that she had "snuck out" of the house to "escape"). They'd been romantically involved since the previous summer. Four months earlier, Smyth said, Erik Menendez confessed to Dr. Oziel that he and Lyle had killed their parents.

During "pillow talk," as one of her attorneys would later call it, Smyth and Oziel discussed the Menendez brothers. She also told the detectives that Oziel raped her. "One of the times we had sex it was definitely rape, because I pretended to be asleep and he went ahead and had sex with me," she said. But they were more interested to hear about the Menendez brothers.

CHAPTER 30

THE BHPD
SEARCH WARRANT

L AUREL OZIEL HAD JUST STEPPED OUT OF THE SHOWER WHEN she heard banging on her front door. It was Thursday morning, March 8. She opened the door and was startled to see Beverly Hills Police detectives, a prosecutor, and a court-appointed special master who handed her a search warrant. They said her husband had evidence, six audio cassette tapes, related to the commission of a felony. Laurel said she had to finish dressing and quickly slammed the door. "Mind if I burn the tapes?" Deputy D.A. Elliot Alhadeff can be heard saying on a police video recording. At his quip, they immediately made Laurel let them in. She was allowed to get dressed after a detective searched her drawers, closet, and even the toilet tank.

Jerry Oziel's car phone rang just after 10 AM as he was driving to his office in Beverly Hills. A bunch of men flashing badges were in their living room, Laurel told him. "I think you better come home."

Oziel called his attorney, Brad Brunon, before contacting the American Psychological Association for advice. They advised that if the search warrant was valid, there was nothing he could do.

California law makes the patient the holder of the confidential privilege with a therapist. The psychologist is obligated to "assert the privilege" if the patient is not there to assert it personally. To protect the confidentiality and to act as a buffer between the police and the doctor, a special master—a court-appointed attorney—is present during the search of any therapist or his property. Under regular procedure, the special master turns over everything seized to the court, under seal, pending a decision on admissibility.

When Jerry Oziel arrived home, the special master explained that they were looking for tapes with information related to the murders of Jose and Kitty Menendez, including statements allegedly taken by the therapist. According to the search warrant, "the tapes indicate[d] the planning of the crimes, and a description as to how the crime was committed." They also demanded Oziel's appointment book and keys to any family safe-deposit boxes.

Oziel wanted to wait for his attorney before answering any questions. When Brunon arrived, there was a short discussion about the warrant's parameters. Then, Brunon told the officials that Oziel was reluctantly "complying under compulsion of court order without choice." After asserting the therapist's privilege, Brunon advised Oziel to turn over the safe-deposit box key and vigorously protest the use of anything they found in the box. Oziel explained to BHPD officials that there was actually only one safety-deposit box.

He turned to the video camera and said, "I would like it to be clear that I had nothing to do with this court order. In no way, shape, or form did I violate confidentiality or privilege, or know anything about this, as is evidenced by the state of undress my wife is in and the fact that I was on my way to do a number of errands. I just want that clear. Did I say that very coherently?" Then he added that he wanted it on the record that he didn't know who had provided the information in the police affidavit.

Zoeller answered that their source was "an individual who was now their witness."

Oziel touched the special master's arm and quietly said, "This isn't funny. I'm scared." Then he asked Zoeller, "Do you know anyone with the witness protection program?"

"Are you concerned with your safety?" asked Zoeller.

"I don't think we need to get into that," replied Oziel.

Next, the search party went to the Union Federal Bank on Ventura Boulevard in Sherman Oaks, where Laurel Oziel opened her safe-deposit box and turned over seventeen tapes. Normally, the special master would hold the tapes pending a court hearing on their admissibility. But back at his home, Jerry Oziel insisted that the group had to listen to the tapes. As they played, he asked the detectives if Lyle and Erik Menendez were in custody yet. They told him no.

"If you don't get these people immediately," Oziel said, "you're going to have a lot more things to investigate."

PART SEVEN

WHO KNOWS WHAT GOES ON WITHIN A FAMILY?

CHAPTER 31

THE ARREST — INSIDE THE BEVERLY HILLS BUNKER

A T A FEW MINUTES PAST ONE O'CLOCK ON A COOL MARCH afternoon, Lyle Menendez's new lifestyle as a millionaire orphan abruptly ended. He had just pulled out onto tree-lined Elm Drive in Erik's tan Jeep Wrangler accompanied by Glenn Stevens and Hayden Rogers. The trio had driven less than half a block when a blue Ford Taurus suddenly stopped short directly in front of them. Lyle angrily backed up while yelling at the driver, but as he did, he hit the bumper of a van directly behind him.

Shotgun-toting Beverly Hills Police officers wearing bulletproof vests jumped out and began to shout: "Get the fuck out of the car! Lie down on the ground!" Lyle carefully shifted the Jeep into park. "Keep your hands up where we can see them!" someone screamed. Hayden was ordered out of the front passenger seat. As he reached for the door handle, another cop yelled, "Put your hands back up where I can see them before I blow your fucking head off!" Rogers slowly raised his hands as another member of the arrest team aimed a gun at his ear, opened the door, grabbed him by the shoulder, and jerked him out of the car.

Lyle was handcuffed and placed facedown in the middle of North Elm Drive. Stevens and Rogers were terrified. This had to be a case of mistaken identity. Glenn Stevens was told to get out of the back seat, but he was so badly shaken, he was unable to move. He kept his hands high in the air, deciding it wouldn't be a good idea to suddenly reach down to lift the seat-belt release since fifteen cops had their guns drawn and pointed at him.

For several minutes, Stevens and Rogers were forced to lie facedown in the street with guns pointed at their heads. Then, one of the detectives put Stevens in the back seat of his car. He asked if Stevens knew what this was all about. At first, the young man was too scared to think logically. Then, it hit him. His close friend had just been arrested for killing his parents.

Lyle Menendez was driven away and booked at the West Hollywood Sheriff's station. Stevens and Rogers were released.

It was just after midnight in a suburb of Tel Aviv, Israel, when Erik Menendez put down the Ayn Rand novel he was reading and went to bed. For the past week, he'd been competing in an international tennis tournament. The next morning, his host was awakened by a phone call at 7:30 AM Tel Aviv time from the tennis center that was sponsoring the tournament. "Something terrible has happened to Erik's brother," said a panicky-sounding assistant. Erik called back immediately before contacting Carlos Baralt and Marta Cano. He reassured them that he and Lyle were innocent. It was all a big mistake. Erik spoke with attorney Gerald Chaleff in California and asked questions about extradition and phone tapping. Within a few minutes, Erik hurriedly packed his bags and left with his coach, Mark Heffernan, on the first available flight to London.

Back in Beverly Hills, officials were confident as they bantered with a room full of reporters at a crowded, late-afternoon news conference to announce the arrest of Lyle Menendez. "We have reason to be happy today," said police chief Marvin Iannone with a broad smile. The political pressure had been equally intense along Rodeo Drive and downtown at the district attorney's office to make an arrest in the notorious case. People living in the country's wealthiest city didn't like the idea of a couple being blown away in their living room on a Sunday night and the case remaining unsolved. Iannone speculated that greed had prompted the two murders. "The motives, of course, are varied, and there was an estate worth millions of dollars," he said. "As in any family, there are a lot of conflicts so I don't know if there was a sole motive or several motives." But why, the chief was asked, hadn't these privileged, apparently pampered young men been able to wait until their parents died? Iannone, a former LAPD commander with thirty-three years of experience, shrugged and replied, "Who knows what really goes on within a family?"

After the news conference, TV crews rushed to the Menendez mansion where Maria Menendez allowed several cameramen inside to videotape family pictures. In her heavily accented English, she defended her grandsons and suggested that reporters look inside Carolco Pictures to solve the mystery of who murdered her son.

Shortly before Lyle's arrest, the board of LIVE Entertainment had met to discuss a settlement proposal with the Menendez family. Complex negotiations had been ongoing for months regarding Jose's company life insurance policies. Before the meeting began, the law firm of Kaye, Scholer, Fierman, Hays & Handler delivered a 220-page confidential report to the board. Carolco Pictures, LIVE's parent company, had commissioned its own investigation after media reports labeled the killings a "Mafia hit." The report concluded "there was no credible information that in any way linked the business of LIVE with the murders of Jose and Kitty Menendez." A motion was made to postpone any decision on the Menendez family settlement.

On the day Lyle Menendez was arrested, I spent the afternoon with Marta Cano at the West Palm Beach office of Smith-Barney where she was a financial planner. A smiling black-and-white picture of Jose Menendez was featured prominently in the middle of a wall full of sales awards. For several hours, we discussed the stock market and her children. As I was leaving, we stood at the elevators, and she expressed her concern that the Beverly Hills Police were "harassing Lyle."

A few minutes later, I checked my answering machine and heard a frantic message from the *Miami Herald*: Lyle Menendez had been arrested in Beverly Hills. Before rushing back to the newsroom in Miami, I stopped back at Marta's office. As she saw me coming down the hall, her face fell. In her typical stoic manner, she told me the arrest didn't surprise her. But she was certain her nephews were innocent. "I refuse to believe they plotted the murder," she told me over the phone later that same day.

When Erik landed in London, he phoned Marta and said he didn't want to be paraded in front of TV cameras when he was arrested. Since Gerry Chaleff had previously represented both brothers in the fall of 1989, it was necessary for them to have separate lawyers. Chaleff recommended that the family hire Robert Shapiro, an L.A. criminal defense attorney experienced in high-profile cases. After consulting with Marta and Erik, Shapiro told Beverly Hills Police that his client would voluntarily surrender after his return from "somewhere out of the country."

An hour later, Erik called again. Marta told him she'd arranged for him to fly to Miami, where she and her son Andy would meet him. Once his flight was airborne, Shapiro notified detectives that Erik was en route to Miami. On landing, Erik was met by two plainclothes police detectives. For Erik and his godmother, with whom he'd always shared an exceptionally close bond, it was an emotional reunion. As they sat waiting for his next flight, she comforted him with an arm around his shoulder.

Erik got off the plane in Los Angeles shortly before 2 AM Sunday, March 11. No TV cameras were there, but Les Zoeller and Tom Linehan were waiting. Erik told them that they didn't have to handcuff him. Zoeller apologized and explained that he had to—it was regulation. Just after 4 AM, Erik was charged with suspicion of murder and taken downtown to the Los Angeles County Men's Central Jail.

Later that day, a half-dozen TV vans plus a crowd of reporters, photographers, and onlookers kept vigil outside the mansion. Inside, the Menendez and Andersen families huddled, exhausted and in shock. They wanted to go outside and talk to the media about the close relationship "the boys" had with their parents. But defense attorneys ordered them not to.

The family room where Jose and Kitty had been killed so horrifically was coming back to life. In the fall, people had avoided even walking into the room, and there had been no furniture. Now, everyone gathered there to watch the six o'clock news and its slow-motion video of Erik and Lyle leaving their parents' funeral.

CHAPTER 32

FIRST-DEGREE MURDER

WITHIN TWENTY-FOUR HOURS AFTER THE ARREST OF ERIK AND Lyle, the killing of Jose and Kitty Menendez was transformed from a local Los Angeles story to an international media sensation. On Monday, March 12, L.A. County District Attorney Ira Reiner held a news conference. With Deputy D.A. Elliot Alhadeff at his side, Reiner announced that two counts of murder involving special circumstances had been filed against the Menendez brothers, making them eligible for the death penalty.

"The two boys became suspects very shortly after the investigation began—in a matter of days," declared Reiner. "They recently became the sole and exclusive suspects."

"If the brothers became suspects right away, why did it take seven months to arrest them?" asked a reporter.

"The Beverly Hills Police Department conducted a very thorough investigation into this case," said Reiner. "This did not take so long in terms of uncovering the evidence."

Reiner dodged most of the questions asked by the standing-room-only crowd of reporters. He refused to comment about any evidence or the affidavit behind the search of Oziel's house. When asked for the motive behind the killings, Reiner suggested financial gain: "I don't know what your experience is, but it's been our experience in the D.A.'s office that $14 million provides ample motive for someone to kill somebody."

A few hours later, Erik and Lyle Menendez made their first public appearance at Beverly Hills Municipal Court, a drab beige building located at the south end of the city government complex. A hearing to read the charges against the brothers was scheduled to begin at 2 PM. The media began lining up outside the court an hour beforehand. When the doors finally opened, a crush of people filled every seat except for two rows reserved for the family.

Finally, at 3:24 PM, the brothers walked through a door at the side of the wood-paneled courtroom. Erik wore a charcoal gray Italian suit with a dark blue tie. Lyle was dressed in a blue blazer, gray slacks, and red tie. Erik appeared ready to nod off. After three days of traveling from Israel, he still hadn't slept. As Judge Judith Stein read the charges, the brothers stood with their hands folded in front of them. They looked at each other and suppressed smiles as Judge Stein announced they were charged with the murder of "'Joe-Say' Menendez, a human being."

"Erik Menendez, you are charged with the murder of Mary Louise Menendez, a human being. Do you understand the charges?" As his mother's name was read, Erik looked from the bench to the floor before quietly answering, "Yes, Your Honor." In marked contrast, Lyle confidently responded that he understood the charges against him. As the five-minute hearing ended, Lyle raised his left hand and waved goodbye to the family before disappearing through the side door. Neither was eligible for bail.

On Sunday, March 25, the night before the brothers entered their pleas, a dozen Menendez and Andersen family members were back in Beverly Hills to show their support for Erik and Lyle. Besides Jose's sisters and mother, Kitty's father, Andy, was there, along with her sister Joan VanderMolen and brother Brian Andersen from Illinois.

Extraordinary tension filled the mansion, where both sides of the family were staying together. Everybody was unanimous in their support for the brothers and belief in their innocence.

The next afternoon, the pack of reporters at Beverly Hills Municipal Court was much bigger than at the first hearing. Erik and Lyle walked out wearing the same outfits as two weeks earlier. Both smiled and joked with their attorneys. This time they were unable to mask their smiles as

Judge Stein read the charges against them in what might be described as her cartoon character voice. Reporters interpreted the grins as a sign of arrogance and disrespect. Many media reports criticized the brothers for appearing lighthearted at these serious proceedings. During the brief arraignment, both brothers entered not-guilty pleas.

There was dissension in the family over who should be hired to defend Erik and Lyle. Both brothers actively took part in the search for attorneys. Gerald Chaleff had already been involved in the case since Lyle confessed to him in November 1989.

Chaleff assured the brothers there were defense attorneys more powerful than Robert Shapiro who would want to represent the case, including his friend, Leslie Abramson. There were dozens of meetings with high-profile attorneys. But Abramson was the one who connected the best with Erik. Lyle thought she was "dynamic, clear, and remarkably intelligent." But he was worried Erik would open up and share too much about their lives. At this early point, the brothers were determined to hide their family's secrets.

The problem with Leslie, according to Lyle, was that she could get you to talk. "With Leslie, it was like sitting down with your aunt or somebody. She was like, 'Okay, tell me what happened. I want the truth.' It did not take her long to get Erik to talk—to break Erik down and have him start telling the whole family history—long before we even knew that that was going to be the case."

Forty-six years old with blonde, curly hair, Abramson was small in stature but a giant in the courtroom, where she was known to always "go to the wall" for her clients. Considered one of California's top death-penalty defense attorneys, by 1990 she had defended 600 felony cases, ranging from drugs and extortion to murder. In 1981, one of Abramson's clients was sentenced to death after being convicted of an execution-style murder at a Bob's Big Boy restaurant. In the years since then, she'd "won" all of the death-penalty cases she tried. In capital cases, it's considered a win if you keep your client off death row. Now she replaced Robert Shapiro as the attorney for Erik Menendez.

During my first meeting with Abramson in early April 1990, she was cordial but aloof. She worried that a writer might "do a Joe McGinniss" [the author of the controversial 1983 book *Fatal Vision* about convicted murderer Jeffrey MacDonald] on her client. In spite of her apprehension, Abramson couldn't resist an opportunity to sell her case. "Dr. Oziel is a very bad guy," she said. "He is a master of manipulation who assaults his female patients." Leaning across her desk, she volunteered that Oziel was married but had many girlfriends on the side.

CHAPTER 33

UNANSWERED QUESTIONS

T HE MENENDEZ BROTHERS WERE IN JAIL, BUT THE BEVERLY Hills Police investigation was far from over. Prosecutors publicly proclaimed they had a strong case against Erik and Lyle, but privately they knew there would be a fierce legal battle before they could ever use the tapes seized from Dr. Oziel in court. The most glaring weakness was a lack of physical evidence linking the brothers to the killings.

Although he wouldn't discuss the Oziel tapes, Les Zoeller insisted there was irrefutable evidence that Erik and Lyle had killed their parents. "I wouldn't have wanted to proceed with the arrests if I wasn't one hundred percent certain," he told me. "I could've arrested the brothers when I wasn't completely certain, but my compassion and personal feelings for the family influenced my waiting." Zoeller said the police had thoroughly checked out all business-related leads. Everything came up empty. "As we hit each dead end, the investigation kept coming back to the boys," said Zoeller. "We're lucky we're in Beverly Hills because in a big-city police department, I wouldn't have had this much time to work a case."

Judalon Smyth told investigators the brothers tossed the freshly fired shotguns out of their car along Mulholland Drive. Detectives conducted several extensive searches in the dense, overgrown brush along the scenic highway, but the only thing they came back with was poison ivy.

Smyth agreed to wear a body wire to several meetings with Jerry Oziel. She also continued taping their phone calls. She'd already been doing that for months, but now she turned the tapes over to detectives. During one call a few weeks before the arrests, Oziel became angry over her constant threats to go to the police.

> OZIEL: If you do this, I swear to you, Judalon, you'll be killed. If you turn . . .
> SMYTH: Well, the boys can't kill me because they don't know who I am.
> OZIEL: Judy, if you turn them in, I absolutely would tell them that you turned them in. I'm not going to let them kill me because you decided to do something crazy.

Oziel was sarcastic in another call just after the brothers were jailed: "Well, you did what you did, and that's what you did." He warned her there was going to be intense press coverage. "I suggest you have no comment," he said, "unless you want a number of things disclosed that you don't want disclosed."

At one point Judalon told the therapist she was recording their calls, but he continued talking with her.

In a call two weeks after the arrests, Oziel told Smyth: "We're going to be stars—not exactly for the right reasons."

PART EIGHT

TRIAL BY MEDIA

CHAPTER 34

THE ESCAPE ATTEMPT

We alone know the truth. We alone know the secrets of our fam-
ily's past. I do not look forward to broadcasting them around the
country.
    —from a seventeen-page letter written by Lyle to Erik,
                                                  June 1990

DOWNTOWN AT L.A. COUNTY JAIL, THE BROTHERS TRIED TO
adapt to their new life. It wasn't easy. After a fight with a guard left
him with a black eye, Erik was placed in an isolated lock-up cell.
Lyle was doing slightly better.

At an April 9 hearing in Beverly Hills Municipal Court, prosecutors
asked for a sample of Erik's handwriting "to compare with new information they'd obtained since the arrest." Investigators were certain Erik
had forged Donovan Goodreau's signature when buying the shotguns
in San Diego.

The admissibility of Dr. Oziel's notes and tapes of his sessions
with Erik and Lyle was at the crux of the murder case. He had actually
recorded one therapy session, on December 11, 1989; the other tapes
were audio notes of his recollections of therapy sessions. On June 8,
1990, Judge James Albracht held a closed hearing to determine whether
legal privilege between a therapist and patients applied. But the biggest
story of the day had begun before court had convened.

During the trip from the jail to Santa Monica, both brothers rode in separate "keep away" sections, small isolated cages inside the jail bus. As was usual during transport, both wore two-foot-long ankle chains, restricting their movements. At the courthouse holding cell, as Lyle changed out of his jail jumpsuit, sheriff's deputies saw that a pair of chain links had been cut almost completely through.

Sgt. James Kagy ordered the brothers to remove all their clothes for a skin search. An inspection of the holding cell turned up nothing. At L.A. County Jail downtown, four deputies searched Erik and Lyle's adjoining cells. Deputies were allowed to "fan through" personal papers, but if they came across legal documents they were not supposed to read them.

Inside Erik's cell, Deputy Robert Birkett found what he called an "escape plan with information about extradition treaties from different countries." Another deputy found a small map with references to "E and L" and a paper that mentioned "Swiss bank security" and the questions "What financial security will we have?" and "How will our girlfriends fit in?"

A second paper contained a list:

- Please explain further the different ways to enter Mexico
- Do you have a secure place for us to stay in Colombia?
- Do you need a visa to go to London?
- Is it safer to travel to Lebanon from London or South America?

Late that afternoon, the sheriff's department issued a press release saying there had been an "escape attempt" that morning by Erik and Lyle Menendez. Defense attorneys called that "ridiculous" and accused officials of removing everything from the brothers' cells as a "fishing expedition." One deputy made the biggest catch of the day: a seventeen-page letter written by Lyle to Erik.

We need to hang in there together, in my opinion. You notice I have not held you talking to Cig or Oziel against you even though my entire life is on the verge of destruction as a result of all this. I feel that we have done what we did together and everything we do afterwards is both our responsibility.

I am not the pillar of strength the papers make me out to be or Leslie thinks I am. I think if dad could give us one piece of advice as we left the house that night in August, it would be never to abandon each other no matter the circumstances.

What we did in August was a mistake from what I can tell and I don't know what to do about it.

In a cryptic passage, he wrote:

We did not do anything for the money. To go our separate ways is to lose any meaning our actions had . . .

Sheriff's deputies immediately gave the letter to the Beverly Hills Police. Also in the seized material was a paper titled "Oziel's fears of the following" that had notes from Lyle to his attorneys concerning strategy for dealing with Dr. Oziel at trial.

Several days later, after the story made front-page news, the L.A. County Sheriff's office quietly announced that the Menendez brothers had nothing to do with cutting their chains and had never tried to escape. Cut chains had been discovered at several other courthouses. Jail trustees, honor prisoners with nonviolent backgrounds who helped move prisoners between jails and courts, had cut the chains as a prank. The *Los Angeles Times* quoted an anonymous Sheriff's office source who criticized the department for not conducting a "more thorough investigation" before releasing details of the alleged escape attempt to the media.

A week after the June 8 hearing, Judge Albracht held another closed session where Erik and Lyle testified for the first time. The other witnesses were Jerry Oziel and Judalon Smyth. At one point Smyth turned to the judge and complained that Jerry Oziel was still exerting mind control over her that was affecting her answers. Erik and Lyle told friends that everything Oziel testified about during the in-camera hearings was a lie. They accused Smyth of distorting the truth. Three months had passed since the arrests and the brothers were depressed that the tape litigation was taking so long.

None of the tapes were privileged, Judge Albracht ruled on August 6. It was a stunning victory for the prosecution. "Dr. Oziel has reasonable cause to believe that the brothers constituted a threat, and that it was necessary to disclose those communications to prevent the threatened danger," he said. Defense attorneys warned relatives that litigation over the tapes would go to the California Supreme Court and cause a significant delay in going to trial. After the ruling, Marta Cano conceded for the first time that her nephews might be guilty.

"I know it definitely wasn't money if they did it. The kids always had everything they wanted and had access to several charge accounts," she said. "Lyle would've become the executor of the estate at twenty-two. Why wouldn't he wait six months until he had control over the estate if they were doing it for money?"

There was another problem for the defense. Since Gerald Chaleff had represented both Erik and Lyle in the fall of 1989 and was privy to confidential information they'd both shared with him, it was decided he should withdraw because of the possibility one brother could turn on the other.

On August 16, the L.A. District Attorney removed Elliot Alhadeff as prosecutor on the case. A press release said he'd been replaced because of a "personality conflict" with D.A. Ira Reiner. Alhadeff, a twenty-five-year veteran of the office, was upset about the decision. A week earlier, the L.A. County Association of Deputy District Attorneys had voted him 1990 Prosecutor of the Year. The group issued a statement that it "lacked confidence" in Reiner's judgment for removing him. Reiner replaced him with Pam Bozanich, a ten-year veteran of the office, and Lester Kuriyama, who'd been a deputy D.A. for six years.

CHAPTER 35

JUDALON GOES PUBLIC

"**I HEARD FROM THEIR OWN MOUTHS THAT THEY KILLED** their parents," Judalon Smyth dramatically told Diane Sawyer on *Primetime Live* in August 1990. It was Smyth's first TV appearance speaking about the case. Wearing a conservative royal blue dress and a string of pearls, she said she'd overheard the brothers' confession down the hall from Jerry Oziel's office because he wanted her to call the police "if there was anything that sounded violent or dangerous."

"Erik said that Lyle made him take the first shot. I suppose that's because Lyle thought that if he didn't make Erik shoot the first shot, that he might not be strong enough to do that . . . They didn't talk about shooting the father a whole lot. They did talk that they had to keep shooting the mother. And they kept shooting her because she would move, and they thought that she might live."

Smyth said that she tipped off police that the brothers had crafted an alibi and dumped the shotguns along Mulholland Drive.

"One of the things that I heard Lyle say that was really disturbing to me . . . was, 'Well, for once, my father would have to congratulate me and give me credit that I planned the perfect murder.'" Oziel told her that Lyle had an "asocial personality" similar to serial killer Ted Bundy, she added.

Smyth claimed it was the brothers' idea to record a taped confession. She hadn't heard the tape, but she said that she never heard an "ounce of remorse or one word spoken about any abuse." Initially, Oziel described Erik and Lyle as "murderous monsters" but later called them the "poor boys."

Jerry Oziel vehemently denied that he'd ever asked her to eavesdrop. "If she was ever in my office, she was in my waiting room," he told me days after Smyth's TV interview. "The door to the inside hallway where the therapy offices are remains locked when people are in session."

Examining the office for myself, some of the physical facts bore him out. From the waiting room, nothing could be heard from Oziel's office. When I pressed an ear directly on the inner office door, it was possible to hear muffled sounds but nothing like the detailed conversations that Smyth said she'd overheard.

Erik told a relative that Smyth's "testimony will be torn to shreds in court." But some in the family saw her appearance as a turning point. "Her interview put a perspective on what I had already heard in bits and pieces from the defense lawyers and the kids," said Carlos Baralt. "There is something there, I told Maria. It's not a complete lie." Cousin Henry Llanio, who had been one of the brothers' staunch supporters, was more blunt: "They're guilty as hell. The kids need to confess and plea bargain. My problem now is the motive."

CHAPTER 36

"NOW WE CAN'T SUCCEED"

WHILE ERIK AND LYLE PUBLICLY PROCLAIMED THEIR innocence, their attorneys knew the truth: The brothers had killed their parents. But they didn't know why.

In the early summer of 1990, Leslie Abramson contacted Dr. William Vicary, a forensic psychiatrist experienced with doing psychological assessments for the L.A. courts. Abramson asked Vicary to evaluate the Menendez brothers.

"When I started, I completely accepted the prosecution theory of the case. I said, these are rich kids who were pissed off at their overbearing, oppressive parents. They killed so they could go on with their lives and have the money."

But he suspected there had to be more. Children rarely kill their parents, he knew, and when they do, they're often victims of terrible abuse. Vicary had a hunch that Jose Menendez was going to turn out to be a monster. Kitty's death was more puzzling. "I couldn't believe the mother had been doing nasty, rotten things to her own children. It shows my own naiveté. It's very rare to kill your own mother."

Vicary wasn't optimistic. At best, he thought he might find something mitigating that could reduce the death penalty to life in prison without parole. Frequently, Vicary evaluated people who were psychotic and out of touch. Upon meeting the brothers, he thought Lyle would be a forensic dream case—a bright patient who communicated easily. In contrast, Erik was a mess: "He was trembling, biting his fingernails, sticking his hands in his mouth, looking down. He had very poor eye contact. He rarely said anything. When he did, it was kind of silly, kind of off the point."

But what you see isn't always what you get.

On the surface, Lyle seemed affable and under control. But he was reluctant to discuss his own psychological pain. "He was very suspicious, almost paranoid. Being in a room with him and interacting was a very anxiety-provoking situation. I never made a single note because I thought that would blow whatever support I was working to establish."

Vicary's first session alone with Erik was in a tiny interview room. Across the table, Erik was chained to a chair. Most of Vicary's notes were of Erik talking about his father. There was the standard outline of his biography: "Came to U.S. at 16 . . . Hertz age 28 . . . RCA Records . . . LIVE Entertainment $1.5M a year." But also: "Could charm anybody . . . stupid joker . . . controlled."

At their next meeting a week later, Erik said that his father "didn't have the ability to love people." Erik said that Jose told them "how easy it would be to get a new family" and "kill your children if they were out of control."

In later sessions, Erik described Jose as a "mental manipulator." Kitty "loved us but hated us." She yelled at her sons that she wished "they'd never been born." Over and over, his father repeated what he could've done "if I'd had your start." They "grew to hate him." At one point, he told his sons that he had "disinherited and disowned them."

In the middle of the night in his cell, in the darkness, Erik said he was startled by his father's voice speaking to him. It sounded "like a stone, like the devil," and he would "do anything not to hear it again." But it constantly reappeared.

The experience was so unsettling that Erik frequently got up in the dark and looked around for his father. Sometimes, the voice would whisper to him in a dream. But other times it would be screaming: "You're stupid!" "You're not worthy of being a Menendez!" "It's your fault!"

When it came to patients hearing voices, Bill Vicary had a test. "Real patients tell you it's just like someone in the room standing next to you talking," he said. "The people who are making it up talk about voices inside their head." Erik thought his father was with him in the jail cell.

Erik initially praised his father. "It was exactly the opposite of what you'd expect for someone that's cooked up some kind of a scheme to portray his father as abusive and a rapist," Vicary said. "The schemer would start out from the very beginning saying, 'My father was a terrible person. He was a bastard. He was terrible. He ruined my life.' Both Lyle and Erik started out in the exact opposite position. They had nothing but nice things to say about their parents." Vicary thought Erik and Lyle had been programmed to depict Jose Menendez as heroic. After the killings, they began to idealize their parents. Their reflections were like a battered individual describing a dead abusive spouse.

Erik described his life before the killings as a "training camp." Vicary was surprised when at their eleventh session Erik told him that being in jail was "relaxing . . . like a vacation." Now, for the first time in his life, he could set his own schedule. And there was one other thing Erik was relieved about: "Now we can't succeed."

In the days after the killings, Erik didn't understand why nobody came forward to punish him. He experienced tremendous guilt. "We had money, but it wasn't success we had achieved on our own," he said. He was tormented about inheriting millions.

"F beat M sometimes with a belt," Vicary noted in the twelfth session. "M always had bruises on legs, chest, abdomen, back . . . said she fell . . . saw when she swam." Erik said Kitty always feared Jose. After listening to his mother cry daily, he persuaded her to get a divorce. "I wanted her to talk to me, hold me," he said.

Eventually, Erik opened up more, giving information "on his terms." It never worked when Vicary tried to ask specific questions. If he pushed, Erik would close up. But eventually, that changed. Erik wanted to talk. "In fact, he wouldn't shut up," said the therapist. "He was under so much turmoil and pain that he developed psychotic symptoms." Vicary prescribed Triavil, a combination tranquilizer and antidepressant, to keep him from going over the edge. As months passed, Erik was struggling in jail. He had trouble sleeping and often woke up early. His appetite was poor, and he'd lost twenty pounds since being arrested. He kept having anxiety attacks and couldn't stop crying. He was in fear of "falling apart."

"F had violent temper, explosive ... usually against M," Vicary noted in their fifteenth session. Erik called his mother delusional because she considered Jose a "great man." She would tell the brothers that "he loves me."

Erik was frustrated that she protected Jose but not her sons. "We couldn't take refuge in our mother's arms," he said. "She wasn't going to piss him off to save us." He believed that Kitty hated Lyle more than him. Jose spent more time with Lyle, whom he favored as his first-born son.

After discovering their mother's suicide notes, both brothers worried about leaving Kitty alone with their father. They thought she wouldn't last long after they both left for college. "Nobody knew what was going on in the family," Vicary said Erik told him. Vicary believed that his visits along with Leslie Abramson's mothering were helping. "He never really had anybody in his whole life that he felt he could tell some of these things to. It was very slow. It was like pulling teeth with him, but over time, I think we really had a good rapport."

"I hated it and couldn't stand it anymore," Erik said, cryptically in the eighteenth session. "'M's family thought we had the perfect family,'" Vicary wrote. "'Everyone thought we had great parents—why didn't we? My father loved me only if I did well.'" In their next meeting, Erik explained his overwhelming need to confess to somebody after the killings. He was increasingly depressed and suicidal. He felt better after talking to Dr. Oziel. He tearfully admitted that he "wouldn't live" if Lyle died. "I love my brother more than anything," he said.

Jose considered his younger son a failure, even though he'd been accepted at UCLA and Berkeley. Erik wanted to join the pro tennis tour for a year, but after his poor play at the Kalamazoo tournament in August 1989, Jose cut off his training program.

The week before the killings was tense. Erik "hated" being around his parents. In the five days leading up to August 20, he slept a total of only twelve hours. When he woke up he'd be shaking. "We lived in a war zone. I couldn't take it anymore." There was another startling revelation in the twenty-fifth session: "F raped M ... tied her to a bed ... Lyle walked in on it" when he was ten.

Frustrated and perplexed, Leslie Abramson pressed Vicary: "Why can't you get more? We need the answers. It's not making sense. This doesn't fit together." The biggest puzzle was Kitty. "We could understand the father being killed if he was an SOB," Vicary said. "What we couldn't put together was why they killed the mother."

Months had passed. Perhaps the brothers had nothing else to tell. Maybe this was it. The lawyers and Vicary met. Did they really believe that? It didn't make sense; there must be more. And there was.

It emerged at their twenty-sixth meeting. "'M I hate you," Vicary noted from Erik's disclosures. "Found out one week prior to killings M knew F molested Erik." In the next session, more details poured out: "F not having sex with M . . . 'Age 6 F giving me massages, said I needed stretching . . . Age 5–6 F massages sore muscles from sports . . . eventually tells me to turn over . . . massages my penis . . . told me it was a tension release . . . told me I needed to release the stress and tension . . . oral sex since 7 or 8 . . . asked me to give him massage and oral sex.'"

With his jaw quivering, Erik revealed more details of the sexual abuse. Jose forced him to swallow after ejaculating in his mouth. Erik became emotional as he told of being raped at age ten. "It was difficult," he tearfully recalled. "I told cousin Andy who promised never to tell . . . F would be furious if anyone knew." Erik had been afraid to say no.

"The first person I ever talked about this with was my priest, Father Ken Deasy," Erik told me. "I wanted it to get out. Once I told my priest, I wanted to talk about it with Dr. Vicary and my family." Third was Steve Goldberg, the twenty-seven-year-old attorney the Baralts had hired to handle the estate. He'd been visiting Lyle and Erik in jail two or three times a week. Although they spent most of their time together discussing business, the brothers had developed a bond with Goldberg.

One afternoon, Goldberg sensed that Erik wanted to tell him something. As he talked with both brothers in the attorney room, they admitted to him that they killed their parents. They then presented a long list of instructions. First, they wanted to confess to their family.

Goldberg called Carlos and Terry Baralt, who immediately flew to Los Angeles. In his office, he told them that their nephews had committed the murders. Then, at the jail, the brothers confessed to their aunt and uncle.

"I could barely get the words out," Erik said. He cried when he admitted the killings and his father's molestation. Everybody cried. Later that day, the Baralts called Marta Cano and broke the news.

When Erik revealed his secret, Leslie Abramson was vacationing in Ireland. On her return she picked up frantic messages from Dr. Vicary. The lawyers wanted to know why the brothers hadn't turned to other relatives for help. Vicary thought that they were both psychologically mixed up and had little self-esteem or confidence. Their emotional maturity lagged behind their chronological age. He estimated that Erik was in the range of age eight to twelve, and Lyle twelve to fourteen.

Shortly after Erik began revealing the molestation, Lyle dropped "little hints" about his own experience. The lawyers suspected there was more. "Initially, there was some gentle exploration with Lyle, but it was like No Sale," said Vicary. "He said, 'It didn't happen to me. Nothing like that ever happened to me.'" Later, Erik told Vicary that Lyle had secretly confessed to him: "Lyle told me something sexual did happen between him and our father, but he's never going to tell anybody. There's no way that's ever going to come out." Vicary began to believe that Lyle was more fragile than his brother.

Lyle's second attorney, Joel Isaacson, left the case. Isaacson was tired of butting heads with Leslie Abramson, who was clearly in charge of what would be a joint defense. Several weeks later, Jill Lansing, who had been the number two chair behind Gerry Chaleff and Isaacson, was named Lyle's new lead attorney. Lansing and Abramson had been close friends since working together in the L.A. public defender's office.

In April 1992, a jury returned not-guilty verdicts for four Caucasian Los Angeles policemen accused in the videotaped beating of Rodney King, an African American man. The judge who presided over the trial was Stanley Weisberg. Riots that followed the acquittals resulted in the deaths of fifty-two people and caused $1 billion in damage.

Weisberg was a former L.A. County deputy D.A. who'd been the lead prosecutor in a 1987 murder case in which twenty-five-year-old Ricky Kyle was accused of killing his wealthy entertainment executive father. During the five-month trial, several witnesses testified that Ricky Kyle had confided he wanted to kill his father. "Before Henry Kyle's death, Ricky Kyle talked about killing his father because he hated him and he was desperate for his money," Weisberg told jurors in his closing argument. "Ricky Kyle did kill his father. He put a bullet through his father's heart, then told people afterward." But the defense presented evidence that Kyle had suffered a lifetime of physical and verbal abuse. They claimed Kyle had shot his father in self-defense. After seventeen days, the jury came back with a verdict of involuntary manslaughter.

The California Supreme Court rejected a lower court ruling in August 1992 that gave prosecutors access to the tapes from all four disputed therapy sessions. The justices agreed that two of the meetings (October 31 and November 2, 1989) were not confidential because Dr. Oziel believed that Erik and Lyle Menendez posed a danger. But the court ruled that the two other sessions (November 28 and December 11) would remain private since no threats had been made during those sessions. The ruling was an important victory for the defense. The December 11 taped session with the brothers' own voices was now off-limits to the prosecution.

In December 1992, a Los Angeles County grand jury returned two indictments for first-degree murder against Erik and Lyle Menendez. The indictments added a new charge of conspiracy, alleging that the brothers bought shotguns and ammunition two days before the killings and also contacted Perry Berman to set up an alibi.

But in a serious blow to the D.A., grand jurors declined to include one of the cornerstones of the prosecution's case: murder for financial gain. The absence of the financial gain special circumstance would not keep prosecutors from presenting greed as a motive, prosecutor Pam Bozanich declared. "I don't think you can ignore it."

"Money is not what this case is about and never has been," countered Lyle's attorney Jill Lansing. "The Porsche and Marina del Rey penthouse were an important part of the prosecution's case in terms of making people not like the kids. The brothers had all the money they needed before the killings."

In a front-page story in the *Los Angeles Times* in early July 1993, shortly before the start of the trial, the defense said that Erik and Lyle Menendez had been sexually molested by their father. Leslie Abramson said she was disclosing "what really happened" because of her concern for the brothers' negative portrayal in the press. Both sons were "subjected to a system of child rearing that was by its very nature abusive . . . They were objects for the gratification and the aggrandizement of the parents," she said.

Defense witnesses would describe Kitty Menendez as an impatient and intolerable woman who flew into uncontrollable rages. "These kids lived in an atmosphere that was like a training camp," Abramson said. "Later it was more like a concentration camp once the really ugly stuff began." She described the deaths of Jose and Kitty as "overkill," saying that the brothers fired in terror.

Abramson and Lansing had debated the decision to go public for more than a year—Leslie for, Jill against. Abramson said they'd been working on the defense since September 1990. But as she feared, what was labeled the "abuse excuse" was cynically seen as a late and desperate ploy to save the brothers from the gas chamber.

On July 8, 1993, a jury of seven women and five men were impaneled for the trial of Lyle Menendez. A week later, six women and six men were chosen for Erik Menendez's jury.

PART NINE

TRIAL BY TWO JURIES

CHAPTER 37

SHOWTIME — OPENING STATEMENTS

JUST AFTER SIX IN THE MORNING ON TUESDAY, JULY 20, 1993, three years and eleven months after Jose and Kitty Menendez were killed, a line for the public seats to the murder trial of their sons formed outside the Van Nuys Superior Courthouse.

By eight o'clock it was a carnival atmosphere. The court allowed only twelve seats for the media, so most reporters were relegated to watching a TV feed in a building a block away. Just before 9:30 AM, Maria Menendez waved a frail finger as the brothers entered the packed courtroom. Two minutes later, Judge Stanley Weisberg took the bench: "The Court will call the case of the People v. Menendez."

There were two juries because some evidence didn't apply to both defendants; for instance, one brother's friend might not testify in front of the other's jury. Erik and Lyle were allowed to stay in the courtroom for each other's opening statements. Both lead defense attorneys wore white. Pam Bozanich, dressed in a dark red suit, began a twenty-eight-minute account of what she said happened August 20, 1989. She described the brothers as "two actors" who had fooled investigators on the night of the killings. The brothers suggested that detectives consider Jose's "seedy" business associates as suspects. They hired bodyguards so their relatives would think they were at risk.

Lyle went on a spending spree that included buying Rolex watches and a $64,000 Porsche. He hired someone to erase the family computer after he unsuccessfully searched for a new will. He told his friend Glenn Stevens that he'd be—"and I apologize for this," said Bozanich—"'fucked' if the police ever got their hands on the audiotapes he'd recorded with Dr. Jerome Oziel."

According to Oziel, the prosecution's star witness, Lyle and Erik "killed out of hatred" and to be free from "their father's domination and impossible standards." They never mentioned to Oziel that the "killings were in self-defense, or that they'd suffered any abuse . . . It will become apparent that this murder was unlawful, unjustified, and wholly premeditated," said Bozanich. "But for a few mistakes they made, this was almost the perfect murder."

Before Jill Lansing began her opening, she posted Menendez family pictures on a bulletin board in front of the jury box.

"On August 20, 1989, Lyle and Erik Menendez killed their parents," she began. "We're not disputing where it happened, how it happened, or who did it. The only thing you are going to have to focus on in this trial is why it happened. What we will prove to you is that it was done out of fear."

Dismissing the prosecution's greed theory, Lansing maintained that the brothers had plenty of money. Lyle lived in a mansion, drove an Alfa Romeo, and had credit cards since age fifteen. "This trial will take you behind the façade of the rich houses and fancy cars, the wealthy friends and the impressive social engagements," she said. "It will take you into the life that was experienced by Lyle Menendez and his brother as they grew up."

Lyle felt responsible for protecting his brother. Erik told Lyle that he couldn't stand the sexual molestation any longer, she said. "Lyle couldn't turn his back on his brother." At the defense table, Lyle began to cry softly.

Lyle was molested between ages six and eight, she said. At thirteen, he sensed that something was going on with Erik and decided to confront his father. Jose promised the abuse would stop. Lyle thought his intervention had worked. Now, he was going to talk to Dad again. But the confrontation didn't go well. Jose Menendez made it very clear that this secret would never leave this family. Lansing explained how in the week before the killings the brothers' "fear had accelerated." Lyle and Erik "believed they were about to be killed, and they acted."

The emotion of the 911 call was genuine. Their story about going to the movies wasn't a "sophisticated alibi." She attacked the spending spree evidence. The brothers didn't know about an insurance policy that would pay them $500,000 within a month of the killings.

When Lyle first talked about the molestation, he told the family, not the attorneys. Then, the defense team had experts evaluate the brothers. Kitty Menendez told Lyle that she never wanted him, and that his birth ended her dream of a career in broadcasting. "She humiliated and degraded him, telling him, 'You get in the way and you ruin my life,'" Lansing said. "Lyle lived in a world of contradictions."

Jose wanted Lyle to become a "corrected version" of himself, "with everything Jose didn't have. He was going to have all the money he needed. He was not going to suffer the degradation of being working class, which was so offensive to Jose." Lyle sat with his head down, crying.

Jose "reveled in his sadism." He called Lyle "inept and stupid." The physical violence included beatings and belt whippings. Lansing described the argument after a tennis match, when Lyle had yelled at his father to shut up. "His father grabbed him by the throat and socked him square in the face, and said, 'If you ever embarrass me again, I'll kill you.'"

"The Menendez family blended sex and violence," said Lansing. "They had no boundaries. The boys showered with their father up to the very end, and their mother, in their teens, was still coming in the bathtub and bathing them and washing their hair."

Jose gave Lyle massages starting at age six. "He told him this was the type of thing that the Romans did. He told him that this is what fathers and sons do, that he was special, that this was a special bond that they had. And he began the sexual molestation." Lyle felt "confusion and fear," but liked the attention until "objects were used which hurt."

Lyle pleaded to his mother for sympathy. She told him, "Your dad loves you. You have to be punished sometimes." After Kitty discovered Jose's eight-year affair, a "crazy woman got even crazier," Lansing said.

"During the last week, Lyle and Erik talked about a mother who was willing to die and willing to kill. They talked about a father who was not going to be controlled by anyone or anything. They talked about parents who can treat their children as objects, who can abuse and use and degrade them. And they knew that these were parents who could kill their children."

In her opening statement, Leslie Abramson promised that Erik Menendez would testify. When the police didn't come immediately after the shooting, she said, the brothers decided to "cover up" their involvement. "After a lifetime of abuse, he didn't want to go to jail," she said. "Erik will tell you why he killed his parents." After returning home the night of August 20, Erik was hysterical, incapable of any response.

"What did they do to their children to bring this about? What is it that was done to Erik Menendez?" Abramson said it began at age six with Jose's "inappropriate touching and arousal of his young son, and escalated in a carefully calculated pattern of grooming the child for his father's sexual gratification." After that there was "forcible oral copulation, sodomy, rape, and the intentional infliction of pain by the use of foreign objects upon Erik's person."

Erik's head suddenly dropped, his chin on his chest as he sobbed quietly. The jury was riveted.

"Witnesses will tell you that Mr. Jose Menendez thought himself a superior being and indoctrinated his children into believing that he was, in all respects, perfect," said Abramson. "All that mattered was being rich." To incestuous parents, she said, "a child is just a thing." When Erik was eleven, Jose pulled on his hair while forcing the boy to perform oral sex on him. When Erik cried the first time that Jose ejaculated in his mouth, Jose slapped him. To torture Erik, "he used a variety of objects: needles, tacks, wooden implements, knotted ropes. These episodes are what Erik called the 'Dark Days.'"

To her sons, Kitty Menendez was "cold, distant, and hostile," Abramson said. The evidence would show that she knew Jose was molesting Erik. She seemed afraid of Jose, and Erik thought she was a victim, too. He didn't tell his mother because he didn't want to burden her with his secret.

"You will have to decide the truth," Abramson told the jury. "You will hear evidence that she never tended to her son while he was throwing up in the bathroom next door to her bedroom, after a sexual episode with his father." The sex happened as often as twice a month.

The Menendez home was a "boot camp," and Kitty was an enforcer. In school, it was grades that mattered, not learning. Both parents intimidated their sons' teachers and frequently did their homework for them. Jose Menendez taught his sons to "cheat, steal, lie, but win!"

Erik idolized Lyle, his only close friend. At age fifteen, Erik prayed for a miracle: He'd go off to college and the molestation would end. After the family moved to California, the sex stopped for some time. But six months later, Kitty discovered Jose's affairs, and Erik watched his mother fall apart.

Kitty always knew the smallest details of Erik's life; he wondered if she had "supernatural powers." After her death, he discovered that she'd secretly been taping his phone calls. Kitty had demanded that Erik find a girlfriend within six months, and when he did, he devoted himself to her obsessively, meanwhile worrying that she'd think he was "different" and maybe gay. He blamed himself for the sex with his father.

Shortly before the killings, Jose used sex with him as punishment. By then, Jose had ended the "propaganda that it was normal . . . It was clear to Erik that now the sex was a show of force and dominance and nothing else, and Erik Menendez hated himself for not being strong enough to stop it." The last time Jose sodomized his son was in May 1989 when he became enraged over a failed class and a poor tennis performance. In the first week of August 1989, Jose became furious again when Erik lost another tennis tournament.

Seven days before the murders, Jose told Erik that he could enroll at UCLA but would have to sleep at home so they could monitor his schoolwork. "Erik Menendez understood immediately what this meant," said Abramson. "The sex was going to continue." Erik was despondent.

Friday morning, August 18, the brothers decided to buy guns for protection. After learning that there was a waiting period for handguns, they purchased two shotguns. On Sunday night, "in pure terror, pure panic," anticipating their own murder, the brothers burst into the family room, firing. Erik believed his parents were "incapable of dying."

"The prosecution is relying on Jerome Oziel," said Abramson. "We will challenge Dr. Oziel. He wasn't present at events, and we will challenge his truthfulness. He had a motive to lie [and he did].

"The prosecution tells you [Erik] did it for money," she concluded. "What do they say when poor kids kill?" Abramson sat down and gently touched Erik's arm.

CHAPTER 38

THE PROSECUTION— GUILTIER THAN SIN?

One kid killing their parents is a bad seed. Two kids killing their parents is a bad family.

—Prosecutor PAM BOZANICH to ABC News,
January 2017

BHPD SGT. TOM EDMONDS TOOK THE STAND TO INTRODUCE the interviews he taped with the brothers ninety minutes after they called 911. The voices were muffled and barely audible, so transcripts were passed out to jurors. Erik displayed no reaction as he listened to his account of arriving home on the night of August 20:

". . . we went inside and I was smelling smoke. After that we saw them and immediately I started screaming, and—and so I went upstairs and Lyle called the police, immediately." Asked if he had ideas who might have done the murders, Erik said, "No, my family has no enemies, but my brother may know."

The next morning Edmonds played his interview with Lyle Menendez, who explained how they missed connecting with Perry Berman.

"I was still a little bit upset, so I told him to meet us at this place and we could get together to do something." Edmonds hadn't asked Lyle to explain what he was upset about. Next, Lyle described their return home: "And I thought it was strange in a way and, you know, I smelled smoke everywhere." Erik had also mentioned the smoke inside the room, but Edmonds didn't follow up on that either.

Edmonds hadn't considered the brothers suspects so he didn't give them gunshot residue tests. Both Erik and Lyle appeared to be traumatized. Lester Kuriyama asked Edmonds if he knew that Erik was an "aspiring actor." Leslie Abramson angrily objected but was overruled.

"Would it be fair to say that as you sit today in court that you have learned you were lied to on that day?" asked the prosecutor. Abramson objected again. At a sidebar, she told Judge Weisberg, "None of this really goes anywhere . . . they can be traumatized and guiltier than sin." This time he agreed.

Kuriyama asked Perry Berman about the phone call from Lyle late Sunday evening, August 20. Berman said that Lyle sounded a "little jumpy" and "anxious." He went to the Cheesecake Factory but the brothers never showed up.

Berman said he met the Menendezes in 1985 in New Jersey when he coached Erik. Once, during a weekly lesson, when Perry fed Erik lobs to improve his confidence, Jose ran out onto the court.

"He basically came down, started yelling at me, feeling that I was making it too easy on his son. He basically didn't understand my reasoning for that, and just basically walked off."

On Jill Lansing's cross, Berman said that in his fifteen years of coaching he'd never seen a parent interfere with a lesson in the way that Jose ran onto the court. It was "shocking."

"Was the Menendez home a relaxed, easygoing, warm environment?" asked Lansing.

"I feel that Mr. Menendez ran his home as though it was a company and he was chairman of the board. He was very strict with the boys. He wanted to have control in every aspect of their lives, either academically, socially, with tennis, with the girls they wanted to go out with, the schools they selected."

"And was there tension in that home?"

Yes, Berman said, adding there was a "sense of secrecy. I believe that they kept a lot [of] what was going on to themselves."

In Sacramento that afternoon, the California Board of Psychology charged Dr. Jerry Oziel with assaulting two female "patients"—the former nannies—while they were his lovers. Oziel was also accused of giving them mood-altering drugs without prescriptions. The charges were filed by Judalon Smyth, who reiterated that Oziel wanted to be called "Dr. Daddy."

The accusations were filed just days before Oziel was to take the stand as the star prosecution witness against Lyle and Erik Menendez. Speaking to reporters, Leslie Abramson said "This guy was a menace to the mental health of the people of California. If we're allowed to prove the true nature of this person, his ethics and total ineptness, the jury will not believe what he has to say." She accused Oziel of blackmailing the Menendez brothers by dictating audio notes after therapy sessions "to give himself a source of future income. He could have called police, but he preferred to have a device to hold over their heads."

But the prosecution would not be deterred from calling Oziel to testify. Pam Bozanich told reporters their case remained strong: "We have uncovered no evidence of physical or sexual abuse. The fact that Mr. Menendez was domineering, controlling, overbearing, and hard to live with is not news to us. You don't kill people you love."

On Monday, July 26, the fifth day of trial, Judge Weisberg ruled that the juries would not learn about the screenplay *Friends*, which had been widely publicized by the media. "The probative value is nil. The potential to confuse issues is great," said Weisberg.

The People then called Craig Cignarelli, who appeared in front of only Erik Menendez's jury. Smiling and relaxed, Craig said he met Erik at Calabasas High School, where they were both stars on the tennis team. They bonded quickly, often sharing their dreams and ideas for the future.

Cignarelli testified that he visited the Beverly Hills mansion ten days after the killings to be with Erik, "just to kind of hang out with him, make sure everything was okay." While he was there, a man with a pregnant wife came to work on a computer in the master bedroom. "He said that his brother had a computer expert come up and erase the family will." Craig said Erik told him that the "original will left all the money to the kids."

Craig had stayed overnight that evening. Kuriyama asked if Erik discussed the killings. With a deep sigh, Cignarelli answered yes.

It began as they stood in the foyer outside the family room where Jose and Kitty died.

"Do you want to know how it happened?" Cignarelli said Erik asked him. "And I said, 'Yes.' And I wasn't really sure where he was going with it.

"He said that he went back outside, and his brother was standing there with two shotguns and said, 'Let's do it.' And they walked inside, and Lyle was standing—or Erik went up to the door on the left, which was slightly open. Lyle went up and put his shoulder against the door on the right. And Erik said he looked in, saw his parents sitting on the couch. And Lyle swung open the door and shot his father, and looked at Erik and said, 'Shoot Mom.' And Erik said he shot his mom as she was standing up yelling."

Then, Craig said that he and Erik played chess and ate dinner.

"Did Erik Menendez ever tell you that he acted in self-defense?" asked Kuriyama.

"No," replied Cignarelli.

"Did he ever tell you that he was being abused by his parents?"

"No."

Months later, Cignarelli said, Erik denied that he had any involvement in the murders, and suggested that they might have been related to the Mob or his father's business.

The direct examination only took twenty minutes. Then, Cignarelli's cool demeanor abruptly changed as Leslie Abramson began cross-examination. Abramson asked if he'd ever seen Jose Menendez get emotional at their matches.

"Not screaming, but saying, 'You need to do better.' Just criticizing him and pushing him to do better, like most parents."

"Do most parents criticize their kids in front of other people?"

"In Calabasas, yes," he replied.

"Tough parents in Calabasas," declared Abramson.

"Let's not editorialize," said the judge.

On direct examination, Cignarelli had testified that Erik had confessed to him "about a week and a half" after August 20, but he admitted in cross that he initially told detectives it had been during the weekend of October 21, 1989. His recollection of the date had changed after reading police reports, he said.

"I told them when the weekend was, and they gave me the exact date."

"How would they know when the weekend was, Mr. Cignarelli? They weren't there."

He believed that prosecutors coordinated the date to when the computer expert was at the house. "I guess they put those two together."

"I see," Abramson said, sarcastically. "So you're putting your story together to match when the computer person came up?"

"I'm not putting my story together . . . I'm just telling the truth! The computer person was there when I was there."

But when he'd met with police in November 1989 he hadn't mentioned the computer expert, he conceded on cross. He couldn't describe him, except that he'd come with his pregnant wife. Cignarelli thought that the expert had stayed in the bedroom and unsuccessfully searched the computer for a file named "WILL."

When Erik showed him the family room, he said Erik told him there had been "skin and blood all over the place."

"It bothered me to be in the house a little bit. But with all the security guards around, it was okay."

"Now you didn't ask Erik, 'Why did you do it?' did you?" asked Abramson.

"No. Everybody comments about that," he said.

"I move to strike that, Your Honor!"

"The last remark is stricken, and the jury is admonished to disregard it," replied the judge.

Cignarelli explained that the confession could have been one of the "mind games" that he and Erik loved to play.

To later trap his best friend, he said he agreed to "act as an agent for the police" and wear a body wire. He denied that detectives had threatened him to do so.

"So there was no downside?" asked Abramson.

"No. The downside was, I was doing this to my best friend."

CHAPTER 39

I DON'T RECALL—
DONOVAN GOODREAU

LYLE MENENDEZ WAS DREADING THE PROSECUTION'S NEXT witnesses, his two closest confidants. Within a month after the killings, Glenn Stevens informed on him to the police while still enjoying Lyle's generosity. But first was Donovan Goodreau. The defense was uncertain what he might say.

Goodreau, now age twenty-three, had become a personal trainer in New York City with some celebrity clients. As he entered the witness box, he was so nervous that as he spelled his name, his voice cracked.

"Mr. Goodreau, sit back and take a deep breath," said Pam Bozanich.

Goodreau recounted his two-month stay in Lyle's dorm room in Gauss Hall, his lie about enrolling in school, and the day Lyle's friends hurriedly packed all of his belongings and loaded them into his dilapidated truck. After leaving for New York, Goodreau realized he'd left something behind—his wallet with his California driver's license. That was three months before the murders. He and Lyle had not seen each other since.

"Were you by any chance in San Diego at any time around August 18, 1989?" asked Bozanich.

"No," said Goodreau.

"Did you buy any shotguns during that period of time?

"No, I didn't," he replied.

Goodreau worked all day at Boxers restaurant in New York on August 18 and 19.

At the request of the Beverly Hills Police, Goodreau provided a handwriting sample—a series of two dozen identically scrawled signatures. The next prosecution exhibit was the federal form filled out to buy two shotguns in San Diego two days before Jose and Kitty died. Goodreau denied that he was involved in the transaction.

"Did you ever give permission to Erik Menendez to use your driver's license?" asked Bozanich.

"No," he answered quietly. But he and Lyle had often borrowed each other's IDs. He frequently used Lyle's Social Security ID to eat in the Princeton dining halls.

Goodreau snuck a glance at Lyle as Jill Lansing began cross. When they'd met, he said, they quickly bonded and spent all their time together. "He didn't have all the money in the world. He was basically on an allowance, like most students there."

Going to Princeton was Jose Menendez's idea; Lyle would have preferred UCLA, said Donovan. Lyle sensed that his father was disappointed in him.

"What kind of similarities did you have in your past?" asked Jill Lansing.

"Oppressive fathers," said Goodreau.

Shortly after Erik and Lyle's arrest, Les Zoeller had told me, over lunch, "There's a very interesting guy you should talk to in New York City who could give you a lot of information." In July 1990, four months after the arrests, I finally met the interesting guy—Donovan Goodreau.

For two hours, Goodreau reminisced about his lost friendship that had lasted just over three months. "I tried to call him after my mom told me about the murders. I must have called Les Zoeller twenty times and left messages asking Lyle to call me," but he never responded.

Lyle had shared with Goodreau the pressure he was under as the son of Jose Menendez. "Lyle and I became very close because we both had dominant, pushing fathers. When we met, we talked for hours about our dads, our hopes, and our futures.

"Lyle said the one thing that would drive him to kill his dad was his girlfriends. He said he was upset that his mom was becoming a basket case because of the girlfriends."

Three months later, on October 25, 1990, Glenn Stevens told me about a conversation he'd had with Donovan several months earlier.

Stevens said Donovan told him that he and Lyle had become such close friends because they had told each other they'd both been sexually abused as children.

"By the father or the mother?" I asked.

"By the father, I assume. Donovan said it as if Lyle didn't go into complete detail with him. He just said Lyle was very pissed off about things that his father had done to Erik, as far as sexual abuse. That's what Donovan told me."

On December 7, 1990, Goodreau told me directly about the molestation. In a taped phone interview, Donovan said that he and Lyle had a long discussion about it at a Chinese restaurant in Princeton. "I'm not gonna lie about the abuse talks, but I won't be the first to step forward," he said. This was two and a half years before the brothers would publicly admit that they killed their parents after enduring years of abuse.

RAND: I heard something this week that sexual abuse might be the kind of defense they try to do.

GOODREAU: Oh, no, no, don't tell me they're gonna do that.

RAND: Yeah, that's what I heard. Nothing definite.

GOODREAU: You know what's gonna happen. Lyle's gonna tell them, well, if you don't believe me, ask Donovan. (laughter) I told him, they're just gonna like have a microscope all over me. Are you kidding?

RAND: I don't think they'd try to pull you in if it's bullshit.

GOODREAU: No, see, the reason he told me that—he did tell me a lot of things about his father and stuff, but it's like I always thought he was doing that to lure me into maybe believing his objective, but he never told me why he was doing it, why he was telling me. It didn't make sense until afterwards. You know what I'm saying—he told me a lot about their past and stuff and it was similar to my past.

> I, too, was molested as a child, and I told him that and I
> guess that opened the gate and he told me and it was like,
> wow!
> RAND: Did he say that he was molested?
> GOODREAU: I, uh, yeah. Lyle and his brother were molested.
> But it's like he didn't—he wasn't clear. He was never clear.

At lunch in New York in October 1991, Goodreau again brought up sexual abuse in the Menendez family.

"Lyle started telling me stories about Jose sexually abusing Erik when he was little. He said they took showers and baths together. The big bathtub in the new house was for sex scenes."

That was consistent with what Erik had mentioned in his interview with me in October 1989.

Donovan speculated that when they'd exchanged admissions of being molested a few months before the murders, perhaps Lyle was setting him up. Had Lyle planned his parents' murders months in advance and planted his best friend as a witness? But if you had, wouldn't you stay in touch with the person who might save you from Death Row? Lyle never returned Donovan's calls to him after the murders.

In the three years since I met Goodreau, he'd been one of my most prolific sources on the story. We'd spoken a few times a month, including a lengthy interview recorded over two days in March 1992. On July 23, 1993, three days before he would testify in California, I phoned him in New York.

Goodreau told me he was "very nervous" that he'd be asked about sexual molestation when he testified. He repeated what he'd first told me in 1990: "I'm not going to lie, but I'm not going to volunteer the information." We also discussed his reunion with Glenn Stevens in October 1989: "He walked over and gave me this big hug, and we walked inside and we were talking and he mentioned it [the abuse], and I almost fell off the seat because I thought I was the only one in the whole world who knew."

In redirect examination, Pam Bozanich asked Goodreau about a call Lyle got from his father one afternoon, after which Lyle had become angry.

"I think we had spoken earlier about his father's relationship with another woman, and I think the phone call triggered something, and he turned and said, 'I could kill my father for what he did to my mom.'"

"Did you feel that he was actually going to go out right then and kill him?"

"Not at all."

That exchange seemed valuable for the prosecution, but it opened the door for Lansing, who may have anticipated it, in recross:

"When you talked about your background, did you talk about areas that you had in common?"

"Yes," Goodreau replied.

"And was it your impression that Lyle admired his father?"

"Yes, very much so."

"And yet there were things about him that he did not admire?"

"Yes."

A year before testifying, Goodreau met with Lansing for three hours in a hotel room in New York and gave a sketchy account of the emotional dinner at the Chinese restaurant. It's possible that the prosecution, who called Goodreau, didn't know about the hotel meeting. Now Lansing asked for a sidebar.

Weisberg said he'd have to hear the testimony without jurors present.

It was just after 4 PM when the two panels were sent home for the day. Lansing then asked Goodreau about having a conversation with Lyle at a Chinese restaurant.

"What I think you're referring to is, towards the end of my stay at Princeton we had had a dinner at a Chinese food restaurant late at night. School was coming to a close. There was a lot of pressure on him, and we were talking about our plans for the summer and the future. And all the chairs were up on the tables around us. And they were just waiting for us to leave, and we just talked about, he started—"

"Let me ask a question."

"Okay."

"Did you reveal something about your own background of a personal nature?"

"Yes, I did."

"And did he, in response to that, reveal something to you about his and his brother's background?"

"No."

I was astonished. So was Lansing.

"Did he ever tell you that he and his brother had been molested by their father?"

"No, he didn't."

"Have you ever told me that?"

"I can't recall that I have."

"Have you ever told anyone else that?"

"I can't recall that I have."

As the exchange sank in, the color drained from Lansing's face.

"You don't remember whether you've ever told me or anyone else that Lyle Menendez told you that he and his brother were molested by their father?"

"I never . . ."

". . . in a Chinese restaurant?"

"I told him I was molested as a child. He never told me he was."

"He never said anything to you about that?"

"No."

"And you have never told anybody that he said anything of that nature? Is that true or not true?"

"It's true that—I never told anybody that I said that. I was under the assumption that by his reaction that he had had problems, but it was only an assumption."

The defense team conferred briefly.

"Mr. Goodreau, did you ever have an interview with a reporter in this case, on tape, in which you made that statement?"

"Bob Rand was the only reporter I interviewed [with] on tape. So it may have been him."

"Don't you think you would remember if you had?"

"Oh, sure."

"So, is it your testimony that you haven't?"

"It's my testimony that I haven't."

"Thank you."

Goodreau was excused until the next morning. As I walked out of the courtroom, Leslie Abramson approached me to say that she was going to have to subpoena my tape. "You'd better do the right thing," she said.

But what was the right thing?

I retreated to another floor to collect my thoughts. Before trial, Pam Bozanich had told me, "We realize there are credibility problems with some of these young witnesses."

I called a friend, attorney Tony Glassman, who suggested that I broadcast the tape that evening on local TV news as a way to avoid a subpoena from either side and be pulled into the case as a witness. I called Sylvia Teague, the managing editor at KCAL, Channel 9 in Los Angeles. I'd met her a few weeks earlier to discuss doing analysis during the trial. Teague asked me to come to the station for an interview and so they could broadcast some of my interview with Goodreau. I had to go home first to get it.

By the time I arrived at the station, it was too late to get the story on their 8 PM news hour. I played a section of the interview for reporter Jim Hill:

> GOODREAU: We were at a Chinese restaurant . . . he says, I know everything about you, you're my best friend. I know everything about you. It was real—you couldn't fake the kind of emotion he was giving me right then.

Goodreau told Lyle that when he was a child, he was molested by a friend of his family.

> GOODREAU: I'm telling the story, I'm all choked up, and then he was in tears. For twenty minutes, he didn't speak.
> RAND: Basically, he said his father had been abusing Erik?
> GOODREAU: Yeah, him and Erik.
> RAND: Lyle also?

GOODREAU: Yeah. He would take baths with him and stuff. Just, oh, man . . . you're just . . . it's weird because you felt—we weren't drinking, we were just sitting there, the whole place was closed, the chairs were up on the table, the guy's waiting for us to leave and he's telling me this. I could've fallen out of the back of my seat. He's telling me about him and his younger brother, and how his brother had been the most affected by it because he's younger and more impressionable.

Hill was tense because of his deadline. After dubbing the audiotape, they added video of me watching Goodreau in court and asked what I thought of his testimony.

"It appears he may have perjured himself," I said.

I phoned Jill Lansing and Michael Burt, the second chair defense attorney for Lyle, to suggest they watch the 9 PM news. Both were excited.

Minutes later, KCAL did a dramatic cold opening: There'd been "high drama in the courtroom" that afternoon during the Menendez brothers' murder trial, said anchorman Jerry Dunphy. Over video of Goodreau, red block letters filled the screen: PERJURY? In the breathless style of breaking TV news, the anchors said they had an exclusive story about a key prosecution witness "who may have lied on the stand."

The story repeated at 10 PM as the lead.

On the way home, my mind spun. Now I wasn't just covering the story, I'd become part of it. During the previous weekend, I'd flown from Los Angeles to Miami to chase down leads. I'd returned late Sunday night and slept just three hours before returning to court, so I was running on adrenaline. In spite of that, it was hard to fall asleep wondering what would happen when Donovan Goodreau returned to the witness stand on Tuesday.

———————

The next morning, I was standing outside the courtroom drinking coffee with Dominick Dunne, the writer covering the trial for *Vanity Fair* magazine. Les Zoeller approached and handed me a subpoena, demanding all of my tapes and notes related to Donovan Goodreau.

Back inside, without the juries present, Pam Bozanich told Judge Weisberg, "Last night on Channel 9 News, Mr. Robert Rand, who's a reporter who's been working on this case for, I think, in excess of three years, played a portion of an audiotape of an interview he had had with Mr. Goodreau, which is what I think the defense wants to show to the court and to Mr. Goodreau today."

My attorney Tony Glassman wouldn't be available until after lunch. If I was forced to testify, he advised me not to discuss anything that wasn't already published or broadcast. Press shield laws in most states protect a reporter's unpublished notes and tapes. But because I'd played an excerpt of the tape for Jill Lansing earlier when preparing a story, Bozanich told the judge that the entire tape should be considered published and I was no longer shielded. At the same time, Bozanich wanted to keep the defense from playing the tape for the juries. She said she'd learned that morning that I'd discussed molestation with Glenn Stevens, who told Donovan, who then completed a circle by passing the information back to me.

"It appears that Mr. Rand, and not Mr. Goodreau, is the genesis of this information," she said. Nor was the source "Lyle Menendez, but was Mr. Rand." What she was saying was that it sounded like I had made it all up, as if I'd started a rumor, and therefore the defense shouldn't play the tape and question Goodreau. She also wanted Judge Weisberg to exclude me from the courtroom because I'd acted in bad faith. She asked for a hearing without the juries present to question Stevens, Goodreau, and me.

The problem seemed to be that the prosecution hadn't seen Channel 9's news the previous evening. In fairness, I hadn't called them. I had contacted the defense attorneys, who had said they were going to subpoena the tape.

"I just have one concern," interjected Leslie Abramson. "That is, the prosecution seems to be taking the position that, if there is a conflict with respect to the source of information that somehow that information doesn't get presented in trial. And our position is, that's a credibility issue, like any for the jury to resolve."

Judge Weisberg disagreed. As for my exclusion, he expressed concern that there was the "potential of familiarity" by jurors with someone who sat in the courtroom daily. Perhaps, he suggested, they'd appraise my testimony differently than from a witness they'd seen for only one day. I was ordered to leave the courtroom.

After being called by the prosecution and sworn in to testify, I found it bizarre to sit in the witness box and look out at the people I'd been covering. Now, Erik and Lyle Menendez watched me along with attorneys, spectators, and other reporters in the packed courtroom. My father in Ohio was watching live on Court TV.

Pam Bozanich was particularly upset that I had played a segment of my tape for Jill Lansing but never asked the prosecution for an interview. I explained that one of the D.A.'s press people had told me that the prosecutors weren't available for interviews until after the trial. After a few short questions, Bozanich demanded to hear my entire two-and-a-half-hour interview with Goodreau. Judge Weisberg suggested that she find out more about the making of the tape.

"Is it your contention that Mr. Goodreau told you that the defendants had been sexually abused?"

"Yes."

My original taped interview with Goodreau was an audiotape, but the video of the KCAL 9 news story was played at the hearing, and the video story contained a section of the audio interview.

Now Bozanich asked me, "In the portion of the tape that we viewed, it appears you are asking him a number of leading questions. Is that correct?"

"I asked him a number of questions. That's what a reporter does."

"And those questions, then, you would not characterize as leading? Is that correct?"

"Objection, Your Honor," interrupted Leslie Abramson. "This is just argumentative."

"Overruled."

"You would not characterize the questions you asked of Mr. Goodreau, which were played on Channel 9 News, as leading? Is that correct?"

"No. It was in the context of an anecdote he was telling me about Lyle Menendez complaining about Jose Menendez sexually abusing Erik and Lyle."

"Do you, in fact, have interviews with other witnesses for the prosecution in this case?"

"Yes."

"And you are refusing to give that to the prosecution? Is that correct?"

"Yes."

"Why is it you will give information to the defense and not the prosecution?"

"I didn't give information. What I was doing was an interview. In the course of an interview, sometimes you reveal information. It's the same thing that I believe prosecutors and police do. Sometimes you reveal information to gain other information. That is what I was doing."

"Are you a police officer?"

"No. I'm a reporter."

"Objection, Your Honor," said Abramson. "This is just argumentative."

The judge still wanted to hear about the making of the tape. Questioning me himself, he asked about my conversation with Donovan Goodreau four days earlier.

"I don't wish to go into that," I replied. "It's unpublished material, and it deals with a source."

"The source being Mr. Goodreau?"

"Correct."

"The same source that you disclosed to the world on Channel 9 News last night?"

"I disclosed a very limited portion of information."

"And you feel that you qualify under the California shield law?"

"Yes, I do."

Judge Weisberg disagreed. "Based upon what has been presented to me, I find that Mr. Rand conducted this interview of Mr. Goodreau at a time when he was neither connected with or employed by any news organization, whether it be a newspaper, magazine, or other periodical publication or press association or wire service; that he conducted this interview solely in preparation for a book that he was writing. He so testified this morning.

"The court finds, in both reviewing his testimony this morning and this afternoon, that that is how and why the interview occurred; therefore, the shield law under section 1070 of the evidence code does not apply to Mr. Rand. It was written to apply to a certain limited class of individuals, and Mr. Rand does not fall within that class . . . Therefore, the court would order that Mr. Rand turn over to the person that subpoenaed the documents the audiotape that is at issue in this case. You're ordered to turn it over to the prosecution. Do you have it here?"

"Yes, Your Honor."

"Okay. That's the order. Turn it over."

After court adjourned that afternoon, ten TV crews and two dozen reporters surrounded me in a half circle. As my colleagues confronted me with questions, I felt like I was watching a movie about myself. When the news conference ended ten minutes later, I was exhilarated and exhausted.

"As far as we're concerned, he was attempting to manipulate the outcome of the case," Pam Bozanich told a reporter afterward.

I was simply being a journalist and publishing significant information. When court adjourned the next afternoon, as I left the courtroom I saw Bozanich, who had a curious look on her face. Maybe it was because she'd listened to my entire interview and realized that I hadn't asked leading questions. Goodreau had freely volunteered detailed information about the molestation.

Three days later, I appeared before Judge Weisberg with an attorney and requested the return of my reserved courtroom seat. The prosecution still wanted me excluded from the courtroom because I was a potential witness. It was the first time in the trial that prosecutors had requested that any witness be kept out. Jose Menendez's sisters had appeared in court daily and frequently were emotional. Three weeks (and thousands of dollars in legal bills) later, the judge allowed me back in.

"Well, the situation has not yet changed but the court feels, at this point, even though the court is satisfied that its ruling was and is correct in regards to Mr. Rand and his status regarding the reporter's shield law, the court will permit him to return to the courtroom."

With the ruling, I could then resume simply covering the story instead of being part of it. But neither I—nor the court—was done with Donovan Goodreau yet.

CHAPTER 40

TRIAL WITHIN A TRIAL — DR. LEON JEROME OZIEL

THERE MIGHT NEVER HAVE BEEN A TRIAL, OR EVEN AN ARREST, without Leon Jerome Oziel. And now, in one witness, the state had someone who could testify to the brothers' dramatic confession to parricide, the remorseless logic of its premeditation, and the absence of any claim by them that the murders were prompted by physical or sexual abuse or imminent peril. To the defense, Oziel was the primary threat to their clients' freedom. For three years, the defense had waged war against Oziel's account of the confessions, claiming that everything Erik and Lyle had said to him were the privileged disclosures of clients to their therapist that could not be admitted as evidence. The defense had won some battles but lost the war. By Wednesday, August 4, 1993, the complex terrain of what could and couldn't be said in open court had been mapped out. Still, both sides would angrily contest every inch of territory.

Lester Kuriyama led Oziel point by point through the confession: Here was no tale of violated, bashed, and bloodied children finally driven to defend themselves. Instead, prosecutors contended that two young men had coolly calculated that the only way to solve their problem of a difficult adolescence was to murder their parents.

"Did you ask Erik Menendez why he included the mother in this plan?" Kuriyama asked.

"At this point? I believe I did . . . They couldn't find a way to accomplish the end of killing the father without also killing the mother. The reason being that the mother would have been a witness, number one, and would have reported them. Number two, they didn't believe the mother could have survived emotionally, anyway, without the father." The boys thought of it as a sort of euthanasia, Oziel concluded.

Oziel depicted a nightmare of reason, a murder so carefully thought through that even their father wouldn't have criticized them for it.

Oziel testified that the brothers had laid out a long list of grievances that, to them, justified their father's death warrant. They included elements of revenge and greed: Their father had turned them in to police for the Calabasas robberies, and Lyle believed there was a chance he was planning to disinherit them. The list didn't include self-defense, except in a general sense that could apply to any child of an overbearing parent.

"He said he didn't want anybody looking over his shoulder, and that's why he killed his parents to begin with," Oziel said.

Oziel said he laid out for them two explanations of murder: "premeditated, involving a sort of plan, a job that needed to be accomplished," or "a crime-of-passion-type killing, where there wasn't any premeditation—grabbing the nearest knife or pistol and in the heat of the moment shooting someone." To describe their own crime, the brothers without hesitation chose the first option.

———

The morning had underscored the need for the defense to throw everything they had at Oziel. And they had lots. Leslie Abramson started with Oziel's résumé, which included abundant references to the term "sex therapist." Then she dragged him through his billing practices. She also hit him with his media résumé, which included numerous appearances on local and national TV.

Oziel said he didn't recall appearing on most of those shows, not even on the national networks. You could almost see the jurors thinking, *Yeah, right.*

By then, Abramson may well have had jurors seeing the witness as a sex-obsessed, patient-gouging, prevaricating media hound. The capper followed: "Now, in 1988, when you first met the Menendez family, did you tell any or all of them that your license was on probation at that time? And it was still on probation, was it not, at the time that you placed the tapes, the notes, the transcribed notes which you've been using here, in the safe deposit box from whence police retrieved it, correct?"

What about those notes? They were spoken into a tape recorder some uncertain amount of time after the confessional sessions took place on October 31 and November 2. Why had he waited so long? Why did he make them when he did? Were they an accurate reflection of the brothers' words, or just Oziel's superimposed impressions? Abramson wasn't shy about providing the larger answer herself: Oziel had fabricated the whole thing.

"During sessions, do you ever take notes?" she asked.

"Well, I would say with some frequency I take notes during sessions and, most particularly, I take notes when something critical is happening as a way of memorializing an insight or a particular issue that I want to make sure that I get down. And if nothing that critical is happening, or if notes would have to be very elaborate, usually I do those notes after the sessions."

Abramson couldn't have known that Oziel would say in open court that he took notes during "critical" sessions, but she pounced as if she'd been lying in wait. She asked if he thought whether his sessions with Erik and Lyle Menendez on October 31 and November 2 were critical. He said yes.

"You didn't make any notes whatsoever during those sessions; isn't that true?"

"I certainly did not."

The rest of the afternoon was one contentious exchange after another. Abramson questioned Oziel about when he told Judalon Smyth about the confessions, and why he told her at all.

Smyth had claimed that she was in the waiting room during the October 31 session, but Oziel categorically denied that. Abramson asked where he was on the previous evening, when he talked to Erik on the phone and made the appointment. At first Oziel said he didn't recall, but when pressed, he said he believed that he returned Erik's call from Smyth's apartment.

ABRAMSON: Did you ask Judalon Smyth to come to your office on October 31 in order to eavesdrop on your therapy sessions with the Menendez brothers that day?

OZIEL: Actually, it was quite the contrary.

ABRAMSON: Well, can you answer that question yes or no, Dr. Oziel?

OZIEL: I don't think I can.

ABRAMSON: You can't answer that? Did you ask her to be there?

OZIEL: No, I didn't.

ABRAMSON: There you go.

OZIEL: I do not recall Judalon Smyth being there, that I saw her. I was in session with Erik and Lyle for approximately four and a half hours, and I would have no way of knowing whether anybody else came into my waiting room while I was in session with somebody. So the answer is, to the best of my knowledge, no, she was not there.

ABRAMSON: Well, if you have no way of knowing, then your answer, I take it, is you don't know?

OZIEL: I don't know. But I do not believe she was there.

It continued when Abramson asked if Smyth was present in Oziel's office after the October 31 session, while Oziel, fearful for his life, called therapists, lawyers, and cops to get advice on how to handle his situation.

ABRAMSON: Was she there?

OZIEL: I do not recall her being there.

ABRAMSON: So are you saying she wasn't there, or are you just saying you don't remember?

OZIEL: I don't believe she was there.

ABRAMSON: Well, you don't believe she was there?

OZIEL: I don't recall Judalon Smyth as having been there, no.

The siege continued the next morning. Abramson had Oziel reconstruct his actions on Halloween night after the brothers left, with the perceived threat of murder over his head. This was fertile ground, enabling ample opportunity to continue her theme that Oziel's testimony was not credible and to introduce a new one: He was a self-centered philanderer.

That set up perfectly when Oziel said he believed that he and his family were in mortal danger, but instead of going home to assure their safety, he went to his girlfriend's house. Oziel objected to calling Judalon his "girlfriend," so Abramson snapped, "Would you be more comfortable with the word 'lover'?"

Oziel explained: "I was afraid that if, in fact, in some way they could have followed me to where I was, they would have found me with my wife and children."

"So you instead went to Ms. Smyth's and put her, based on what you're telling us, in danger?"

"Actually, at the time, I didn't think that Erik and Lyle would have been going to Ms. Smyth's. Erik knew where I lived. My most immediate concern was that the highest probability was that they would go to my house. And for that reason, I didn't go to my house."

Abramson got the zinger: "I thought I just heard you say you thought they might follow you."

Although Oziel said he didn't invite Smyth to listen in at his office, he did admit that he relayed the confession to her that night, which raised more questions.

Oziel justified violating his patients' confidentiality because he thought he was in danger, but his relationship with Judalon Smyth meant that she was in danger as well, Abramson pointed out. At that point, Erik and Lyle knew nothing about Judalon.

"Couldn't you have just decided, rather than reveal what your patients had been telling you, to have nothing to do with her at that point?"

No, Oziel said, he thought that Judalon's "obsession" with him meant he couldn't stay away from her. He also feared that the brothers might break into his house and find various things relating to her, like personal letters, business agreements, and, most importantly, a signed confidentiality agreement relating to her tape duplicating services, an arrangement he feared might suggest to the boys that Judalon knew their secret.

Abramson asked how many days Oziel stayed with Smyth. Several, he said.

"Were you hiding out?"

"Pretty much."

Abramson let that sink in.

For the rest of the morning, she kept hammering at Oziel's reasons for revealing the brothers' confession not only to Judalon, but to anyone. She tried to suggest that his actions after October 31 were inconsistent with someone in fear of his life—the legal justification for a psychologist breaking his patient's confidentiality.

"Isn't it true," she demanded, "that over the course of your relationship with Ms. Smyth you frequently threatened her, to control her behavior by telling her, 'Aha, I'm going to tell Erik and Lyle that you know their secret, and they'll come kill you.' Didn't you do that?"

Oziel, looking wounded, shot back, "Quite the contrary."

But Abramson had tapes. After Smyth had gone to police to persuade them to arrest Oziel, she'd recorded their conversations, both with a body wire and on the phone. Now Abramson was relishing the result, dishing out Oziel's own words for the doctor to swallow like spoonfuls of castor oil.

"On the tapes that Ms. Smyth made for the police, can your voice be heard threatening that she'll die if she goes to the police?"

Oziel spit out his medicine: "No. My voice can be heard warning her that I thought Erik or Lyle would kill her if she went to police."

And then Abramson played the tapes that contradicted Oziel's testimony for jurors.

It was quitting time, Friday afternoon, but the rumble was just getting started. The jurors had the weekend to ponder two relationships: Oziel's love/hate affair with Judalon Smyth and his all-out war with Leslie Abramson.

On Monday, Abramson pressed Oziel on the days just after Lyle's threats. Oziel said he'd taken a vacation with Judalon, prompting Abramson: "And how did you explain that one to your wife?"

And why did he come back? "Did the threat automatically disappear at the end of the weekend?"

Oziel was still squirming when Abramson opened a new front: "By the way, Ms. Smyth was not only your girlfriend, she was your patient, was she not?"

"Absolutely not!"

Did he ever consult with her over the phone? Did he ever diagnose her?

Absolutely not and absolutely not, Oziel insisted.

Abramson then handed the baton to Michael Burt, who produced a letter, signed by Oziel, used to excuse Smyth from a small claims court appearance. It referred to a phone consultation and made a diagnosis: "Judalon Smyth was incapacitated 8/30/89 by a chronic stress-induced panic disorder, as reported to me by her via telephone."

Oziel, eyes flaring with anger, then almost certainly made things even worse when he debated whether it was his own signature. Then, his memory apparently refreshed, he explained the letter away as a favor to a friend. Burt pounced. "When you told the jury you did not diagnose her, that was false testimony, was it not?"

"If this is construed as a diagnosis," Oziel responded, "then it would have been false testimony. If it's not construed as diagnosis, it wouldn't be."

"Well," Burt noted, "you didn't sign the letter 'L. Jerome Oziel, Concerned Citizen,' did you? You didn't sign it 'L. Jerome Oziel, Boyfriend,' did you? You signed it in your professional capacity."

Next, Burt produced a press release by Oziel from his news conference in October 1990: "Judalon Smyth relentlessly pursued a committed relationship with me, which I rejected." It also described the nature of her interest as an "unreciprocated fixation."

Oziel stood by that statement. Burt then presented a phone bill. Within a few days in September 1989, a time when Oziel had testified he'd wanted nothing to do with Smyth, he'd called her dozens of times, once talking for more than four hours. Other times he left insistent messages on her answering machine.

"So who's being obsessive here, doctor?" Burt asked.

Prosecutors then introduced a bundle of florid love letters that Judalon had written to Oziel. Once it became clear that Judalon wanted him to leave his wife for her, Oziel said he continually tried to break off the relationship but she constrained him by suicide threats, and then, when he did break it off, an actual suicide attempt. Oziel testified that tapes of his calls to Judalon that might appear to support the defense theory that he was obsessed with her were actually motivated by fear: He was afraid she'd go to police and put his family in danger, and he was afraid she might kill herself.

The defense countered Judalon's passionate prose with Oziel's own, handwritten in January 1990: "For like a nymph she strides from the forest at day break dressed in white where no other man had truly known her, Judalon."

"Is that a poem which you wrote to Judalon Smyth at a time which you've testified you were trying to break off the relationship?" Burt asked.

"It wasn't a poem I wrote to Judalon Smyth," Oziel protested.

As the day closed, it became obvious that Oziel would still be on the witness stand the next morning. Abramson told the judge, "I'm going to be briefer than I thought. I'm frankly sort of sick of him."

By the sixth and final day of his testimony, it seemed that even the national audience on Court TV was weary of this slugfest. Done with trying to discredit Oziel by a thousand cuts, Burt went in for the essence:

"Did you make the tape recording [of your notes on the confessions] for the purpose of creating a false record so that you could use the tape to extort money out of the Menendez brothers?

"Isn't it true that over the course of your relationship with Ms. Smyth, you frequently threatened her, to control her behavior by telling her, 'Aha, I'm going to tell Erik and Lyle that you know their secret, and they'll come kill you?'"

Oziel denied it all.

"Do you remember," asked Burt, "an occasion where you and Ms. Smyth were in her bedroom and you were singing some songs to her in an Elvis Presley imitation voice? . . . And you said, 'Elvis is alive and singing songs in my bedroom. That's good. They'll put you away in a loony bin for sure.' And Smyth saying, 'I'll send them the videotape.' And you saying, 'Yeah. Right. I'll kill you, or I'll just leave a message for Lyle.' Do you remember making that statement?"

Oziel said he'd been joking.

Burt went on to something less humorous: "You say, 'You already did something really stupid, really, really stupid.' And she then says, 'Well, the boys are in jail and I'm not dead, and you said if I went to the police I'd be dead in two minutes.' And your answer was, 'Guess what, it's going to be a little bit longer.'"

That wasn't a threat, Oziel said. "I was expressing anger towards her for putting myself, my wife and my children, and, I perceived, her, in danger."

"And do you remember saying," Burt continued, "'Judalon, you don't know what you're talking about . . . There was 14 million dollars involved in this.' Do you remember . . . that it was your understanding that the Menendez estate was worth approximately 14 million dollars?"

"I don't recall making the statement. But I—you know, I might have made the statement."

Burt took one more shot: "Have you talked about writing a book about your experience in this case?"

Oziel admitted that he had. Burt suggested he was hoping to make a lot of money.

"Money wasn't even anything I thought about," Oziel said.

"Never entered your mind? That would be strictly out of an educational and humanitarian goal?"

"What entered my mind," said Oziel, "was to discuss what it's like to be a witness in this kind of situation and how, actually, being a witness is in many ways like being put on trial . . . So it's like this experience, actually, Mr. Burt, that we're having right now."

CHAPTER 41
THE PROSECUTION RESTS

I N THE THREE YEARS AND FOUR MONTHS FROM THE MENENDEZ brothers' arrest to trial, the media had made this a big case, a crusade, even, because they saw a need for justice for two spoiled rich kids who were in a hurry to inherit their parents' money. However, a Los Angeles County grand jury in December 1992 hadn't seen it exactly as clearly. They'd refused to return an indictment that Lyle and Erik had murdered for financial gain. Now, near the close of the prosecution's trial presentation, they hadn't yet nailed down a motive.

Dr. Oziel had told prosecutors in December 1992 that the brothers were inspired to kill after watching a "BBC movie special" a few weeks before August 20, 1989. Nobody had figured out what that was. Investigators called the British Broadcasting Company to check its schedule. Les Zoeller phoned Scotland Yard to ask if any similar killings had taken place in England. Prosecutors checked old *TV Guide*s.

Oziel's reference to such a movie seems to have come from audio notes of his October 31, 1989, session with Erik; however, the transcription of them had no specific reference to BBC:

He then walked into the office with me and began to reveal in elaborate detail, all of the events leading up to and, following the actual murder of his parents. He specifically informed me that during this television show which dealt with a son murdering the father that he and his brother, Lyle, had begun to talk about how similar their father was to the father presented in the television show.

Then, Lester Kuriyama told the judge the previous Saturday his daughter wanted to see *The Addams Family*. When his wife went to get the video, right below it on the video store shelves, in the *B*s, was the *Billionaire Boys Club*.

"Eureka!" said Leslie Abramson, rolling her eyes at the ceiling.

Kuriyama's wife rented the movie and raced home. He said, watching it "sent chills up my spine. The similarities between this case and that movie are astounding!"

NBC first aired the made-for-TV movie in 1987. Here were the similarities Kuriyama noted: The club leader, Joe Hunt, had discussed the "perfect murder." The Mafia and drug cartels initially were suspects. Hunt had used going to the movies as an alibi. The son of the second *BBC* victim wanted to inherit the $30 million estate of his father, who had political enemies outside the United States; in Iran, Hedayat Eslaminia had been a high-ranking official for the Shah of Iran. Erik Menendez had said that Castro might have killed his father.

"He gets all these ideas from this movie," said Kuriyama. Dr. Oziel claimed that Erik called Lyle over and said, "Look at this movie. This is like our dad."

Leslie Abramson's face displayed mixed astonishment and anger.

More: Joe Hunt drove a Jeep. Erik bought one after the murder. Hunt wore a Rolex; so did Erik. During his dinner with Craig Cignarelli in November 1989, recorded by police, Erik suggested they form a group that would make them millions of dollars.

"Kinda like in *BBC*," said Cignarelli. "Kinda like in *BBC*," repeated Erik, who was friends at Beverly Hills High with Amir "Brian" Eslaminia, the younger brother of Reza Eslaminia convicted in the BBC case. And the capper: NBC rebroadcast the movie, which ran four hours over two nights, on July 30 and 31, 1989, a Sunday and Monday night, three weeks before August 20.

Kuriyama wanted to show the video to the jury.

"Sell popcorn?" quipped Weisberg.

"The People are trying to use that for the most prejudicial of possible reasons to show that Erik is a killer like the people in the *Billionaire Boys Club*," answered Leslie Abramson. "It's a more specious theory even than the screenplay theory, to base a jury's determinations on a fictional account."

Then she dropped that the brothers weren't even in Los Angeles on the two days in question.

"Well, he did see the movie, so he must have been around here somewhere," said Kuriyama.

The judge agreed with the defense. The movie would not be shown.

"I guess we cancel the popcorn," Abramson said later.

On the days Kuriyama claimed they'd been watching the *BBC* movie, the brothers were at a tennis clinic at the Saddlebrook Country Club, a resort north of Tampa, Florida. Tommy Thompson, the director of coaching, told me that Erik had been there for several weeks, and Lyle joined him for the last ten days of July 1989.

"Erik was a great kid—personable and worked very hard," Thompson said. "Lyle was quieter and more reserved. The brothers stuck close together while they were here."

The clinic had a grueling routine: on the courts from early morning until late afternoon. The brothers were in the Junior Division and were required to be in their rooms by 9 PM with lights out at ten. There were no TV sets in the rooms. The movie that Kuriyama suggested inspired the brothers to kill their parents aired on NBC in Tampa from 9 to 11 PM on July 30 and 31.

"I don't think the people are going to believe that Lyle and I could do this after watching a movie," Erik told me in a conversation from jail on the evening that the prosecution rested. "Maybe you go out and rob a store—you say, let's go do that. But you don't do this. Brian Eslaminia knows I never saw the *BBC* movie, because I discussed it with him."

Erik thought that the prosecution's theory "should be that the molestation happened, but Lyle and I weren't afraid. We just hated them so bad—that this is why it happened."

Lyle agreed, he told me. "I guess they are going to stick to the evil bad-seed kid theory. Clearly, their best theory is hatred, and I don't think that is going to hold up, either, because the events surrounding August 20th, within a few months before and after that, don't support it.

"There is too much—there were too many good things going on in my life for me to toss it for that reason. I'm not a guy who hated, and I'm not a guy that even expresses anger very well, and hopefully, my own feelings—the mixed feelings about the whole thing coming out—will make a difference for the jury, although it may not."

"Where are the witnesses that talked about hatred?" Erik asked. He suggested that the defense present a chart of four categories: Hatred, Money, Molestation, and Fear, listing witnesses who supported each theory. "And where is the balance going to line up? You should actually put a weighing scale on the table, and put a marble for each side. They have the burden of proof. They have to really prove it."

The brothers had kept up on public opinion by reading the hundreds of letters they received weekly, plus a friend of theirs, Norma Novelli, had recorded Court TV's commentary and call-in shows, which she played for them over the phone.

"The defense tried to put on a cheap version of *Divorce Court*," Pam Bozanich told reporters after the prosecution rested. "And now, they're going to put the parents on trial. Since [the parents] are dead, they can't say much about it, can they?"

Leslie Abramson saw it differently: "Now, we start talking about what really happened."

CHAPTER 42

THE DEFENSE

A S THE DEFENSE OPENED ITS CASE ON MONDAY, AUGUST 16, THE focus was to show in the smallest possible strokes how two decades of life in the Menendez household contributed to what happened on the night of August 20, 1989.

The first prosecution objection to defense testimony came two minutes after the first witness, Jose Menendez's sister, Marta Cano, was sworn in. Jill Lansing asked if Marta and Terry Menendez were treated differently growing up than their baby brother. Judge Weisberg sustained the objection, and, at a sidebar, defense attorneys vigorously argued for the admission of Jose and Kitty's family history.

"If children come from a home where the parents were raised in safe, caring environments, the likelihood of abuse of the child is substantially less likely than children who are raised in a home where there is violence and abuse and various forms of childhood trauma," Lansing said. "It would be our purpose, with not only this witness, but with one other witness [Kitty's sister Joan VanderMolen] to go very briefly into childhood experiences."

"It's our argument that it's too remote and irrelevant to the issues to be raised in this trial," countered Pam Bozanich.

"I have to agree with the prosecution," said Judge Weisberg. "We're getting into an area that is so remote that it's not relevant to any issue in this case. To put the childhood of the father, or the victim, on before the jury just doesn't have any relevance."

Leslie Abramson quickly jumped in: "The People have raised the specter, and will no doubt raise it again, that our clients' claim of abuse is totally fabricated, and we think we should be entitled to show that the character traits of their father, that they will testify about, were observable even when he was a small child, which is what this witness is able to testify to . . ."

The judge disagreed. "To go back to the childhood history of the victim is totally irrelevant," he said. "It doesn't prove anything."

"That means all the experts are wrong when they say abuse is multigenerational?" asked Abramson. Weisberg acknowledged that the testimony by defense experts, to be presented after the brothers took the stand, could go into these areas. Menendez and Andersen relatives, however, would not be allowed to discuss family life from the 1940s and '50s. The ruling was a major setback for the defense strategy of exposing Jose and Kitty's family secrets.

Over persistent prosecution objections, Cano was allowed to describe the relationship between her brother and his sons. "Lyle wasn't allowed to express his opinions. He was told what to do," she said. As a young boy, her nephew always seemed "very tense and very frightened." There was little warmth between father and son.

"He was more inclined to be tender with Erik. He did not see Erik the same way he saw Lyle. Lyle was for his own image. Lyle could be as successful and powerful as he was."

To present an overview of child abuse, the defense put on John Briere, a University of Southern California psychiatry professor.

"Men abused as children don't tell people about it," he said. "They feel they're going to be judged harshly." Among his other points: Young male victims worry that people will consider them homosexual or inadequate. Research said that married men with available adult sex partners were just as likely as others to molest children. Abused children suffered from hypervigilance, a "constant dread of danger"— similar to the "learned helplessness" associated with battered women's syndrome.

On cross, the professor conceded that a "normal childhood" couldn't really be defined. Evaluators were at the mercy of what they were told.

"What if the person was arrogant? asked Bozanich. "Would that be sort of the opposite of low self-esteem?"

"You may know this," said the witness, "arrogant people actually have very low self-esteem."

"And some arrogant people are just arrogant," snapped Bozanich.

─────────────

The next morning, Allan Andersen, the thirty-one-year-old, bearded, younger son of Kitty's brother Brian, took the stand. He had spent three summers with his cousins in the 1960s and '70s. Andersen said that Erik and Lyle were instructed by their parents not to show emotion because it was a sign of weakness. His Uncle Jose and Aunt Kitty themselves often engaged in violent arguments and displayed irrational behavior. When Kitty got angry, she'd clench her knuckles and grit her teeth until her neck veins bulged. Standing up, Andersen demonstrated her rage for the jurors. Sometimes, "in a frenzy," she'd walk to the kitchen sink and smash glass cups and saucers. "I would yell, 'Kitty!' and she would snap out of it. It was frightening."

Jose, he said, would whip his sons with a belt until they were bruised. He'd also drag them into their rooms and leave them locked inside for hours.

"As soon as Jose took either one of the boys into their room, the door was locked behind them, and Kitty made clear you did not go down the hallway," he testified. "I saw him grab the brothers when they didn't want to go. Just lifted them off their feet. Kitty would turn the TV up and you heard 'Fuh-tsshhh'—the sound of the belt." Andersen also heard many late-night emotional fights between Jose and Kitty. The next morning, he'd notice bruises on his aunt's arms and neck.

Andersen didn't witness any sexual abuse, but in retrospect, he said, there were possible indicators. The brothers and their father took showers together after playing tennis; that was "kind of strange." He remembered Erik as a "sweet child" at four. Two years later, he was withdrawn and introverted. Andersen was shocked by the change. Young Lyle took out his anger by ripping apart his beloved stuffed animal collection.

Andersen's last encounter with the family was ten days before the killings. Erik came with Kitty to see Andersen's new baby. Kitty looked like a "puppet on a string," he said. "She had no frame of mind. Her eyes were bloodshot and pale, and she was dressed in a very unusual way."

The next witness was another cousin, thirty-two-year-old Kathleen Simonton, daughter of Kitty's sister, Joan. Simonton testified that she'd spent part of the summer of 1976, at age fifteen, with her aunt and uncle. Her parents had told her that the Menendezes were the "perfect family, successful and well-to-do."

Simonton also described her aunt's so-called frenzies. "Her intensity and rage could be very scary," she said, becoming emotional. Kitty was angry with her for smoking and wearing a bikini as well as poorly vacuuming and folding the laundry—her responsibilities that summer.

"You couldn't predict how to avoid trouble. You became invisible and didn't create waves." Lyle wasn't allowed to cry. Erik, who kept to himself, was quiet and "made to feel dumb." He was frequently asked why he couldn't be more like his brother. She also remembered Jose taking his sons down the hall into their rooms, and being ordered to stay away when that happened.

"Were these bad boys?" asked Jill Lansing.

"Oh, no," said Simonton.

A third cousin, Kathleen Simonton's thirty-four-year-old sister Diane VanderMolen, was the first defense witness to tell jurors about sexual abuse in the Menendez family. Diane was rosy-cheeked and eight months pregnant. As a teenager, she spent summer vacations with the Menendezes, whom she called "very special to our family." Six years later, at age twenty-three, she worked for the family as a housekeeper and gardener. In the 1970s, Diane had felt welcome at the house. Her later visits weren't as pleasant. She became emotional as she explained how Kitty became angry and flew into "immense rages" several times a week.

VanderMolen said there was all sorts of "weird" sexuality in the house. One night after dinner, Jose was with the boys upstairs. Then, eight-year-old Lyle came to her basement room and said he wanted to touch her "down there . . . My impression was he was afraid. He became more serious and said he and his dad had been touching each other in the genitals. I went to get Kitty and told her, but Kitty didn't believe me." After that, Kitty dragged Lyle, bewildered, upstairs to bed.

"It was never discussed after that," VanderMolen cried softly. "I convinced myself I was in the wrong." Both Erik and Lyle cried as they listened to her testimony.

Kitty lectured Diane several times in front of the brothers about the damage that children can cause to a marriage. They could "drive a wedge between a husband and wife," she warned. Yet unusual things also happened between the boys and their mother. When the brothers were ages eleven and fourteen and their father was out of town, they'd argue over whose turn it was to sleep with Kitty. Also, Kitty would say she had to help Lyle wash his hair when he took a bath. That would take fifteen minutes, VanderMolen said.

In a hearing without the juries, Leslie Abramson dropped a bombshell: Lyle had molested Erik when they were eight and five years old.

Both brothers would be taking the stand to testify about the abuse. "I swear and promise, scout's honor, my client is going to testify," said Abramson. But Judge Weisberg warned the defense: "The whole issue is being blown out of proportion—that somehow there's a linkage between the molestation, if there was one, and the killings."

"It does not surprise me to hear the court say that," said Abramson, embittered. "It horrifies me, but it does not surprise me." In a response loaded with potential significance, the judge declared, "The fact that there was a molestation doesn't constitute a legal defense."

Outside the courtroom, Abramson complained to reporters that Weisberg was "treating this case like a liquor store robbery. But this case by its very nature requires evidence not relevant in the ordinary criminal trial."

In the following days, the defense presented a parade of the brothers' friends, teachers, and coaches.

Charles Wadlington was their first tennis coach until Jose fired him after five years. The tall, patrician-looking man testified that Jose wanted his sons "trained very, very hard, and pushed as hard as they could go."

Jose told him it was their "family tradition to excel," and believed that his boys could become number one–ranked tennis players.

"He wanted them to play for results, and I wanted them to play tennis as an art form and for the beauty of the game. I would try to explain to the father how to best train a child so that they can progress and not only win but also develop as a person."

"Did he want you to teach the boys methods of cheating?" asked Michael Burt.

"He had me teach them all psychological ways to disrupt the opponent, both subversive and openly," Wadlington replied.

On cross, Lester Kuriyama asked how Jose Menendez compared with other tennis parents Wadlington had observed over the years.

"He was what I consider the worst parent of the people that I had coached, and most of the high-achieving students' parents were demanding, but he took it a step further. He was the harshest person I had ever met." He'd never seen Kitty Menendez smile or compliment her children. She was "usually sarcastic and hostile."

Wadlington called the boys' schedule "cruel." They practiced daily at 6 AM—even when they were sick and it was raining.

"Why did you continue to coach them if so much that you didn't approve of was going on?" asked Leslie Abramson.

In one of the most poignant moments of the trial, tears ran down Wadlington's cheeks as he struggled to stay composed. "Because I cared for them," he sighed deeply. "Well, I thought I was about all they had as a friend."

CHAPTER 43

SISTERS IN CONFLICT

Marta Cano began to notice that Kitty Menendez's mental state was deteriorating in 1985. "Kitty was sort of incoherent," Cano testified. "She was very tense and very nervous, and she seemed to glare at things and just stay quiet and not respond to things that we were talking about." When Marta asked what was wrong, Kitty said she'd run out of Valium.

Two months before the murders, Marta was at Erik's high school graduation. Kitty rear-ended a car at a stoplight while driving home.

"After she hit the car, what did she do?" asked Leslie Abramson.

"Well, the car turned on the road to stop to talk about the accident, and she just put the accelerator on and asked Erik to look back and see if [the driver] had seen the license plate."

"So she ran from the scene?"

"Yes." She was terrified that Jose would find out she'd had an accident.

Abramson asked if Cano ever saw her brother give orders to his children.

"He did that all the time."

"And how did they respond to that?"

"They just obeyed. It was a command."

"Did you ever see either one of them argue, fight, refuse, disobey?"

"Oh, no."

"You say that, 'Oh, no.' Are you sure? Never?"

"Jose was not the type of person you could answer to."

"What about you? Could you answer to him?"

"No."

"Did you see adults try to answer him back?"

"Yes. And they would be humiliated and ridiculed."

"In front of his children?"

"In front of everybody."

When Erik was younger and lost a competition, Jose would humiliate him in front of others, she said. "He would tell him he was a sissy. It was about time that he became a Menendez. That he was not worth his last name, that he should be ashamed of his average, mediocre performance."

Cano said that Kitty never defended Erik and was not an attentive mother to either of her sons. When Lyle was a baby, Kitty wouldn't "kiss and coo" him. "She did not like Lyle. She seemed to resent him." Even at age two, when he was hungry she let him fend for himself.

"Lyle would go and climb on a chair and get on top of the counter and get his cereal and rip off the box and pour it out, and it was just a disaster," she said. Kitty wouldn't help, even if she was in the room.

"Did she make a move to grab the baby so he doesn't fall off the counter?"

"No."

"Nothing? Did you make a move?"

"Yes, I did."

"That's when she stopped you and said he can fend for himself?"

"That's correct."

Abramson showed Cano a photo of two-year-old Erik hanging from a chin-up bar with a terrified look on his face. In the picture, Jose stood off to the side, laughing. Cano became emotional looking at the photograph. She admitted she'd initially told detectives the family was "close and loving."

"Did you tell the police about the treatment that you saw your brother and sister-in-law impose on their children?" Abramson asked.

"I didn't tell anybody."

"Why didn't you tell that to the police in 1989?"

"Because it would break the image that I know Jose and Kitty always wanted to give, and I had no reason to do that."

"Even after your brother and sister-in-law were dead, were you conscious of the notion of not bringing any negative scandal to your brother and sister-in-law?"

"Of course. There was a very beautiful image of what the Menendezes had been, and I didn't wish to change that. I wish I had never had to change it."

In a blistering cross-examination, Pam Bozanich tried to force Cano to say that she hadn't been fully candid with Les Zoeller.

"The boys were not at stake at the time," said Marta.

"So, since they're at stake, it's then that you will paint this picture?" Bozanich prodded.

"I didn't lie to him. I just deviated portraits of image."

"When you were asked by detective Zoeller if you knew of any problems within the family, you said no," said Bozanich.

"He was referring to other kinds of problems."

"Well, did you think that the things that you've told this jury about, do you think those were problems?"

"Those were mistreatments and definitely were issues. But I didn't see them as problems in reference to threaten my brother's life."

Later, Bozanich asked Cano whether she had anything nice to say about her brother. She answered, he was an "admirable person" who "controlled every business negotiation he would encounter," and had "total dedication to his children." But that became a "sick type of obsessive dedication."

"What about Mrs. Menendez? Is there anything about her that you liked?"

"I admired her. She was a tremendous athlete. She was very strong. She could pick up a Christmas tree and move it from one place to the other . . . I admire the fact that she was intelligent, and she was a handyman, and she could put together a barbecue."

Alicia Hercz, the former neighbor of the Menendezes in Princeton who had visited Kitty at the mansion three weeks before the killings, was also

Lyle's Spanish teacher in 1984 and '85. At a parent-teacher conference, she said that Lyle's classroom performance wasn't nearly as good as his papers. Both Kitty and Jose became confrontational and intimidating. Hercz later discovered that other teachers also suspected Lyle's parents were doing his homework.

"Kitty could be fierce in her stance about things," said Hercz, "She could be needy at other times, pathetic, kind of suspicious of people, unorganized, spacey. All kinds of contradicting things." Jose, whom she called Joe, was "extremely good at intimidating people. He was abusive. Could be cruel to people, even in a social setting, controlling. I found him destructive at times. If a party was going on, he had an edge about him, or a something about him that could almost destroy the mood. Very cruel, very sarcastic."

When Lyle was about to graduate from high school, Hercz said her husband asked him about his future plans. "No matter what my husband asked, Joe would answer, not Lyle. He just sat there."

She described Lyle as "a loner. Sad. Pathetic. Lonely. Morose . . . Had no sense of humor. Was a very unusual child." The last time Hercz saw Kitty Menendez, her friend seemed "strange. The strangest I had ever seen her."

———————

Sandra Sharp taught Spanish to both brothers at Princeton Day School. Erik practiced tennis so much, she testified, he had difficulty completing his homework. Jose called her a "terrible teacher" because she couldn't teach Spanish to his children, who "obviously had a Cuban gene."

Sharp said that only Jose attended Lyle's parent-teacher conferences. He had low expectations for Erik, but Lyle was "perfect. He was going to be the best tennis player in the United States . . . And he expected perfect grades because he had a perfect son. And that I better be the perfect teacher, so that his son could get the perfect grade."

———————

Shortly before she was sworn in, Teresita Baralt told me that she had mixed feelings and was "torn both ways." Terry loved her younger brother. And she loved her nephews. Lyle was her godson, and their relationship had always been close. Defense attorneys hoped her testimony would be impassioned. "They want me to say one thing, but I have to say what I believe," she said.

On the stand, Baralt was nervous as Jill Lansing questioned her. For almost half of the twenty-nine years since the Menendezes had fled Cuba, she and her brother lived in the same house or nearby. Frequently, the Baralts and their four daughters vacationed together with the Menendezes.

She described Lyle as a "very fast baby. He stood up at five months by himself. He walked at seven or eight months. He rode his bike by three and a half, no training wheels. I mean, this kid was coordinated."

"Erik was extremely attached to his mother. And Kitty was not an affectionate person with the kids. But she would have kind of, you know, when you look at a child condescendingly. Okay? That was the relationship."

Young Lyle was jealous of all the attention that Kitty gave Erik. "Kitty had a rapport with Erik. She never had a rapport with Lyle. I know that sounds awful, but that's the way I saw it." Kitty thought that Terry was "overprotective" with her children. "She thought that when you leave children alone, they learn to defend themselves."

As a youngster, Lyle had a bed full of stuffed animals. "There was no space for Lyle in the bed," said Baralt.

"Did they seem important to him?"

"Very much so."

In her toughest criticism of her brother, Baralt said that Jose could be "harsh" and "say things in a way that makes you feel like you want to disappear." His "cut you to shreds" voice would go lower and slower when he was angry.

"I did not see them being abusive to the children. I just saw their ways of parenting to be completely different from mine." Always, there was a relentless urgency to excel. "Whatever you did, you had to be the best at it," said Baralt. "Trying was not good enough. And to grow up with that kind of pressure is very hard on children."

"Did it appear that Jose had total control over Kitty?" asked Lansing.

"The world liked to think so. That was not so. She just learned to be very good in public—there were no more open fights. She just stayed quiet, but not in private."

Baralt didn't know that Kitty had a drinking problem but noticed "her cup of coffee always included a half a cup of Galliano." When Jose walked in, Kitty would whisper, "Put it away," and say, "He doesn't like it when I drink."

And Kitty kept other secrets. She never said anything about her search for Jose's lovers, or her three years of therapy.

"You learned a lot of things after they died that you didn't know?"

"Yes. And I wish I had known more. I could have helped."

On cross, Pam Bozanich asked for an example of something nice Jose had done for his children. Baralt told of how he stopped a soccer game to rescue Lyle when he broke his collarbone.

"Did your brother love his sons?"

"I think he did. You can love somebody and still hurt them, you know."

CHAPTER 44

A COMPELLING WITNESS

ERIK AND LYLE MENENDEZ NORMALLY SPOKE WITH EACH OTHER while they were being transported to the trial. But on Friday, September 10, Lyle told me there was "deep silence" on their drive from jail to court. "The defense calls Joseph Lyle Menendez," announced Jill Lansing at five minutes before two o'clock. When the brothers entered the packed courtroom, Lyle, dressed in a pink shirt and navy crew-neck sweater, walked directly to Lansing. The testimony began with Lyle's recollection of "good memories" of his father and his mother. Then Lansing got blunt.

"Did you love your parents?"

"Yes," he choked out hoarsely.

"And on August 20, 1989, did you and your brother kill your mom and dad?"

"Yes."

"Did you kill them for money?"

"No."

"Did you kill them to pay them back for all the bad things they did to you?"

"No."

"Why did you kill your parents?"

"Because we were afraid."

When he was growing up, Lyle explained, sports were "everything to my dad, and that was my whole life at the time."

"And was doing what your father wanted of you important?"

"That's what made him happy, and that's what I wanted to do."

"Why'd you want to make him happy?"

"So he would love me."

Lyle could barely be heard through his own sobbing.

At six years old, his daily swimming practices with older kids left him nauseous. He begged his mother not to make him go. She threatened to tell his father. When Jose came to the workouts, he'd hold Lyle underwater to make him build endurance by fighting for air. Young Lyle wasn't allowed to make friends because that might compromise his competitiveness.

"I was the most important thing in his life, and what I did was serious," said Lyle. "My brother was unimportant . . . I had to be doing something. I was achieving something, something of importance. And it was very different."

Kitty resented the time that Jose spent training the brothers. "She would say that I ruined her life," he said. She complained that Jose had forced her to have children she didn't want. "Why can't you be more like your brother?" she yelled at him. If he tried to respond, she'd snap, "Shut up! I don't want to hear it! You're stupid. I hate you!"

The courtroom was in a state of emotional shock when the judge called the first recess after about forty-five minutes. In addition to Erik and the family, several jurors and reporters had been crying. As I walked outside, Dominick Dunne asked me to follow him down the hallway so we could talk alone. Dunne looked pale as he told me, "I can't believe I am going to say this, but I think I believe him." It was a complete surprise since Dunne had always been a staunch cheerleader for the prosecution in *Vanity Fair*. Usually, we were on opposite sides of the case—particularly during our debates on Court TV. But at this moment, as personal friends having a private conversation, we both agreed that we had just witnessed some of the most gripping, dramatic moments either of us had ever seen in a courtroom.

After the break, the emotional testimony became even worse.

"Did your dad used to have talks with you about sex between men?" Lansing asked.

Yes, said Lyle. It began as after-sports massages when he was six or seven years old. As the massages became more sexual, he said, Jose compared it to "Greek soldiers having had sex with each other before going into battle so they would have a stronger connection." His father called it "bonding." Jose warned him that "bad things would happen to me if I told anybody, and I told him I never would."

Lyle frequently buried his head in his hands and cried as he divulged a progression of sexual contact: fondling at age six; oral sex on his father at age seven ("He would put me on my knees, and he would guide all my movements"); sodomy with a toothbrush or shaving brush at age eight ("He'd have a tube of Vaseline and just play with me"). By then, Lyle was doing the same to five-year-old Erik in the woods behind their house. From the witness stand, through tears, Lyle looked at his brother and apologized. Erik turned away and sobbed.

Choking on his tears, Lyle recalled the first time his father raped him.

"Did you cry?"

"Yes."

"Did you bleed?"

"Yes."

"Were you scared?"

"Very."

"Did you ask him not to?"

"Yes."

"How did you ask not to?"

"I just told him that I didn't want to do this, and that it hurt me. He said he didn't mean to hurt me, that he loved me."

"Was that important to you, that he loved you?"

"Yes. Very. But I still didn't want to do it."

Lansing showed the jurors nude photographs she said that Jose had taken of Lyle and Erik as young children, bending over and showing their genitals. In the framing of the pictures, their heads were cut off. Jose had shown movies of pornographic violence to an audience that included his young sons and neighbors.

Lyle said that he'd complained to his mother: "I told her to tell dad to leave me alone—that he keeps touching me."

"What did your mom say?"

"She told me to stop it, and that I was exaggerating, and that my dad has to punish me when I do things wrong. She told me that he loved me."

That evening, an exhausted Lyle told me that "he had already made peace" with his decision to reveal his family's secrets. "I felt I had finally betrayed my dad," he said in a call from jail. One member of Lyle's jury went home and cried for hours.

As the trial resumed on Monday, Lyle testified that at age thirteen, he worried about confronting his father with his suspicions of what he was doing to Erik. He was afraid that Jose would "beat me up" or get "incredibly angry" and hurt Erik. Still, he decided he had to do something. To prepare, Lyle turned out the lights and played the Lionel Richie song "You Are" over and over as he tried to concentrate.

"My dad had taught me to do this, and I tried to just relax because I was just so tense."

"Did you tell your mom what you thought was happening to your little brother?" asked Lansing.

"No."

"Why not?"

"My mom wasn't going to do anything about it."

After Lyle talked with Jose, Erik told his brother that "things had gotten better." He didn't admit he'd been molested but left Lyle with the impression everything was "resolved."

Lyle wet his bed through his teenage years, which outraged both Jose and Kitty. Jose would taunt him: "You're a sissy just like your brother." Sometimes his punishment would be a beating. His mother would "rub my face in the sheets. She refused to change them. I'd sleep on the floor."

"She was never gentle and affectionate with me," he said.

"Did she ever act like she loved you?"

"I felt that she hated me—that's what she told me all the time."

Until he was age eleven, Kitty often went topless in front of him, and showed him pictures of herself in lingerie. When he was thirteen, she still gave him baths, washing him "everywhere." She invited him to her bed and wanted him to fondle her. "I took it to be love," he said, and "she was enjoying it." But he was not. When he stopped sleeping with his mother, "we had arguments and problems over that for a long time . . . really my whole life."

She would beat and kick her sons, and dragged Lyle around the room by his hair. Once, she chased him with a kitchen knife. After cutting herself one evening, she blamed Lyle by smearing her blood on his face and not letting him wash it off. She characterized all his girlfriends as "gold diggers, bimbos, sluts, and country girls."

"I thought his testimony was compelling, just like watching Sir Laurence Olivier act is compelling," said Pam Bozanich outside the courtroom. So far, she'd heard nothing that justified homicide.

———————

After a one-day recess when he was treated for the flu, Lyle told more details about his stuffed animal "family" and the oddities of his real family. In a soft voice he explained that his stuffed animals "got me through the day, taking me out of where I was to this other world of friends . . . they were soft. They made me feel safer. As I got older, it was embarrassing to me because stuffed animals are for little kids. But it was very important to me," he said.

Lyle gave examples of his father's controlling behavior: Jose broke up the relationships with several of his high school girlfriends. Jose introduced him to another girl, a beauty queen—as Kitty had been. Lyle's mother began taking pills when she discovered that his father had a mistress. Erik found a note she'd written apologizing because "she couldn't handle the shame" and that she "was sorry she had to take this way out and she was leaving."

"I thought it was clearly a suicide letter," said Lyle. "She wasn't leaving town." He suggested that she should consider divorce. Kitty became enraged and accused him of trying to break up her marriage.

She showed him the thirteen pills she took daily, explaining that she "needed them to get through the day." That was the first time she'd ever acknowledged having a problem. In the summer of 1988, Erik told him that Kitty had bought another rifle. "She was very much out of control. She was extremely unstable and seemed to be . . . very mad at the world."

One week after taking the witness stand, Lyle described the emotional night when he and Donovan Goodreau exchanged confessions of sexual molestation.

"After some amount of him crying and having a hard time getting it out, he told me he'd been molested. I felt very bad for him because I knew how it felt." Lyle said he wanted to comfort the man he called "my closest friend ever" who was in "tremendous pain." He confided that the same thing had happened to him and Erik. "I wanted him to know it didn't make him anything strange or weak."

"Why hadn't you told anybody before?" asked Jill Lansing.

"Partly fear of my dad for sure would be one reason I never would. But . . . you know, I had stuffed animals. I had these problems with girlfriends. And I felt so much lesser than my dad. It was just one thing after another. And I wanted to take—put this out of my mind. And my dad never brought it up. So I didn't ever tell anybody."

"Did it make you feel better to tell him?"

"I think we both felt a lot better. For sure."

Later that day, at last, Jill Lansing asked Lyle Menendez about the night of August 20, 1989.

Unlike his earlier testimony, Lyle spoke in a monotone about the days leading up to the shootings, losing his composure only when talking about the actual shooting.

"At some point that summer, less than a week before your parents died, did things start to change in your family?" asked Lansing, Yes, Lyle replied. It began with a confrontation with his mother.

"When my mom goes off, she talks about your whole life," he said. "She brings everything into it. You're born and ruined her dreams . . . and you're ungrateful, spoiled—it just builds, and she works herself into this frenzy where she's just completely out of control."

Several nights later, he confronted his father about the ongoing molestation of Erik. Jose told him to stay out of it. Flustered and agitated, Lyle threatened to tell police and the family.

His father's ominous reply—"We all make choices in our life. Erik made his. You made yours"—frightened Lyle.

"I thought we were in danger. I felt he had no choice. He would kill us. He'd get rid of us in some way. Because I was going to ruin him."

On Sunday evening, August 20, the brothers wanted to go out, but Kitty told them they couldn't leave. Jose ordered Erik upstairs to wait for him, and then led Kitty into the den and locked the doors behind them.

"I was sure that was it. I just freaked out . . . I thought they were going ahead with their plan to kill us."

"How did you feel then?" asked Lansing.

"Just hard to describe how I felt, but like I had to run as fast as I could and my life was sort of slipping away, and that we were going to die."

The brothers got their shotguns, and "burst through the doors" of the den. Jose was "coming forward . . . standing," and Lyle fired "directly at him. I believe he fell back . . . Things were shattering, the noise was phenomenal . . . It was just chaos. I couldn't tell who was firing at who. I was just firing my gun."

"I never wanted to have to do what I did here. I felt drained since I've done it. I felt like I betrayed my dad to some extent," Lyle said on the last day of his direct.

"Why, after all he did to you, do you want people to think well of your father?" asked Jill Lansing.

"I just miss the connection I had with him, and I loved him, and I felt, I guess, very guilty, and seeing my grandmother and people hurt."

To conclude, the defense confronted the problem of Dr. Jerry Oziel and the brothers' confession. Lansing referred to the murders as "the time when your parents died" as she led Lyle through a series of denials, contradictions, and explanations. Oziel had testified that Lyle discussed committing the "perfect murder," but Lyle insisted that "we never talked about the perfect stuff."

He also contradicted Oziel's testimony that the brothers said they'd killed Kitty because they pitied her. Lyle said it was Oziel who'd said "we'd probably done her a favor." He insisted that neither he nor Erik told Oziel they'd done the killing for money because "we thought we were out of the will." Why hadn't they told their therapist about the sexual abuse in the family? He "just didn't want to," Lyle replied.

He denied telling Oziel they'd killed for hatred. "I said I hated him for dying, and there were times I hated him for some of the things he did to my mom."

"What do you mean you hated your father for dying?"

"Well, for a long period of time I was—it sounds bad, but I felt like it was my dad's fault that this had happened."

Lyle denied that the murders were premeditated. "Then, suddenly, it was over . . . My parents were taken away," he said in a low voice. "It was just my brother and I. We never got our act together in any way up until the time we got arrested."

Leslie Abramson declined any examination on behalf of Erik. Throughout the afternoon, she had draped a motherly arm around Erik's shoulder whenever they spoke. As the juries left the courtroom, she put her arm around Lyle.

CHAPTER 45

LYLE'S CROSS-EXAMINATION

"**Y**OU WANT THIS JURY TO ACQUIT YOU, DON'T YOU?"

"I would like to be able to go home and start my life over."

On the first day of Lyle's cross-examination, Pam Bozanich repeatedly attacked his credibility, forcing him to admit previous lies to detectives, prosecutors, and reporters. Throughout the onslaught, Lyle remained composed and poised. He acknowledged in a slightly hoarse voice that the jury might not believe he was now telling the truth.

Challenging Lyle's allegations of abuse, Bozanich asked, "Is there anything I can ask you, or say to you that's going to get you to say those allegations are untrue?"

"They are true," said Lyle.

Bozanich reminded jurors that the defendant was responsible for killing the "two people who could come in and say they're not true."

Lyle said that he and Erik were terrified and believed their options were limited. "Nobody in my family would stand up to my father. I didn't want to go to the police. I didn't want to run away."

Jose's motto, said Lyle, was "lie, cheat, steal, but win." His testimony was truthful now because the "decision was made to say exactly what happened, the bad details as well as the good things. There were times I lied to people. I hope people understand."

"Why is it that you continued to lie about your involvement in the crime?"

"I didn't want to go to jail, or I didn't want my brother to go, either."

"You almost got away with it, didn't you?"

216

"You characterize it that way, and you think it's funny. But my brother's and my life was very miserable for six months before we got arrested, and obviously wasn't better after we got arrested. And it isn't good now. And it never really has been great," he said, emotion rising in his voice. "In some ways, getting arrested was a relief. And the changes that have happened are a relief. And I don't know what's going to happen at the end of this case. And we may go off to prison—very likely. But, you know, some good things have come of it."

Like the poised tournament tennis player he was, Lyle Menendez swatted Bozanich's questions back across the net.

Kitty's rages left him "confused," but he insisted, "I loved my mother."

"When you put the shotgun up against her left cheek and pulled the trigger, did you love your mother?"

"Yes."

"And was that an act of love, Mr. Menendez?"

"It was confusion. Fear."

"What did you think she was going to do to you?"

"At that point, I wasn't consciously thinking anything in particular. I was just reacting . . . something I saw or something that I heard freaked me out even more, and I ran out, and I was afraid."

"You were afraid she might live, weren't you?"

"No. It wasn't that she might live. It was just a caving-in kind of fear that I was not really in control."

"Did you feel the gun touching something fleshy that moved when you pushed it?"

Lyle covered his mouth with a fist and shook his head, no. If he really loved Kitty, demanded Bozanich, why hadn't he called for paramedics after the shooting?

"I was just thinking that we were going to die. It was like survival mode . . . I was expecting to be fired at."

As for Jose, Lyle said that he desperately wanted to be a part of his father's life, but "I didn't confront my father at all."

"When you had a gun, you confronted him just fine," Bozanich said tersely.

"We were afraid . . . We didn't know what was going on. We thought they were going to kill us."

He added in a low voice, "I never disrespected him, except for the one time."

———————

Throughout the day, Bozanich let the witness expound on his answers, a tactic for which she was later criticized. It never occurred to Lyle to "just leave" because his life was going well. "You've suggested many times I could just tell my dad to screw off . . . I wanted to be part of my dad's life. I felt that I needed him to keep me going," he said. "We were a family—I was brought up that way, and I wasn't just going to leave. It's just not easy."

"So you liked your life," Bozanich said sarcastically.

"At that time I felt it was going better than it had in all the previous years."

Jurors listened again to Lyle's sobs and his brother's screams on the 911 tape reporting the murders.

"Mr. Menendez, in that tape, you're crying quite a bit," said the prosecutor.

"Yes."

"At the same time you're crying, you're lying, aren't you?"

"Um, yes."

He acknowledged other lies: He didn't tell relatives about the abuse or the murders. He didn't tell the police about the abuse because "I didn't think they'd understand. We had just shot my parents, and regardless of the reason, we were going to go to jail and our life would be ruined."

After the shooting, he and Erik had waited for the police. "When they didn't show up, my brother and I decided that if it was possible, we didn't want to have to explain what happened. We had just shot our parents, and we didn't want to go to jail."

"You wanted to get away with it, right?"

Lyle didn't answer that with a yes. Instead, he repeated that he and Erik tried to hide their guilt because they didn't want to tell anyone about the abuse, and they didn't think anyone would believe them. He described Kitty as "totally unpredictable," except that "she was consistent in her hatred and resentment" of him.

"It seems impossible to believe my dad would choose to get rid of his sons . . . But that's what we believed. He was willing to kill me to preserve what he had built for himself."

"You were your father's proudest creation?"

"Yeah, I guess so."

"You were his namesake?"

"Yes."

"You were a Menendez?"

"Yes."

"You really believed your father was going to destroy you?"

"Yes, ma'am."

That evening, Court TV's commentators scored the day as a win for the defense.

————

On the second day of cross, Bozanich focused on the spending spree. "I was kind of down and depressed and wandering around from store to store," said Lyle.

"So you thought that [an] 18-karat gold Rolex would go nicely with your funeral suit, is that right?"

"No, I didn't. Again, I really didn't think much about money in my life. I just bought things spur of the moment all the time. This was just another thing."

"So what you did is you killed your parents and began to spend their money, right?"

"Well, that is something that happened, but I don't think characterizing it that way puts it in the right context."

Bozanich set traps and sprung them. Lyle said that the shootings left him "numb and exhausted and very, very in shock." He remembered "glass shattering," "huge noises," and "firing as many times" as he could. But he also acknowledged that he remembered to pick up all the shotgun shells.

Lyle testified more about tensions that had escalated that weekend.

"Closing the doors to me was the last thing that caused me to totally freeze and panic and realize it was happening . . . I thought they were armed ... I thought they were in the process of killing us. I thought they planned this in advance."

"This is what really happened, Mr. Menendez?"

"This is what really happened."

Bozanich was incredulous that the brothers were able to make all the stops they claimed in the sixty-seven minutes between the shootings at approximately 10 PM and the 11:07 PM phone call to Perry Berman. "I didn't want to get a ticket, obviously, but I was driving fast," said Lyle. He admitted he never searched the house for the weapons he believed his parents had. He thought Kitty had a handgun with a silencer that might have come from one of his father's underworld connections. When they bought the shotguns in San Diego, it was not part of a murder plot—it was for self-defense. Their only concern was surviving.

On the third day, the stress of Bozanich's cross showed on Lyle. Frequently he slumped in his chair or sighed loudly. His answers seemed more spontaneous, less rehearsed, and perhaps more telling.

Bozanich demanded more details of the night of the murders.

"I really don't have any particular memory of why I did some of these things that don't make particular sense ... I remember bursting into the room. I remember some very vague things, and then I remember it being over."

Bozanich showed him a picture of the coffee table in the family room and pointed out what was on it: a glass, a bowl with a spoon, a Michael Jackson audio cassette, a cigarette lighter, and some papers from UCLA.

"What on this coffee table was threatening you?"

"Nothing."

"He didn't threaten you? He didn't have a weapon? He didn't do anything out of the ordinary?"

"Well, yes, he closed the doors."

"The last straw?"

"It was the last straw. It was the last thing I remember before I panicked."

Bozanich did a tomahawk chop as she declared, "You went into that room and started firing your weapon before you even knew what your parents were doing, didn't you?"

"Yes. We were in a panic . . . I just remember going in, it was dark . . . someone was coming toward me on the right, like a shadow." And Lyle just began firing wildly.

Bozanich asked if Jose was getting up. He "was not rising. He was standing. I just kept firing. I'm not sure at what point I realized the person to my left was my mother."

Lyle said he remembered putting the 12-gauge shotgun to the back of Jose's head and pulling the trigger.

"Was he seated or standing?"

"I guess I was over him. Because I was over a little to the side of the couch . . . I didn't put it up against his head on purpose . . . It was just a rush, and me firing."

"When you went to the area behind the sofa and unintentionally put the gun against your father's head and pulled the trigger, where was your mother?"

"In my mind, she was sort of sneaking around the side of the coffee table."

Bozanich pounced. Her voice rose. The courtroom murmured.

"You said your mother was sneaking. Did you think she was going to do something sneaky to you when she was crawling behind the coffee table?"

"No, I thought we were in danger, still." Seeing her crawl past the coffee table "caused me to freak out and run out of the room.

"When I went outside to reload, I was confused and afraid and I wasn't thinking even that those were my parents. I was thinking, 'Danger,' and going through the motions."

When he returned, the room was "filled with smoke. You could not see well at all. I could barely see that area, that freaked me out, and I ran over to it."

"And then you pulled the trigger?"

Lyle sighed deeply.

"Yes."

As Lyle Menendez approached the stand on his ninth and final day as a witness, he nodded and smiled at the jurors. Nobody acknowledged him.

In redirect, Jill Lansing gave Lyle another chance to describe life in his home. It was "very unpredictable," a place where there was "not a lot of normal communication." The brothers learned to read facial and behavioral clues, tones of voice, and body postures that signaled impending punishment or violence.

"My dad controlled people with hand signals. But it was more than that . . . you could read his face, just whatever he was doing—if he changed into tennis clothes right away, or if he stayed in his business suit, or if he went over and watched TV . . . I wanted his approval so bad that even shaking his head sort of made my heart sink."

Lansing asked if his expensive tennis lessons and private schools were part of "everything that any kid could have wanted."

Lyle answered that he was lacking in "emotional things" as well as "time to play with friends and just things other kids do . . . I was just doing the best I could."

"Based on all of the things you learned about your parents in your life, in terms of their behavior, when you saw the things they were doing in that last week, did you believe that they were going to kill you?"

"We believed they were," said Lyle.

Bozanich, quick on her feet, returned with a vengeance for a recross.

"Mr. Menendez, what hand signal did your father give to you before you put a gun to the back of his head and pulled the trigger?"

"He didn't give me any."

"And what signal was your mother giving you when she was sneaking away near the coffee table before you went out and reloaded?"

"Nothing . . . I was just afraid at that point."

Then Lansing:

"Did the signals come before you entered the room?"

"Yes."

In a final attack, Bozanich asked Lyle, "And it's your testimony here today that you didn't kill your parents for the money—is that correct?"

"Definitely not."

Every day that Lyle was on the witness stand, he carried a different letter in his pocket from one of the abuse survivors who told him nobody had believed them when they were growing up.

CHAPTER 46

STRANGE SINS— ERIK TESTIFIES

"**L**os Angeles County Jail," Erik Menendez replied when Leslie Abramson asked where he lived.

Erik, wearing a light blue oxford cloth shirt with a maroon paisley tie, looked younger than his twenty-two years.

From there, Abramson immediately cut to the chase: "What do you believe was the originating cause of you and your brother ultimately winding up shooting your parents?"

"Me telling Lyle that, uh"—his face reddened as he burst into tears—"my dad . . . my dad had been molesting me."

Bit by bit, Erik told the jury how his father molested him when he was age six and continued abusing him until shortly before the shootings. If he told anyone about it, "He told me he'd tie me to a chair and beat me to death."

There were four forms of abuse, and Erik had given a name to each: Knees, Nice Sex, Rough Sex, and Just Sex. Some versions included "pins and tacks that Dad would stick in me" during oral sex.

Two women on Erik's jury looked ashen as he described the molestation.

Erik testified that although he knew the abuse was "extremely abnormal," he didn't "want to be humiliated." It was "partly my fault in that I never stopped him. I let him go on . . . I thought I was a coward. I hated myself for it."

When he was seventeen years old, he said, he tried to refuse: "He walked into the room, and I said no." His father "threw me on the bed and went to get a knife and put it at my throat."

Erik dreamed about going away for college, maybe to Princeton with Lyle. Kitty wanted him to attend UC Berkeley or Brown University. He settled on UCLA, but in mid-August 1989, Jose told Erik that he would live at home, not in a dorm.

"The one thing I had been living for was suddenly taken away from me, and I didn't care about life anymore." He considered suicide, by cutting his wrists, hanging, or driving off a cliff. Then Lyle had the fight with Kitty that revealed his toupee, and Erik decided to share his own secret.

On the evening four days before the murders when Jose burst into Erik's room and threw him down on the bed, his father was "more angry than I had ever seen him." This time, Erik struggled and managed to escape. He ran downstairs and saw his mother, who said, "I've always known. What do you think, I'm stupid?"

On the way home from the shark-fishing trip on Saturday, August 19, Erik said Kitty told him, "If I'd kept my mouth shut, things would have worked out in the family."

Abramson asked what that meant.

"Things had not worked out in the family, and she was going to kill us . . . I thought they were going to kill Lyle and I. It seemed clear."

On his second day of testimony, Abramson asked Erik about the night he and Lyle shot their parents.

It was "real, real eerie . . . it was horrible." The room filled with smoke, and his memories were vague. Pressed for details, he answered, "I don't know. I don't know. I just walked into the room. I just started firing, and I don't know, and I didn't think about these things. I didn't think where was this, where was that. I just started firing, and I don't know."

When the noise ended, "The fact that my mom and dad could be killed—it just seemed impossible to me."

Abramson asked, "Did you think they were immortal?" Prosecutors objected, and the judge told Erik to answer in his own words.

"They were so powerful and so overwhelming in my life, I thought they could never go away and never not be in my life."

The abuse started, Erik said, when Jose massaged him while he was wearing underwear. Then came naked "mouth massages"; Jose told his son that they were sharing as soldiers had in "ancient times—the Romans and the Greeks."

At first, Erik said, he liked the special attention from his father. But a short time later, "I didn't like what was going on. I thought it was really dirty."

It didn't stop. When he was eleven, his father forced him to perform oral sex: Knees. In sixth grade, Nice Sex began, mostly massages with hands and mouth but also forced anal sex. A year later, Jose began Rough Sex. By candlelight, his father had him perform oral sex while Jose stuck him with pins and tacks. It was a lesson, Erik explained, in absorbing pain without crying out. Sometimes, Jose forced him to kneel on the sharp edge of his bed while he raped him in front of a mirror. When they lived in New Jersey, Jose forced sex on his son two or three times a month. When the family moved to California, when Erik was age sixteen, the sex stopped for a few months but then resumed.

On the night of the murders, his father ordered Erik upstairs to his bedroom. "I thought he was going to kill me that night. And I thought he was going to have sex with me first."

Instead, an argument exploded. Lyle screamed at his father, "You're not going to touch my little brother!" Jose replied, "I do what I want with my family. It's not your little brother. It's my son." Kitty watched with a "stony, sort of hard look." Erik remembered how scared he was. "I felt my stomach twist my bowels."

When Jose and Kitty went into the TV room and closed the doors, the brothers thought they had weapons inside. "I thought I was going to die . . . It's happening now."

Outside, the brothers each took a shotgun—"a stupidly big thing"—loaded them with shells, and returned inside. The TV room was mostly dark. "All I remember is firing."

Leslie Abramson asked what was in front of him.

"My parents."

On the third day, Erik told the jury of his overwhelming depression after his parents were dead. He had images in his mind that he couldn't lose of the smoke-filled TV room after the shootings. He also had recurring visions of the goriness. "Anything could spark it. Anything would remind me, and I would see them in the room . . . I was feeling very bad about killing my parents . . . It was confusing, the guilt. Thinking about what kind of person I was tore me apart, and gave me a lot of pain."

By confessing to Dr. Oziel, "I knew I had really betrayed my brother's trust."

Speaking more about the abuse, he said he called himself the "Hurt Man." Friends and relatives heard him say it but didn't know what it meant. Jose gave him a private name, too: "Faggot." Although Jose ridiculed homosexuals, he insisted that sex with his son had nothing to do with homosexuality. Erik never dared talking back to his father's name-calling, but he often dreamed of saying, "Then what the hell are you?"

On the fourth day of testimony, Erik tried to explain why he hadn't told his therapist about the abuse. He hadn't wanted to tarnish his father's memory. "I was just much too ashamed to deal with it. I wanted to keep it as secret as possible, bury it, throw it in the ocean, make it disappear. I thought they were great people I had killed, and . . . I loved them more than I had ever loved them at that point."

In cross-examination, Lester Kuriyama pressed Erik on details about the murder scene.

"Now you surprised your parents while they were watching television and blasted them until your pump shotguns were empty of ammunition, correct?"

"No, sir," said Erik. The TV was on, but his parents weren't watching it. As the brothers barged into the room, he thought his parents were standing. "I shot everything I had, mostly shooting at my mom."

Then he heard something that "freaked me out. I guess I would call it a moaning, because she was dying."

"You were so freaked out that you went to your car, and you had ammunition in a box, and you handed that ammunition to your brother?" Kuriyama demanded.

Erik said he was "scrambling around for shells," and handed one to Lyle. "I knew he was going back into the room. I knew what was going to happen."

"You just instinctively knew your brother was going to return to finish killing your mother?"

"Yes."

Kuriyama then pointed out that for firing wild, the brothers had been "deadly accurate." Jose had been hit six times, Kitty approximately ten. "Mr. Menendez, there were only two shots that missed."

"Apparently."

Kuriyama pressed for more details about buying the shotguns.

Erik had testified that before they bought the guns at a Big 5 Sporting Goods store in San Diego, they went to a Big 5 in Santa Monica. To set the scene there, Kuriyama asked dozens of questions, including about the handgun display in a glass case.

"I think it was a two-shelf container . . . there were guns on the top, that's what I remember seeing," Erik said. "I specifically remember seeing the ones that did not have a revolver." He also remembered that BB and pellet guns were "over to the right . . . the real ones were more in the center, where I was." Erik picked out a gun, although he couldn't remember the caliber or color. Then they learned that the state had a fifteen-day waiting period to purchase handguns, so they left without buying.

"Now you're telling the truth about everything in this case, aren't you?"

"I'm telling the truth to the best that I can," said Erik.

"And even though you lied in the past, you're telling the truth now, aren't you?"

"Yes, I am."

"Did you truly go to the Santa Monica Big 5 store on the morning of August 18th to buy these handguns?"

"Definitely. Without any doubt. I did."

The deputy district attorney then calmly informed the witness that the Big 5 stores had stopped selling handguns three years before he was there.

Erik fumbled a response: "Ah, Mr. Kuriyama, there were guns there, and we did look at them." Kuriyama theatrically let him dangle.

———————

When court resumed for Erik's sixth day of testimony, the deputy D.A. continued his attack. Erik insisted that he went to a gun store in Santa Monica but conceded it might not have been a Big 5.

Kuriyama pressed for more details of the murders. "Mr. Menendez, when you were shooting at your mother, did she simply stand in front of you and take all the shots that you were administering to her?"

"I don't know."

"You have no idea what she was doing?

"I didn't see her. As soon as I started firing, I didn't see anyone."

"How could that be?"

"I guess because the room was dark, and because there was so much noise and there was so much fire. And maybe because I don't want to remember."

———————

"Mr. Menendez, you say you'd been molested for twelve years, correct? Is that your testimony?" Kuriyama asked the next day.

"Yes, that's what happened."

"All the way up till when you were nineteen years old?

"Up until my father died."

"Are there any witnesses to this molestation?"

"Was anyone in the room?" Erik asked.

"Yes," Kuriyama responded.

"No."

"In fact, the only person who could deny or contest your claims is your father, right?"

"My mother and my father."

"And both of them are dead, right?"

"Yes."

Asked if they'd killed Kitty to keep her from testifying against them, he answered, "I doubt she would have been a witness against us at any point. I think she very well might have killed us and killed herself. Just poisoned everyone."

That was another opening for Kuriyama. "You wanted to kill your mother, didn't you? As badly as you wanted to kill your father?"

"I hadn't thought about the difference. I only thought that they were going to kill us, and at the last moment, we killed them."

Two days later came this:

"Now, you've testified, sir, that your mother was going to kill you that night?"

"Yes."

"That's still your belief, is that correct?"

"Well, if I knew they did not have weapons in that room when they walked in that room, I would not have walked in the room. I don't know what my belief to this day is. I can't be sure that's my belief to this day."

CHAPTER 47

THE RETURN OF DONOVAN GOODREAU

T HERE WAS INTENSE DEBATE AMONG REPORTERS IN VAN NUYS AS well as people around the world following the trial on Court TV. Did the sexual molestation really happen? There are rarely eye-witnesses or videos to document incest. Even today, abuse victims are often hesitant to reveal their devastating secret to anybody.

Marta Cano's son Andres was sworn in after Erik finished his tes-timony. Growing up, the tall, handsome twenty-year-old student at the University of Central Florida was always close with his cousin. Occa-sionally, Andy spent weekends or time during summer vacations with the Menendezes. Rarely was Erik allowed to stay overnight with the Canos.

Once, when Erik was twelve and Andy ten years old, Cano testified they were playing war games in a field when Erik asked Andy: Did his father ever give him massages?

"At that point I got the feeling—I'm sure he let me know this—but he was actually trying to find out if these massages were normal," said Cano. "And my response to him was that I wouldn't know. I didn't have a father around. My parents were divorced then. And I really couldn't help him."

"Was there something else he told you about the massages, like where they were?" asked Leslie Abramson.

"Well, he told me his father was massaging his dick . . . He wanted to know if this happens to every kid with a father-and-son relationship."

Andy wanted to ask his mother, but Erik made his cousin swear he never would reveal the secret to anyone. A month later, the cousins continued their conversation.

"I asked him why didn't he let his mother know," said Andy.

"She'll get mad at my father," Erik told him.

Later, Erik told him that the "massages were beginning to hurt." To Andy, it didn't make sense. Besides the "massages," Erik never said anything else about being molested. Later, Erik told his cousin that he wanted his father to "stop everything he was doing to him." Erik seemed nervous and again insisted that Andy never divulge his secret. Andy agreed by making a "pinky promise."

A year later, while playing with Erik, Andy scraped his leg and noticed a jar of Vaseline in his cousin's room. "I figured it was a type of ointment that you put on scratches . . . I picked it up, and Erik immediately told me to put it back down . . . He said, that's not what it's for."

On cross, Lester Kuriyama asked, "Your cousin was a good friend of yours?"

"Yes. He was. And is," replied Andy, firmly.

"And I believe your mother testified that she would lie for the brothers. Would you also do that?"

"I'm not lying for him now, and I wouldn't lie for anybody under oath, Mr. Kuriyama."

"You would not?"

"I would not, Mr. Kuriyama."

Marta Cano smiled at her son.

During redirect, Cano testified that the first person he'd ever told about Erik's massages was Leslie Abramson, and that was five months after the brothers confessed the molestation to the family.

The defense recalled Donovan Goodreau, a reluctant witness for them, to corroborate the brothers' stories of sexual abuse. After prosecutors had forced me to turn over my interview with Goodreau in July, they'd decided not to play the tape for the juries.

Jill Lansing asked Goodreau about the "mood of the conversation" at the Chinese restaurant the night the friends had exchanged confessions of being molested.

"I had known Lyle for several months up to that point and we had spent a lot of time together, bonded as friends, and got to know each other very well," he said timidly. His voice was composed, but he rocked back and forth in the swivel chair.

"I felt really close to him and I felt like, you know, he showed an interest in me and wanted to know everything about me, and also I felt the time was right for me to tell someone."

After hearing Goodreau's secret, Lyle got "pretty quiet" and "seemed somewhat emotional about it."

"Were you shocked at how emotional he was?" asked Lansing.

"Oh, yes. Absolutely. You never know what to expect when you tell someone something like that."

"And did that cause you to believe that something similar may have happened to Lyle?"

"Absolutely."

Pam Bozanich objected to the question as leading. The judge ordered the answer struck.

"What did that cause you to believe?"

"That he may have had similar experiences."

"And did he say anything to you about having had a similar experience?"

"Not that I recall. No."

"Did he say anything to you about his father having molested both him and his brother?"

"No. I would have remembered that."

"You would remember that if he'd said that?"

"Yes."

"Did you ever tell anyone else that Lyle had told you that he had been molested by his father, and his brother had also?"

"Obviously I heard the tape, so I know that I may have mentioned it later on."

"And to whom did you mention it?"

"Bob Rand."

Jill Lansing approached the witness stand where a portable cassette tape player sat. Goodreau drank water while bailiffs passed out transcripts to jurors and reporters of my March 1992 interview with him.

"Mr. Goodreau, do you remember when you testified on July 26, 1993, as a prosecution witness, you said that you had never told anybody that Lyle Menendez had made this statement to you?"

"Yes."

"So I take it you were mistaken at that time, is that correct?

"Obviously."

Lansing played a segment from the interview in which Donovan explained how Lyle had revealed his own molestation to him. At first, Goodreau stared at the tape player; then he turned and watched the jurors. Lyle went back and forth from reading the transcript to staring at his former friend.

"Having listened to the tape now, does that refresh your recollection?"

"No. I heard the tape last time, and it doesn't help me. I know I said that, but I just can't recall all the events surrounding it."

"Okay. Well, do you think when you told Mr. Rand that in March of 1992 you were telling him the truth?"

"I really can't recall why I would have said that, whether it was the truth or not."

Goodreau repeated that since the brothers' arrest, the primary people he'd spoken with about the case were his and Lyle's former roommate Glenn Stevens and myself.

"Now, is it your testimony that Bob Rand told you that Lyle and Erik had been molested by their father?"

"Oh, no. I'm not saying that at all. I'm not sure where I heard it."

"Is it your testimony that Glenn Stevens told you that Lyle and Erik had been molested by their father?"

"It may have been. It may have been Bob Rand."

As his testimony kept going in circles, Lansing read a section of the transcript in which Goodreau told me he was surprised that Stevens also knew about the molestation: "And Glenn just freaked me out, because I thought Lyle—I thought I was the only one who'd heard about that or knew about that, and all of a sudden Glenn told me the same thing. He said, 'Did you know about the molestation and all that?'"

"Do you remember that?" Lansing asked him.

"No."

"Do you remember telling Mr. Rand that?"

"Not—not clearly, no."

"But if your voice is on the tape . . ."

"Obviously."

"Then it would have been something you said, is that correct?"

"Sure."

Lansing read more from the transcript:

"And he brought it up again. And I'd almost forgotten about it. And he brought it up again. And I just couldn't believe it. I said, 'Really.' I said, 'I didn't know about that.' And it was kind of strange for him to tell me, because I was wondering under what circumstances he would tell Glenn . . ."

"Now, that's referring to Lyle telling Glenn—is that correct?"

"Yes."

"But at the time that you were all at Princeton together, was your relationship with Lyle much closer than Lyle's with Glenn?"

"Absolutely."

"And then the tape goes on to say: 'And you know, I thought he was having problems, you know. Lyle was scared, too. The house at Calabasas had this huge bathtub, and he was like fearing this thing'—do you remember saying anything about a bathtub?"

"No."

"But if your voice is on the tape, you would have been the one to say it, is that correct?"

"Yes," Goodreau replied, continuing the game of cat and mouse.

"What's your testimony with regard to Mr. Rand? Did he tell you that Lyle and Erik had been molested by their father, or did you tell him?"

"I have no idea."

"Well, when you listened . . ."

"Obviously, I told him. But it seems like there was a couple places where he seemed to be leading me, and I'm unclear about whether I may have come on to that assumption myself or have been . . ."

Goodreau was now parroting the prosecution's theory that I'd set him up with "leading questions."

"So are you suggesting that Mr. Rand gave you this information?"

"I already answered that earlier," he said softly. "I have no idea where I may have come up with that."

"So you're not saying Mr. Rand gave you that information?"

"I'm not sure if he did or not."

"And you're not saying Glenn Stevens gave you that information?"

"He may have also. I'm not sure."

The Menendez family in 1988, one year before the double murders of
Jose and Kitty Menendez at their mansion in Beverly Hills, California.
From left: Twenty-year-old Lyle, a student at Princeton University;
parents Kitty and Jose; and seventeen-year-old Erik.

The public was stunned by the emotional testimony of Lyle Menendez. Jurors, reporters, and family members were all seen crying during the first hour of Lyle's testimony on September 10, 1993. A TV pool feed arranged by local L.A. stations and national networks live from the courtroom was broadcast around the world.

The testimony of Erik Menendez was equally as dramatic as that of his brother, Lyle. An international audience watched the gavel-to-gavel TV pool feed daily, following every development as if it were a novela.

An unruly six-year-old Jose Menendez with his sisters, Marta (*L*) and Terry (*behind*), and their mother, Maria, in 1950.

Lyle and Erik's paternal grandmother, born Maria Carlota Llanio (*top row, R*), competed on the Cuban Olympic swimming team in the 1930s.

The Menendez and Llanio families in Cuba in the early 1950s. Young Jose Menendez (*front row, second from L*), cousin Henry Llanio (*front row, far L*), and Jose's parents, Maria Menendez (*center row, second from R*) and Jose Menendez "Pepin" Pavon (*top row, R*).

Fourteen-year-old
Jose Menendez at boarding
school in Kentucky in 1958.

Debutante Marta Menendez
(later Cano) in Havana
at age fifteen.

Baby Erik with his godmother, Marta Cano, who remained supportive of both of her nephews throughout the lengthy criminal trials.

Maria Carlota (Llanio) Menendez in the mid-1980s.

OAK LAWN
INDEPENDENT
YOUR "OWN" LOCAL NEWSPAPER
Thursday, September 20,
Thirty-second Year —
Oak Lawn,

Youth 17, Killed When Motorcycle Crashes With C[...]

Mary Louise Anderson (left) being crowned "Miss Oak Lawn" by Village President Fred Dumke (left) in recent beauty and talent pageant. Standing are, l. to r., Nikki Lou Best, first runner-up, and Jean Tenegal, second runner-up. At right is Al Krugerer, commander of Johnson - Phelps VFW Post, which sponsored the pageant.

Crown 'Miss Oak Lawn'

Named "Miss Oak Lawn" in 1962, a popular Mary Louise Andersen was known to her family and friends as "Kitty." In 1963, she met and married Jose Menendez.
(OAK LAWN INDEPENDENT *newspaper, Oak Lawn, Il. Lysen/ Gavin families*)

Kitty Menendez
in the 1970s.

A 1962 picture of eighteen-year-old Jose Menendez and older sister,
Terry (Menendez) Baralt (R), with their goddaughter, baby Marta,
the daughter of Marta Cano (L).

Jose Menendez with sons Erik (L) and Lyle (R). The photo became a
controversial piece of evidence in the first murder trial in 1993. Arguing
that years of parental abuse led the brothers to kill their parents, the
defense claimed the photo showed Jose Menendez's hand in
an inappropriate position in Lyle's lap.

Erik (*far L*) and Lyle (*far R*) with their cousin
Andy Cano (*center L*) in a family photo in the 1970s.

Three generations of Menendezes: Young Lyle
with his father and grandparents, Pepin and Maria.

The Menendez family of four in Princeton,
New Jersey, in 1983, attending cousin Andy Cano's
First Communion celebration.

Jose Menendez gave Lyle (*L*) and Erik (*R*) intensive tennis lessons
from a very young age. This photo of father and sons was taken
in Princeton, New Jersey, in the mid-1980s.

While at RCA Records, Jose Menendez hobnobbed with
musical celebrities, including Kenny Rogers, Barry Manilow,
the Eurythmics, and Rick Springfield, pictured here with Menendez.

Jose Menendez (*L*) at a 1985
Menudo concert in São Paulo, Brazil.

Jose Menendez (*center*) with Grace Slick and other
members of Jefferson Starship in the mid-1980s.

Pepin, Lyle, and Jose Menendez
in Princeton, New Jersey, in 1985.

Erik and Lyle at Erik's
high school graduation in June 1989.

Kitty, Erik, and Jose at Erik's graduation
from Beverly Hills High School in June 1989.

The last known picture of Kitty and Jose Menendez, taken
outside their Calabasas, California, dream house in early August 1989—
a couple of weeks before they were killed by their sons.

The Menendez case became an international sensation that was a major story in the United States and other countries. Rand's articles appeared in the *Miami Herald*, *People*, and *Playboy* as well as many foreign magazines.

eles Char...

DAILY 35¢
DESIGNATED AREAS HIGHER

RDAY, JANUARY 29, 1994
THE TIMES MIRROR COMPANY / CCY / 104 PAGES

THE SUNDAY TIMES | October ...

Magazine

PLUS 40 PAGES OF MEN'S
STYLE AND FASHION

Menendez Case Ends in a rial; D.A. to Retry Brothers

■ **Courts:** Jurors were irreconcilably split, with some holding out for lesser manslaughter charge. Prosecutors will again seek first-degree convictions. Judge schedules hearing to set new trial date.

By ALAN ABRAHAMSON
TIMES STAFF WRITER

The Menendez murder case ended Friday without a single verdict as a second jury was declared deadlocked, the jurors hopelessly polarized over whether Lyle and Erik Menendez were coldblooded killers or long-suffering victims of abuse within their family's gated Beverly Hills estate.

Van Nuys Superior Court Judge Stanley M. Weisberg declared a mistrial in the Lyle Menendez case Friday afternoon, ending the two-month trial, separate jury for younger brother Erik Menendez was declared deadlocked two ... ago in the Aug. 20, 1989, ... gun slayings of their wealthy ... rents.

Prosecutors promised to try the ... brothers again for first-degree murder

BLOOD BROTHERS

James Dalrymple on the murder trial that shook Beverly Hills

METRO NEWS

Author Robert Rand holds tape recorder at trial media center. He was ordered to surrender two tapes.

KEN LUBAS / Los Angeles Times

Lyle Menendez Went on Spree After Killings, Witnesses Say

AN ABRAHAMSON
STAFF WRITER

Within a week after his parents were killed, Lyle Menendez went on a ... spree, shopping for a ... a house, a restaurant and ... nd hiring a bodyguard, a ... gun.

... ventured out ... usine, trailed ... in a second ... that could ... n emergen- ... day night.

hearing over information about the defense.

Donovan Goodreau, 26, who used to share a college dorm room with Lyle Menendez, testified Monday that Menendez never said he had been molested.

But in March, 1992, Goodreau told author Robert Rand, who is writing a book about the Menendez trial, that Lyle Menendez ... sons. Rand p... interview on ...

the alleged abuse that is important to the defense.

dent at Princeton University, had just returned to New Jersey from California and said his life was in "severe danger," Wenskoski said.

He and a partner provided 24-hour-a-day service and accompanied Lyle Menendez on his many shopping trips, even a 1...

test ride in a...

THE KILLING OF ...SE MENENDEZ

article by ROBERT RAND

A BRUTAL CRIME, A FAMILY WITH SECRETS, THE SHADOW OF THE MOB, A SHRINK WITH A LOOSE-LIPPED GIRLFRIEND—NO WONDER BEVERLY HILLS CAN'T STOP TALKING ABOUT THE MENENDEZ MURDERS

Deux femmes
défendent Erik et Lyle
Menendez,
assassins de leurs
parents à Hollywood.
Un meurtre
dont ils avaient écrit
le scénario !

LE CRIME QUI GLACE

Lyle Menendez (*R*) with his roommate Hayden Rogers outside of Chuck's Spring Street Café, the chicken wing restaurant Lyle bought in Princeton, New Jersey, in the fall of 1989. (*Courtesy* The Daily Princetonian)

Judalon Smyth went to the police and said her lover, the brothers' therapist, Dr. Jerome Oziel, had an audiotape of Erik and Lyle Menendez confessing to killing their parents.

Rand on the set in September 2017 with actress Heather Graham, who played Judalon Smyth in NBC's series *Law & Order True Crime: The Menendez Murders.* Josh Stamberg played the role of Rand, who has covered the Menendez story since 1989.

Rand took this photo of Dr. Jerome Oziel (*center*) and his wife, Laurel, who held a news conference at the Beverly Hills Hotel on September 13, 1990. Oziel denied that he had ever asked Judalon Smyth to eavesdrop on therapy sessions with the Menendez brothers.

No ... ooo ... ooo!

He turns the body over and looks into her dead face. SIRENS. He runs
quickly toward the hole in the fence and leaves as police cars approach
with sirens on full and flashing lights.

10.   EXT. CEMETERY

The day is cloudy and foreboding. A Santa Ana wind is blowing from the
North. CAMERA PANS a group of about fifty surrounding a coffin
suspended above ground. HAMILTON CROMWELL stands at the head
of the coffin. His eyes are red and he begins to cry but succeeds in
gaining control.

                    HAMILTON

          My father was not a man to show his emotions.
          I know that he loved his family and his close
          friends very much. I can only hope that he
          loved me as much as he loved all of you.
          Sometimes he would tell me that I was not
          worthy to be his son. When he did that, it would
          make me strive harder to go further, to prove
          to him that I was worthy just so I could hear
          the words, "I love you, son." (Tears well up
          in Hamilton's eyes.) Nothing I have ever done
          was good enough for this man and I never
          heard those words. But I know he thought
          them.

The coffin is lowered into the ground. As the service concludes, JOE
EDDISER, a young man of eighteen, approaches Hamilton and puts his
arm around him.

                    JOE

          We'll survive, buddy. Your father would
          have wanted you to. He knew what a great
          man you would become .. even greater than
          he was. A warrior who has lost his parents is
          still a warrior.

                    HAMILTON

          (Stopping to hug Joe tightly) What would I do
          without you? without your comforting words?
          I need you, Joe. Don't ever go away.

11.   EXT. FOREST

003583

A page from the unproduced screenplay *Friends*, written by Erik Menendez and
his friend Craig Cignarelli. In the script, which Kitty Menendez helped type,
a character named Hamilton Cromwell kills his parents and inherits
$157 million. The script was not admitted into evidence during the trials.

(07/05/89) There is a notation that she feels what she is hiding is sick and embarrassing. He said it possibly referred to her earlier life but that it is more likely that it refers to her adult life. His reasoning was that what happens to you as a child, by the time you become an adult no longer seems sick and embarrassing. As an adult you have a sense that you were not responsible for what happened to you as a child. However, if the secrets came from adulthood, then it would be sick and embarrassing since you would be the one responsible for it.

Kitty Menendez told her therapist she was hiding "sick and embarrassing secrets" about her family six weeks before she was killed by her sons. (An excerpt of the transcribed therapy notes appears here.)

The Most Official Sex I.O.U.

PRINTED AND PUBLISHED BY CON ART GRAPHICS

This I.O.U. is to certify that
Judalon Rose Smyth owes Jerry Oziel
500 sex acts to be paid in full
over the period of 105 years or Life,
whichever comes first. Until this I.O.U.
is paid in full the giving and the acceptance
of this I.O.U. grants exclusive Rights
to any and all sexual activity on both
parties side until the debt is satisfied.

Signed Judalon Rose Smyth
DATE 11/25/89

WITNESS Shanti Oz
WITNESS ISHI KITTY

Judalon Smyth wrote an IOU to Dr. Jerome Oziel for 500 sex acts. The girlfriend of the therapist claimed she overheard the Menendez brothers' murder confession four months before they were arrested in March 1990.

On January 28, 1994, the Los Angeles County Superior Court announced
two hung juries in the concurrent murder trials of Lyle and Erik Menendez.
This photo depicts the famously outspoken Leslie Abramson with Rand to
the left. District Attorney Gil Garcetti immediately announced he
would retry the case and there would be no plea bargain.

Erik Menendez (*L*) and his cousin, Andy Cano, at Erik's wedding in prison in 1999. Andy was a key defense witness in both trials who said twelve-year-old Erik had told him about being sexually molested by his father.

Lyle Menendez's aunts Terry Baralt (*L*) and Marta Cano (*R*) attended his second wedding in prison in 2003.

Rand discussing the Menendez case with Joe Fryer on
NBC's *Today* on September 2, 2016.

Dateline NBC correspondent Keith Morrison interviewed Rand in August 2017
for the two-hour special, "Unthinkable: The Menendez Murders,"
which aired on November 17, 2017.

At times I wish I could talk to her about things, you know? Some day...Especially dad and I but the way she worships him And tells him every thing I so afraid she'll tell him whatever I say. I just can't risk it. ~~strikethrough~~ Lyle got in a huge fight with her over why we couldn't spend christmas with the rest of the family and mom freaked out and said if he wanted to go he could go alone. I just don't know why she wants to hurt him like that. Lyle wanted to stay but dad wouldn't let him. So now I'm stuck here alone I've been trying to avoid dad. Its still happening Andy but its worse for me now. I can't explain it. He so ~~overweight~~ that I can't stand to see him, I never know when when its going to happen and its driving me crazy. Every night I stay up thinking he might come in. I need to put it out of my mind. I know what you said before but I'm afraid. You just don't know dad like I do. Hes crazy! hes warned me a hundred times about telling anyone Especially Lyle. Am I a serious whimpus? I don't know I'll make it through this. I can handle it, Andy. I need to stop thinking about it.

Anyway I hope your doing good, Hows your new girlFriend, Allican? She sounds pretty great, when do I get to meet her? I can see why you don't want to leave PortoRico! Ha Ha. I hear your playing alot of soccer. thats great, I love soccer to bad I had to

New evidence in the Menendez case in the form of a letter written in 1988 from Erik Menendez to his cousin, Andy Cano, now deceased. The letter was discovered among Cano's personal effects by his mother, Marta Cano, and Rand in March 2018.

Lyle Menendez (*L*) and Robert Rand at Richard J. Donovan Correctional Facility in San Diego, California, in May 2018.

A sketch by veteran courtroom artist Bill Robles moments before the clerk read the "guilty of first-degree murder" verdict to Lyle (*L*) and Erik (*R*) Menendez on March 20, 1996. Following their conviction, a penalty phase was held to determine if the brothers would receive the death penalty or a sentence of life without parole—it was the latter. The Menendez brothers have been imprisoned since their arrest in 1990. (*Illustration by Bill Robles*)

CHAPTER 48

THE THERAPY EXPERTS

FOLLOWING THE BROTHERS' TESTIMONY, THE DEFENSE BROUGHT in psychological experts to explain why Erik and Lyle could have believed that their lives were in danger during the days and hours leading up to the murders.

Dr. Ann Tyler, who treated abuse victims and trained people how to identify child molestation, had spent thirty hours interviewing Erik and read most of his records. "Although physical injuries inflicted by parents heal," she said, "minds do not."

Dr. Ann Burgess, a University of Pennsylvania professor of psychiatric mental health nursing, testified about the "neurobiology of fear," explaining how the brain "rewires" and "remaps" itself after psychological trauma. The effects of fear are easily "rekindled," she said, after a child is traumatized. Abuse victims have a faster biological reaction to fear than someone who has never been traumatized. Fear releases additional stress hormones, such as adrenaline, into the brain. Another result of repeated psychological trauma is hypervigilance, which she defined as constantly searching the environment for anything that appears to be dangerous.

Burgess interviewed Erik for more than fifty hours, read statements by witnesses, and concluded that he had been sexually molested. She believed that the abuse continued up until his parents were killed and that Kitty had facilitated the incest. Erik had a "rescue fantasy" that his life would somehow change and the abuse would end when he went away to college.

"And what happens to children who are in these sorts of trapped situations when their rescue fantasies collapse?" asked Leslie Abramson.

"It will certainly increase their anxiety. There is now no opportunity for them to think of a way out, and it throws them right back into the confusion of what is going to happen."

The most effective psychological expert was Dr. Jon Conte, a University of Washington social work professor who spent sixty hours with Lyle and found him "credible." Conte lectured professional groups on how to distinguish real claims of child abuse from false ones.

"[Lyle] wasn't eager. He wasn't overly dramatic about it. It was quite painful. He had a lot of shame. He was talking the way I've heard many young men his age, and men older, talk about an experience in which they're sexually abused by a father."

When some victims talk about their abuse, Conte said, they reexperience their emotions. But others who have separated from the pain retell it in a matter-of-fact way.

"The absence of emotion that appears consistent with a description of a traumatic event doesn't mean that the person is making it up. It just means that the person has separated from, or somehow tried to cope with the feeling of the pain that goes with it.

"And I think one of the most compelling things, for example, was talking about how much he wanted his dad to love him, and this was important to his dad and his dad liked it, and he wanted to make his dad feel good. I mean, those are the kinds of thinking and effects that a victim who has a relationship with the offender will, in fact, engage in."

Conte was amazed at how Lyle used stuffed animals. "He had large numbers of them, and he gave them personalities, and he acted out scenarios with those stuffed animals, kind of issues in his life . . . he, in a way, was doing play therapy. The difference between Lyle's acting out his issues with stuffed animals and play therapy is that there was no therapist there to help guide the process, to help talk about the feelings that the stuffed animals had, or to maybe figure out ways that the stuffed animals could work out the scenario in a different way."

Conte said there was building anxiety in both brothers the week before they killed their parents. The first event was Kitty ripping Lyle's hairpiece from his head. Erik hadn't known that Lyle wore a toupee.

"This was an event of great emotion. And so, in the spirit of, or consistent with that emotion, Erik tells him a secret about something very painful and traumatic."

At age thirteen, Lyle had suspected that his father was abusing Erik, and confronted him. "His dad said nothing is going on, and if anything is going on, it would stop. So, his view of his father is suddenly challenged."

On Thursday, August 17, Lyle rehearsed a speech he would give to his father when he arrived home. Conte said that was significant because Jose had taught him, in years of dinner-table drills, to be concise while speaking. Lyle made his speech but didn't think he performed well.

"Then when his father says, you know, 'This is none of your business. And what I do with my sons,' which is a very strange way to say this—he's talking to his son. He's talking in a depersonalized way, almost talking to him as if he's an object or a piece of property."

"What's the effect on Lyle's fear level or anxiety level at that point in time?" asked Jill Lansing.

"Well, it's very high. And his dad says things to him like, 'We all make choices.' I mean, it's a threat. It's ominous, as Lyle hears it."

Next, Conte said, Erik went to the guesthouse and told Lyle that their mother had always known about the molestation of Erik.

"Well, I think, again, it's the dismantling of another secret. It suggests that Mom allowed another bad thing to happen to these kids. I believe this is, then, the first time the brothers begin to put all these cues together and say, 'They're going to kill us. They're going to get rid of us.'"

At that point, Lyle suggested running away, but Erik may have been more realistic. "Erik says, 'No, it's not going to work. Dad's got all these contacts,' which Dad does. So they kind of go back and forth talking about what their options are." The brothers knew that Mom had sleuthing skills, too, Conte said. She had tracked down Jose's long-time mistress from credit card receipts and had tapped Erik's phone.

"Now, they have this discussion Thursday night," interjected Lansing. "Running away is ruled out. They make a decision that they're going to go buy guns the next day. Is that your understanding?"

"Yes."

"And what would their anxiety level be at this point?"

"This is an exceedingly unusual step for kids to take," said Conte. "We're going to go out and buy guns to protect ourselves from our own parents. That's done, and I believe at a high level of arousal."

"Is there a component of confusion, or is Lyle certain at all times of exactly what's going on?"

"No. I think he's constantly trying to figure out, 'Am I reading the cues right? Is the danger right? No. It's not possible. Couldn't be.' They ride to San Diego; one of them believing they're going to be killed, and the other one saying it couldn't possibly be."

Conte said that many battered kids crawl back into their parents' laps, hoping for a change.

"Lyle, I think, operates a lot of his life on the feeling that if he just does right, he's going to please Dad. And he doesn't have much evidence that he can please Mom, but he certainly has the hope that Mom will. So, yeah, I think there's incredible ambivalence in believing that your parents would kill you. Lyle gets a sense that this is much bigger than he had realized before . . . He had no idea when his brother had made the first disclosure that the sexual abuse was as extensive as it was."

"And what does this do to Lyle's perception of who his father is?"

"It shocks his view of his father. I think it also increased his own sense of responsibility in needing to protect his brother." When Kitty told them, "Things might have worked out in the family if Erik had kept his mouth shut . . . she's talking in the past tense. That sort of communicates to Lyle that whatever it is has been decided, that there is great risk."

"Do you have reason to believe that Lyle Menendez may have perceived reality differently than someone who had not lived in that family, would have seen cues differently, would have read the situation differently than someone who didn't live there?" asked Jill Lansing.

"Yes."

"And you cannot say whether he was misreading them because of the experience, or he was reading them more accurately than other people would, is that correct?"

"That's correct," said Conte.

CHAPTER 49

MORE FAMILY SECRETS REVEALED

PRIVATELY, THERE WAS EXTREME FRUSTRATION AND FRICTION between Jose Menendez's two sisters and their mother. All three had never wavered from their public expression of their support for the brothers. Marta Cano and Terry Baralt's testimony was critical to the defense's presentation of a troubled family's history. But away from the courtroom and the media, there were ongoing arguments between Maria Menendez and her daughters.

When the family first learned about Erik and Lyle's allegations of abuse in 1990, Maria Menendez refused to believe it. She continued to tell reporters that the Mafia had killed Jose and Kitty—even after the brothers confessed to the family. Two years before the trial, Maria told Marta she wanted to hire people to "break the brothers out of jail," regardless of the cost. Her plan was to take Erik and Lyle somewhere far away so they would never have to reveal any of the Menendez family secrets.

During the trial, Marta, Terry, and Maria were all staying in the mansion in Beverly Hills. Maria told Marta she didn't believe her grandsons. "My mother was very angry," said Marta Cano. "She told me, 'You will kill your brother twice.'" After an angry argument one day, Cano left and checked into the same hotel with the defense psychological experts. One morning, Marta had breakfast with the therapy witnesses before court. She wanted to learn more. They asked her who controlled Jose when he was growing up. Marta replied that her mother always controlled everything Jose did when he was a baby and young boy. "They told me the person who controls a child is the person who abuses a child," she said. "I told them no."

Maria Carlota Menendez was born on December 8, 1917. She grew up in a house in Havana with twelve uncles. Marta believed her mother was molested when she was a little girl by one of the uncles—an alcoholic in his twenties.

Marta believed Maria didn't love Pepin and was forced into marriage with him by her parents because they didn't approve of a man she was dating. In their wedding pictures, neither are smiling. Maria's social circle included people much younger than herself when she was in her thirties. The younger friends were people Maria knew from her participation as a member of the Cuban Olympic swimming team. The family believed Maria may have had romantic relationships outside of her marriage.

When Jose was born in 1944, Marta was two and Terry was four years old. Jose became the focus of Maria's life. He could do no wrong. Maria told Pepin that Jose was "hers." Nobody else in the family was allowed to discipline her baby son. "Jose was an unruly baby," said Marta. "He was always causing problems and allowed to do anything he wanted. My mother was obsessed with him."

When Jose was around three years old, Marta said her father began placing Jose in Maria's bed every morning before he left to drop off the girls at school on his way to work. This routine continued daily until Jose was age six.

In private conversations with the therapy experts, Cano learned that an abuser will typically abuse a new victim who is the same age as when they were abused. When Marta was five years old, she stood in a doorway one day and saw her mother begin to play with three-year-old Jose's penis. Maria ran her fingers back and forth across it. His penis became erect. Maria laughed, turned to Marta, and said, "Isn't that cute?" She remembered her mother fondling her brother's penis on multiple occasions—frequently when she changed his diaper. Marta felt awkward each time.

Marta Cano believed the abuse of Jose by her mother began during the period when he was placed in her bed daily. When he turned five, Maria sent her son to a school that didn't start until 1:30 PM. Maria was home alone with Jose until he had to be in class. Cano believed the molestation of her brother continued for several years after Jose started school.

Jose Menendez was kicked out of three schools before he entered second grade. The defense therapists told Cano that an abused child is restless. Jose was allowed to do anything he wanted. Jose and his father were not close growing up because Maria dominated all aspects of the boy's life.

"My mother would say Jose never did anything wrong no matter what he did," said Cano. "He had the wild behavior of abused kids, the defense experts told me. After I told them the details about our life growing up, they said they believed my mother had abused Jose."

There was also a major division in the Andersen family during the trial. Kitty's sister, Joan VanderMolen, became estranged from her brothers, Milton and Brian. Joan believed Erik and Lyle. The Andersen brothers didn't.

"There was no way Jose was going to let this secret destroy his career, and I think Kitty was caught up in the whole thing," Joan told me. "She was a victim as much as anybody. I don't think she would have hurt her kids for anything in the world, but I don't think she would have been able to stop Jose from doing whatever he had in mind. Not that it was going to happen that night, but I truly think something was going to happen sometime. We would have had a couple of grieving parents, and he would've gone on with his world."

VanderMolen said that Erik and Lyle had grown up being told they were better than other people.

"I'm sure as Jose moved up the ladder, it wasn't the picture Kitty had painted for herself. It was important for Kitty to think that others knew she had a happy home. It breaks my heart that she thought that and couldn't do something about the situation she was in. She always told me everything was wonderful."

Joan told me she believed that her sister, ten years younger, may had been abused when she was a young girl. When Joan was age seventeen, she married and left the house. During the year after Joan left home, Kitty was suddenly enrolled in a boarding school. Members of the defense team believed Kitty's mother figured out that something had happened and decided to send her away.

CHAPTER 50

PRIVILEGE DENIED—
THE "THERAPY TAPE"

T HE EPIC LEGAL BATTLE OVER THE ADMISSION OF A TAPE-
recorded therapy session with Dr. Jerome Oziel lasted three years
and went as far as the California Supreme Court. In August 1992,
the high court had admitted Oziel's audio notes of two therapy sessions,
saying Lyle Menendez had threatened him—something Lyle insisted
never happened. But following the brothers' testimonies, Judge Weisberg decided the recording with Oziel and the brothers themselves from
December 11, 1989, could be admitted because Erik and Lyle had by
their admissions on the stand made their mental state a central issue in
the trial.

On November 12, 1993, in possibly the riskiest action of what had
already been an extremely aggressive defense, Leslie Abramson played
the tape—a piece of evidence she had fought hard to exclude from the
trial. What wasn't known at the time was that attorney Gerald Chaleff
and Jerry Oziel had met privately for an hour before the tape recorder
was turned on. To put things in context, defense witness Dr. Jon Conte
attacked Oziel and said the recording was not a therapy session. "It
appears to be a script," he testified.

In the opening of the sixty-one minutes of taped conversation,
Oziel guided the discussion to where he apparently wanted the conversation to go: "The other sense I felt, or I had, is that you felt totally
trapped . . . what's really wrong with your family is that there wasn't a

family," said Oziel. And: "Your dad was like the enforcer, and your father didn't communicate honestly with your mother, and your mother was terrified of your father."

In the tape, Erik and Lyle said that they killed their mother "to put her 'out of her misery' and that their father deserved to die because his infidelity had driven her to despair." There were passages where the brothers referred to their mother's suicide notes, and then Lyle saying, "I still think Mom's was a suicide." Erik can be heard crying throughout the recording.

Oziel asked if the brothers thought they were "sparing their mother," whom he described as "horribly depressed," a "shell of a person," and "pitiful."

"There was no way, never could she live without my father," replied Erik.

"I kept thinking it over. Almost as if it was true," said Lyle. "Almost as if I was like an instrument of hers in killing herself. That's where we sort of feel like, you mentioned before, that we were doing her and us a favor. In putting her out of her misery."

"I had it in my mind that I would be the turning point. If my mother kills herself, I would hate my father for life," added Erik.

Later, Lyle said "Erik and I . . . would share what was happening in the family. And it was obvious my mother was deteriorating. We didn't want to get to a point where my mother would kill herself. And my father, we were left to deal with my father. I couldn't let him get away with this."

Lyle told Oziel the brothers had to make a decision. His life had been a "basic training course," and he and Erik were fighting for survival.

When Oziel asked if money had been an issue, Lyle replied "that didn't enter into it too much."

"He used money and power to control you . . . I mean, isn't that really, isn't that really what it was about, killing him?" asked Oziel. "I mean, wasn't it about the . . . the amount of absolute control and the ruthlessness?"

ERIK: I don't like hearing these things about my father.

OZIEL: What are you feeling?

ERIK: Upset.

OZIEL: And hurt? Sad? What? You wanna tell me?

ERIK: Well, I had pushed him outta my mind. My father and my mother were, were two people that I loved, and I just don't wanna hear anything about 'em. It doesn't matter what they were . . . I had no other choice. I would have taken any other choice.

Erik said he loved his father but he "had no choice to do what I did, and I hate myself for doing it. And I understand why it was done, but somehow in my mind I can't rationalize it, because [crying], because the love that I had for him and my mother . . . And no one understood."

Oziel frequently appeared to be leading the brothers, who often expressed mixed emotions during the recording:

ERIK: Eventually it had to happen. It was basically ruining my life, and I guess Lyle's. And he was putting my mother through torture, and it got to a point where, where, it, ah, he was amazing. He would do great things for me, and, he would, I wouldn't understand why. I know that she loved me.

Oziel confirmed the brothers knew they had been cut from their parents' will before August 20, 1989: "I remember when your mom called and told [you] that your dad was disinheriting you, because he didn't like how you were behaving and that he thought you weren't being respectful enough."

Erik said that after the killings, he and Lyle hadn't spoken much about their feelings because their parents had raised them not to share emotions. They did admit to each other that they were depressed. "The whole family works behind closed doors," said Lyle.

Oziel asked Erik to tell Lyle that he was worried about him, but Erik balked and started crying. "We hate that hugging shit by the way. We fucking hate that," said Lyle. He admitted he'd been "close to suicide" himself.

LYLE: What Erik and I did took courage beyond belief. Beyond, beyond strength. There was no way I was gonna make a decision to kill my mother without Erik's consent . . . I didn't even wanna influence him in that issue. I just let him sleep on it for a couple days . . . It had to be his own personal issue.

Lyle was surprised the brothers had actually carried out the killings.

LYLE: Honestly, I never thought it would happen. Even though I had thought about it. Ah . . . it was done so quickly, and so, sort of callously almost, because, one, we, if you thought about it too much, the feelings of not having your parents around would get in the way of what was more import- ant. All the little good things that are in our relationship, and I think one of the big, biggest pains he has is that you miss just having these people around. I miss not having my dog around, if I can make such a gross analogy . . . I miss not having my father, and it's almost worse after I find out more and more about how he was such a genius.

After the tape was played, the defense recalled Dr. Conte, who said, "The essential idea that Mom was killed out of mercy I consider to be psychologically naive and not consistent with anything else that was said." The lack of any discussion of molestation on the tape didn't shake Conte's belief that there had been abuse within the family. "Many vic- tims of child abuse are in therapy for years and years and never reveal their abuse," he said.

Later, Abramson had Dr. Ann Burgess analyze the tape line by line. Burgess quoted Lyle: "My father should be killed. There's no question . . . he's impossible to live with for myself . . . based on what he's doing to my mother."

"That's a metaphor for brother," Burgess said. She thought Oziel was "manipulative and controlling." She testified there was a pattern of

Lyle repeating back the words of Oziel, who continually "introduced his own theories."

After court, Leslie Abramson tried to put a positive spin on the day. "It certainly doesn't talk about money. It doesn't talk about *BBC* movies. It doesn't talk about perfect plans. It talks about a very crazy, dysfunctional family and is, in my opinion, clearly orchestrated by the Great Satan," coining a new nickname for Jerry Oziel. "And it ultimately makes absolutely no sense."

The *Los Angeles Times* noted in its front-page story that on the tape "the brothers never mentioned sexual abuse or self-defense—now the cornerstones of their defense against murder charges."

"I think it speaks for itself," said Pam Bozanich.

CHAPTER 51

THE SOAP OPERA
OF JUDALON SMYTH

THE LONG-ANTICIPATED TESTIMONY OF JUDALON SMYTH WAS postponed again when the birth mother of a baby being adopted by Leslie Abramson and her husband, *Los Angeles Times* reporter Tim Rutten, went into labor. Aidan Connor Rutten, a seven-pound, five-ounce boy with blond hair and blue eyes, was born in a Los Angeles hospital. Court was recessed for several days.

Judalon Smyth, whose spirit had haunted the trial for a tense week three months earlier, finally took the witness stand in person on a clear Friday morning in November of 1993.

No way around it, this was going to be nasty. As a witness for the defense, Judalon Smyth had but one purpose: to destroy Dr. Jerome Oziel's credibility. If the prosecution were to salvage any value from Oziel's testimony, they had to persuade the jury that Judalon Smyth was a vindictive flake.

Aided by phone bills and audio tapes, defense attorney Michael Burt began by leading Smyth through her version of the affair with the therapist: Oziel pursued her, called her all hours of the day and night, and exploited her vulnerability.

"Our relationship would flip-flop between therapy and that I was his ideal person romantically," she testified. "I told him I wanted to be married and have children. Oziel said I needed one-on-one therapy . . . his fees were $160 for forty-five minutes. I said it wasn't in my budget."

Smyth laughed in a way that suggested they found a way to work out the fee. She said "our patient-therapist relationship" began in June 1989 and continued until "I escaped" on March 4, 1990. "The therapy was sometimes in the office and other times he came to my house," she explained. "It was not officially like I was a patient."

In addition to mixing the therapeutic relationship with a sexual one, Smyth testified, Oziel also violated other patients' confidentiality almost casually, regaling her with tales from his private sessions.

With that as a platform, Burt tried to anticipate one of Smyth's liabilities—the fact that in late October 1989, at a time when she claimed to have broken up with Oziel, they took a weekend trip together to Arizona. He knew her response would not be the most persuasive element of her testimony, but no sense in leaving it for the prosecution to exploit.

"Why were you going to Arizona with him if you had broken off the relationship?" Burt asked.

"Because on Saturday, when I hung up the phone and didn't want to talk with him or go to Arizona, he raced to my store and did a big number on me, and somehow I ended up going to Arizona . . ."

But once again, Smyth said, she told Oziel it was over between them. "He didn't believe it," Smyth testified. "He laughed a lot, and just did his manipulation . . . trying to keep me in the relationship."

And then, on October 30, Erik Menendez called to make the fateful appointment. Again, Smyth was drawn back in. "He asked me to go and be there for him; that this was like the one last thing I could do; and that if I did this, that it would show that all the work that he had put in on me wasn't for nothing; that if I, you know, did this, that it would show I had learned something."

Burt concentrated on two elements of Smyth's story of the October 31 and November 2 sessions with the Menendez brothers detailed after the fact in Oziel's audio notes. (This was the only therapy information ruled admissible by the California Supreme Court because of threats allegedly made by the brothers.)

The first was straightforward: Oziel lied when he said he hadn't violated the brothers' confidentiality until after he had allegedly been threatened. Smyth stated, in persuasive detail, that she had been present for the first session, urged by Oziel to attend even before any confession had been made. The most oddly compelling evidence corroborating Smyth's testimony was an unlikely scrap of paper with cryptic notes scrawled across it. In Smyth's handwriting were the words, "I'll pick it up" and "Does the public lot close at a certain time?" In Oziel's handwriting, scrawled across the bottom, were several phone numbers and the words "Jim and Judy."

Smyth explained the note this way: After the boys had left, Oziel called his wife to tell her to get the kids out of the house. "He told her that he was going to be moving into my house and that she was to pack a bag for him . . . He kept saying that either he would pick up the suitcase or I would pick up the suitcase . . . And when he said that, I saw it as an opportunity to get out of there, so I wrote: 'I'll pick it up.' . . . Around ten, it started to occur to me that I had parked my car in the public lot next to his office . . . He was on the phone, and I couldn't verbally ask him [if the lot closed]. So I wrote it down; and indeed, the lot had locked at 10 PM, and my car was there until the next day."

"Jim and Judy" was what Oziel had scrawled when speaking with his wife—the names of the friends with whom he would be staying, along with their number. The other numbers were for Erik and Lyle. The intricate detail of Smyth's testimony and the awkward minutiae of the slip of paper combined to create a powerful sense of reality to which any juror could relate.

But if the first aspect of Smyth's testimony was on relatively solid ground, the second was treacherous territory. The defense had to somehow defuse the time bombs of Smyth's statements to the police, in which she swore she had personally heard the brothers admitting to some of the more cold-blooded elements of planning the murders and threatening Oziel. Burt and Abramson were in the awkward position of putting a witness on the stand whose earlier statements, given under penalty of perjury, helped prove the state's case against their clients.

Under Burt's examination, Smyth was saying that she could make out very little of what the brothers had said in the two sessions. She said she'd heard Lyle angrily rebuking Erik for confessing, but she had not heard him threatening Oziel, either directly or by inference. The one "threat" she had overheard, she testified, was Lyle saying, "Good luck, Dr. Oziel." Oziel claimed that statement was made in a menacing way, but Smyth testified that the comment was made without any verbal inflection, and that she saw no reason to interpret the comment as a threat until Oziel "told me I just didn't know what a threat was."

All of this was at odds with what she had told police three years earlier. Smyth's explanation for the discrepancy was twofold. First, she said, she had told police that, for convenience sake, she would simply lump together what she had heard herself and what Oziel had told her about the part of the sessions she hadn't heard. Second, at the time she had given her statement to police, she had still been "programmed" by Oziel, and she hadn't been able to distinguish between what she had really experienced and what Oziel had programmed her to remember. Now, thanks to deprogramming, she had her "real" memory back.

Perhaps in many jurisdictions, defense lawyers would have shrunk from the idea of putting a witness with that kind of testimony anywhere near the stand. But this was, after all, Southern California in the early 1990s, and the issue of mind control and "neuro-linguistic programming" would get an extensive hearing. Besides, the defense may have reasonably concluded, the more disgusted the jurors got with the whole bizarre Jerry and Judalon saga, the more they might want to purge the entire epic—including the confessions—from their minds.

Meanwhile, Burt sought to develop the defense theory, introduced during the Oziel Ordeal, that the doctor had coldly fabricated his account of the confessions—or at least the more damning elements—for the purpose of controlling the women in his life and extorting money from the heirs to the Menendez fortune.

"Were your hands shaking during that time when you were in the office with Dr. Oziel?" Burt asked Smyth.

"Yes," she responded. "He pointed out that my hands were cold and shaking. And then he said that when your hands are cold, that that indicates stress. And then he made a big deal about how his hands weren't . . . 'Feel how warm my hands are. See? No other man you know could handle this this well. Am I bothered? Am I worried?' And he was just like, oh, he's the big protector."

"And later on," Burt continued, driving the point home, "when you had a tape-recorded interview with him at the request of the Beverly Hills Police Department, you said to him: 'I don't think you're afraid of the boys' . . . And he said to you, on tape: 'I don't think I'm afraid of anybody.'"

Smyth went on to testify that on Halloween 1989, after Erik had confessed and Oziel was claiming to be in fear of his life, he did not appear afraid, only eager to "get control" of the brothers.

"He claimed to me that if he could just see them one more time, he could get control of them."

Court adjourned for the weekend at 5 PM. Judalon took the elevator downstairs to watch the TV reporters do their stand-ups, analyzing her testimony for a national television audience. It was already dark on this mid-November evening, but in the dim electric glow of the courthouse, Judalon Smyth was wearing Laura Biagiotti designer sunglasses. She looked very Hollywood.

Monday morning, Smyth took the stand and Burt picked up where he had left off: the control issue.

Smyth said that after the November 2 session with both brothers, Oziel told her he felt that he was getting the control he wanted, but to be certain he was in control, he still felt he needed a tape of them actually confessing to the details of the murder.

Burt then played the tape Smyth had recorded secretly of her conversation with Oziel in which he made the remark, "There's 14 million dollars involved."

On the tape, Smyth responds, "So?"

To which Oziel says: "Figure it out."

Then the topic of testimony turned from the sinister to the surreal when Burt asked, "Did Dr. Oziel attempt in any way to hypnotize you?"

"Yes. I actually wasn't aware of the depth of what he was doing to me until the body wire, because during that time when he says 'thorns,' I had a total blank. And when Detective Zoeller went back to the police station he called me up and he asked me what 'thorns' meant."

The word had been implanted in her mind posthypnotically by Oziel in an attempt to control her thinking, said Smyth. Whenever Oziel wanted Smyth to do what he wanted, he would repeat the word "thorns." It was a wild idea, and a bit risky, from a strategic point of view, to suggest to the jury that the witness for the defense was some kind of zombie being controlled by one-word voice commands—bringing to mind the book/ movie *The Manchurian Candidate* from a few decades prior.

Judalon's impossibly tangled relationship with Oziel didn't help matters. She testified that, in spite of trying to get away from him, she moved into his home in December 1989 because she was scared of Lyle and Erik. "I was in Oziel's house until March 1990, when I escaped . . . it wasn't romantic, but there was sex . . . Laurel [Oziel] and I were good friends."

At this point, two of Erik's jurors smiled and gave each other looks. Even for Californians, this was weird stuff.

On Tuesday morning, the defense introduced Oziel's billing records, indicating that after the confessions, he had charged the brothers thousands of dollars for therapy sessions, many of which they could not possibly have attended. Smyth testified that she overheard Oziel on the phone with Lyle, telling him that he hadn't seen any money from him and that he wanted somewhere around $7,000. "He was pressuring him," Smyth said.

Burt referred to it as a "plan where Dr. Oziel would set up phony appointments . . . and bill them for those appointments."

Smyth said that Oziel told her he was telling the brothers the phony appointment plan was "for their own good," so it would look like they were in therapy.

Having done their best in a tough situation, the defense left Smyth to the prosecution. Pam Bozanich wasted no time getting to the dramatic conflicts in her testimony. Smyth had contradicted herself not only in her earlier sworn statements but in her dramatic national television interviews on *Primetime Live*. Smyth steadfastly maintained her line of defense: She had been brainwashed by Oziel.

The prosecution had a theory of its own: "Miss Smyth, would it be fair to say that when you went to the police on March the 5th, 1990, your primary motivation is you wanted Dr. Oziel prosecuted?"

Smyth didn't even hesitate. "Correct. He was the one who committed crimes against me, not Lyle or Erik Menendez."

Smyth freely admitted that she was outraged at the way her complaints against Oziel were handled, that she was specifically angry at the L.A. district attorney's office, and even implicated Bozanich herself as a coconspirator against her desire to have Oziel arrested and tried for—among other crimes—kidnapping and rape. Smyth's theory was that the prosecutors were so intent on making Oziel an effective witness against Erik and Lyle, that they had no interested in pursuing charges that would diminish his credibility.

Judalon Smyth insisted repeatedly that she believed Oziel had wanted her dead, and offered that belief—and not a craving for publicity—as the reason she had gone public with her story. "I wanted some public knowledge that Oziel intended to kill me so that when I showed up dead, they would know where to look."

"And when you sued him for money, were you also looking for protection?" Bozanich asked.

"I was not interested in the money. Lawyers are the ones interested in the money," Smyth shot back. "I was interested in proving that I was telling the truth, that Dr. Oziel was a liar, and that I had been terribly victimized and had real criminal acts committed against me that no one was paying any attention to."

When Bozanich asked if Smyth still feared that Oziel was trying to kill her, she said: "I do believe that he intends to kill me. I was very concerned about coming to this court because he would have knowledge that I would be here . . . I have given up my right to vote to protect myself so that Oziel cannot find me. You don't know the lengths I've gone to . . ."

Despite the harsh, emphatic responses she was eliciting, Bozanich showed no signs of discomfiture. She was getting what she wanted: raw, seething vitriol of—she would later try to demonstrate to the jury—a woman scorned.

"It was your desire, is it not, to discredit Dr. Oziel by your testimony?" Bozanich asked.

"It is my desire," Smyth responded, head high, "to set the record straight and to tell the truth."

"Okay. So when you told Judge Albracht [in a 1990 closed hearing] that you heard these threats, when you signed your affidavit that you heard these threats, it was not your desire to tell the truth?"

Bozanich proceeded to pound on Smyth's desires—particularly the one to revenge herself on Oziel—until the judge was moved to say enough already: "It's clear she doesn't like Dr. Oziel. You don't have to prove it any more than you have."

But Bozanich did still have to prove *why* Smyth didn't like Oziel: "Ms. Smyth, isn't it true that the reason you're saying these things about Dr. Oziel is because you were in love with him, and he was married, and he wouldn't divorce his wife and marry you?"

After the tortuous charting of a relationship from hell, there was something almost comforting about that simple formulation: finally, a familiar psychic landscape, a motive as old as man and woman.

"No," Smyth boomed. "That is not true at all."

"But you wanted to marry Dr. Oziel at one time?"

It was the other way around, Smyth said. "Dr. Oziel wanted to marry me, not me him."

"But you wanted to have children, and you indicated to police . . ."

"I did not want children that looked like Dr. Oziel."

The courtroom, tense for three days, dissolved in laughter.

CHAPTER 52

DON'T TURN AWAY FROM THE PAIN

" I HATE TO SAY IT'S ALL OVER, BUT I GUESS THAT'S IT," SAID Leslie Abramson to the bench. It was 5:20 PM on Friday, December 3, 1993. There had been 101 witnesses and 405 exhibits over 85 days of testimony for two juries to consider. It had taken twenty weeks, from summer to nearly winter.

Now, outside the courthouse, it was spin time. "We haven't talked about the crime itself for a long time," said Pam Bozanich. "I think we might point out that there are two dead bodies involved in this case. That might be part of our argument."

Then Abramson: "For a case with a simple theme, which is why these boys killed their parents, it has a tremendous amount of overly complicated evidence, uselessly complicated evidence in some ways." But the time had come to "get back to the big picture, which is answering that question—Why? And I'm optimistic that we've presented the answer to that question. Now whether the jury accepts the answer or not, I never, ever know."

Tuesday, December 7, was not a night for sleeping. The next morning, and the week that followed in the glare of television cameras, would define the lawyers on both sides and determine whether their clients were greedy killers or victims who feared for their own lives. But a few tense hours still remained before closing arguments would begin, and there was still work to be done.

Prosecutor Pam Bozanich was on the phone to her father. Smarting from the emotional intensity of the defense's final days of testimony, she had decided to inject some emotion of her own. Few outside the family, and certainly not the Menendez jurors, knew that Bozanich's dad had been abused by his father, and yet had gone on to become a productive citizen, a loving and gentle father who never so much as spanked his daughter. With his permission, she would use that, unfolding the story slowly but not revealing her relationship to the abused child until just before she sat down. It might reach jurors in a way a mere reprisal of the evidence could not and show that abuse is no excuse for murder. It felt right.

Who wouldn't want to win the biggest case of her career? But this was more than that. She sincerely believed that "the boys" had concocted the abuse story to create confusion and sympathy among the jurors, while *her* family had endured the real thing. And, as a woman, she could especially relate to Kitty Menendez, a victim of all the Menendez males. Someone had to speak for her.

Thirty miles away in Cheviot Hills near the 20th Century Fox Studios, defense attorney Jill Lansing tucked in her young daughter, and paced. There was a chill in the night air, but the sky was clear with stars. Lyle had done his part: He had bared himself to the jury, revealing secrets he had guarded for years in a desperate attempt to save his and his brother's life.

Well, the facts were the facts, she told herself. A jury was not going to be *that* swayed by the argument. Still, it was her last chance to underscore what for her was the only issue: Were the brothers afraid when they acted? If so, there was a chance for a manslaughter conviction or a hung jury—maybe even an acquittal.

Why, she asked herself, did she care so deeply about these two young men? Why should she feel sorry for them? Maybe because she was a mother, and picturing painful things being done to a child, any child, was difficult.

From his one-man cell deep inside the jail on Bauchet Street just off skid row in downtown Los Angeles, Lyle Menendez could see no stars, inhale no fresh night air. When he looked up from his bunk, he saw only bars and bare ceiling and lights that were never turned off. When he closed his eyes, there was no peaceful darkness—only the constant din of the overcrowded jail, light seeping through his eyelids, and pictures alternately flashing of his enraged father, the veins in his neck throbbing, and the blood-soaked death scene, where all but the television set playing the Cecil B. DeMille movie *The Ten Commandments* was silent. He was frightened, because of the consequences he faced. And he felt both exposed and relieved. It was nearly over.

The next morning Pam Bozanich walked confidently into the courtroom. On the bulletin board she pinned up a single photograph, Exhibit #7, of the bloody crime scene picture showing Jose sprawled dead on the couch with Kitty nearby on the floor.

Lyle Menendez, wearing a crew-necked green sweater over a crisp white shirt, was brought in from a holding cell. He did not look at the photo. Then the "gold" jury, the panel that would decide Lyle's fate, was ushered in.

Looking straight at the jury box from the podium, Bozanich began her final argument, her usual strident manner suddenly low-key. "This has been a very long trial, and I will make mistakes in citing to you the evidence," she told them.

Since the prosecution rested its case in chief seventeen weeks before, the defense had turned the case into "anything but a murder trial. But the exhibit on the board is why we are here," Bozanich said. "We are not here to discuss whether or not Dr. Oziel should be sued for palimony by Judalon Smyth. We are not here to try Mr. and Mrs. Menendez for being bad parents. We are not here to try Jose Menendez for being an alleged—not a convicted but an alleged—child molester. And we are not here in the psychological malpractice trial of Dr. Oziel."

She led the panel through the four possible convictions: first-degree murder, second-degree murder, voluntary manslaughter, or involuntary manslaughter. She explained the differences, reminding them that "there is no theory by which you can acquit this defendant. There's no legal theory by which you can find Lyle Menendez not guilty . . . The only theory that the People are going to urge on you is this theory: premeditated, cold-blooded, calculated murder."

The defense will argue that there was no premeditation, she told them, and then she quoted from the imminent jury instructions: "The true test is not the duration of time, but rather the extent of the reflection of a cold, calculated judgment. A decision may be arrived at in a short period of time."

She referred to the December 11 tape, on which "you hear Lyle Menendez, unprompted by Dr. Oziel, talking about planning and planning to kill. And he talks about the fact that he gave his brother a couple of nights to sleep on the decision to kill Mom. And implicit in that is that it was a decision to kill Mom that was coldly and carefully arrived at.

"Now, what the defense wants you to do is convict their client of voluntary manslaughter, or better yet, of involuntary manslaughter, based upon this particular instruction, which is: 'A person who kills another person in honest but unreasonable belief'—now, keep in mind, it's got to be an honest belief—'in the necessity to defend against imminent peril'—keep in mind the word 'imminent' here—'to life or great bodily injury, kills unlawfully, but does not harbor malice aforethought, and so, is therefore, not guilty of murder.'"

The brothers bought two Mossberg shotguns in San Diego on a Friday, accumulated ammunition from several stores on Saturday, and called a buddy on Sunday to arrange meeting up on the night of the planned murders, she said. They killed for more than just the money, Bozanich explained.

"What they wanted is their lifestyle. They wanted freedom, and they wanted to be free from the idea that their father would somehow disinherit them. The prosecution doesn't need to prove motive, only that it was a premeditated murder and not a murder in the heat of passion or with this 'honest but unreasonable belief.' All right?"

As for the relatives who testified for the defense, "They had motives of their own: 'Well, we can't bring them back, so let's save their sons.'"

If the Menendez homes were such houses of horror, she asked, why did these relatives send their kids there to stay for weeks or months?

Of Jose and Kitty Menendez, she said, "Obviously, these people were flawed. They loved their children, but they pushed their children and perhaps they pushed—well, I think it's obvious they pushed their children too far, because their children killed them."

If, as the defense claimed, the defendants were acting out of fear and fright and almost on automatic pilot, she asked, how did they have the presence of mind to pull it off? With the police watching, how did they have the cool to collect the spent shells they had picked up and put in the car? "The defense will argue," she said, "that their actions prove their belief that they were about to be killed was genuine; the People say it proves it was their acting that was genuine."

Lyle Menendez, slumped in his chair, showed little emotion, occasionally leaning over to his attorneys to whisper, "Not true."

But what if both brothers were victims of sexual abuse? Bozanich asked. A horrible crime, yes, she acknowledged, but even "if you believe in the sexual abuse, that doesn't mean that the defendants are not guilty of murder, because they are two separate things. The sexual abuse in this case, whether you believe it or not, was disavowed by both defendants as to why they killed their parents. And it's the People's position that sexual abuse is here to make the parents look so bad that you don't care that they're dead." She added, "We don't execute child molesters in California."

She asked jurors to try to imagine—looking at the photo of the gruesome murder scene—what it must have smelled like and felt like in that darkened den. She said the defense brought in witnesses "so you would lose sight of the evidence . . . the defense doesn't want you to remember this . . . Now I've only put up one exhibit here because this is not a complicated case. This is what happened. These two people were sitting there watching television, and they got slaughtered by their sons . . . This one picture is all you need."

She dismissed the defense's child abuse experts as "spin doctors," skilled in "ivory tower analysis" and "psychobabble." The People, she said, chose not to "dignify" their claims by calling its own child abuse experts.

Defense experts "try to persuade jurors they can't as common citizens understand the evidence."

She hammered home the fine line between bad parenting and psychological abuse, and that neither justified murder. "We don't execute people in this state for being bad parents."

The prosecution had proven that Lyle Menendez lied repeatedly to everyone, before and after he was caught, she said. "What makes you think [he] would stop lying now . . . in order not to be convicted?"

She reminded jurors of the multiple shots, the fifteen or more wounds, the reloading of the gun, and the last shot at Kitty Menendez: "Now, remember, Lyle Menendez, when he said—and I'm sure he sincerely regrets this—'My mother was sneaking away.' This woman was shot from behind."

She concluded with this: "[Lyle Menendez] is guilty of two counts of first-degree murder. He is guilty of conspiring with his brother to commit these murders, and he's guilty of killing two people in first-degree murder and he's guilty of doing it by lying in wait and taking his parents by surprise in order to accomplish his goals. Thank you."

"I stood before you a number of months ago and said to you, for the first time that it was ever said to anybody in public by the Lyle Menendez team, that Lyle Menendez had killed his parents and that he had done it out of fear and after a lifetime of abuse . . . I have no idea how you view this case now." Jill Lansing spoke so softly that jurors leaned forward to hear her.

"I said in the beginning that the only issue for you was going to be why. And although Mrs. Bozanich has indicated correctly, it is not up to the prosecution to prove motive, it is here to this degree: You need to decide what was going on in Erik and Lyle Menendezes' minds that night before you can decide what kind of crime was committed."

It was self-defense, she said, although not in its purest sense. "The best that you can do in this case, from our perspective, is a manslaughter, because that is an unreasonable killing in good faith . . . It is our position that Erik and Lyle Menendez, on August 20, 1989, for reasons which may not make sense to you given your life experiences, but made sense to them, believed their parents were going to kill them.

"This is not a trial of the parents, that's true. But it is essential that you understand the world in which they lived. And it was a world exclusively controlled by their parents. It was a world created by their parents. And it is that world that you need to understand before you can evaluate whether small gestures and words here and there really could have made them believe that they were about to be killed."

She asked that jurors not penalize the brothers for having been born into a wealthy family. The killings were not motivated by greed, nor hatred, nor a desire to be free from parental control, nor an attitude of vigilantism.

Nor were they planned: "If you are planning to kill someone, does it make any sense to have done it here in this way at this time?"

Most of the prosecution's case was subject to two interpretations, said Lansing, reminding jurors that in such a situation the law required them to adopt the one that pointed to innocence. Were the brothers making social plans, or setting up an alibi? Were they at the bow on the boat trip out of fear, or to hatch the murder plot? Were Lyle's complaints of headaches and stomachaches a ploy to avoid school, or corroborative of abuse?

Admittedly, "Lyle Menendez lied to a lot of people about a lot of things before he got to this courtroom, but he didn't lie to you here," she insisted.

Lansing reiterated the testimony of the child abuse experts about the short-term effects of sexual abuse—bed-wetting, sexual aggressiveness at an early age, anxiety and depression—and long-term effects such as hypervigilance, fear, and panic and depression as a reaction to stress. Lyle Menendez had them all, in spades.

She reminded the panel about growing up Menendez: Jose's lessons in mistrust, the fights, the bruises left by beatings with a belt, the dinner quizzes, the humiliation, the tension, the private father-son molestation sessions, the day-long tennis drills . . . "Kitty was as frightening as Jose. She wasn't some battered, meek, covictim." And she defended Lyle's "gross analogy" between missing his dog and his father: Yes, it was inappropriate to say that, "but it is very interesting that he grew up with a dog, who he loved, but was vicious."

She wasn't asking jurors to say that "what they did was right or even . . . reasonable, but if they were genuinely afraid, then the crime that they have committed is manslaughter. And if they went into that room intending to kill, then it is voluntary manslaughter; if they went in, in a blind panic, and started firing without the necessary mental state, without the intent, then it is involuntary manslaughter."

Lansing's voice was becoming hoarse, but she continued.

To Lyle and Erik, the events of the final week in the lives of Jose and Kitty Menendez seemed laden with ominous overtones, she said, noting that jury instructions provide that if someone is violent you can expect violence, and if someone threatens you, you can act sooner against him than you would against someone who has never threatened you. In a household where threats and violence were commonplace, a loud show-down over the molestation, sudden orders not to go out, and a time change in a scheduled fishing trip signaled impending doom. The brothers discussed running away but decided it wouldn't work.

"They believed the decision had been made. Maybe you wouldn't have." Then, Sunday night, when Jose came out of the den, grabbed Kitty, and shut the door, they were convinced.

It was only while waiting for the police, waiting for what seemed like a very long time, that they began to think, "Maybe we don't have to tell."

As she wound up her argument, her voice was barely audible above the hum of fluorescent lights.

"It is our position here that after a lifetime of terror, these children were frightened; after a lifetime of threats, these children felt threatened; after a lifetime of a world filled with uncertainty in which you survived by your ability to read cues, they read cues and they read them wrong . . . It may be hard for you to believe that these parents would have killed their children; maybe it wouldn't be hard. But is it so hard to understand how these children believed their parents would kill them? It is hard sometimes to look at pain, and we look away. We close our eyes in movies. We don't read the newspaper. We don't watch the news.

"I ask you now not to turn away from the pain, and to see it for what it was and what it did to Lyle Menendez. I ask you to return a verdict of guilty of involuntary manslaughter."

———————

The next morning, Pam Bozanich shared the secret that had kept her up at night.

"I'm going to tell you a story right now," she started softly. "The story is about a man who I know. And this man grew up in an abusive environment . . . in a home where his father beat him constantly, and he beat his mother as well . . . When this young man turned seventeen . . . he ran away."

The defense objected. Overruled.

Bozanich continued. The man joined the Navy, and when, thirty-five years later, his dying father asked him to make peace, he refused.

"The defense in this case is extremely objectionable," Bozanich said. "For all the people who have been beaten within an inch of their lives, for all the children who have been scalded with hot water as punishment, who've been burned with cigarettes, who have been locked in rooms for days at a time, years at a time, and not fed . . . for all those children who were severely abused, for all those children whose parents put them in the hospital in truly life-threatening situations, this defense is an offense. And for those children who got out of the house and made lives for themselves and became productive members of society, this defense is an offense.

"Individual responsibility, responsibility for one's actions, is the hall-mark of becoming an adult. And in our society, we say adults are eighteen years old."

At the time of the murders, the brothers were adult men, not "the boys," as the defense persisted in calling them. That is part, she said, of the "best defense Daddy's money could buy for his adult sons."

And just because their actions were open to several interpretations didn't mean jurors should abandon common sense.

"One thing I'd like to point out about this case is these particular defendants had never been put in the hospital due to a beating by their parents. They had never been threatened—if in fact, Mr. Menendez, who appears to have had a Latin temper—told people he was going to kill them, he never threatened them with a weapon."

As for the family, "I'm not going to tell you this was a wonderful Ozzie and Harriet family where everybody was happy . . . But the picture that's been portrayed by the defense is warped. It is slanted. It is there to get a result, and the result is to convince you that these murders were justified."

She suggested, instead, that they keep in mind two photos on the board—one of young Kitty Andersen looking glamorous in a strapless evening gown, the other of her mutilated body. "This woman was . . . a victim of her husband and a victim of her children."

Lyle stared down at the table and avoided looking at the pictures of his mother.

She noted that Lyle Menendez tried to explain away everything that the prosecution couldn't prove, and then congratulated himself on admitting what could be proven anyhow. Bozanich was racing, the low-key style of the day before replaced by her usual rapid delivery.

"Whether or not the brothers were abused is immaterial to the charges," she insisted, noting that "it was Dr. Oziel who first planted the abuse idea."

Without evidence, the defense suggested that Kitty Menendez had been sexually abused, Bozanich said, adding that there was more evidence of "another secret in the family"—Erik's suspected homosexuality.

"These people were cold-bloodedly slaughtered by their two sons"—"spoiled, vicious brats," she called them, whose parents supported them while they "screwed up." And "whatever they had done to their sons during their lives, they didn't [deserve this]."

She took a deep breath. "And I'd like to say one final thing. The man that I described to you in my opening remarks, the man who ran away from home, the man who would not go to his father's bedside, the man who made something of his life in spite of the abuse—that man was my father."

CHAPTER 53
CHOOSE YOUR VICTIM

WHO WOULD THE JURY HEAR? PROSECUTOR LESTER KURIYAMA'S style was straightforward, unadorned, and unemotional, and he would be pitted against a criminal defense attorney whose theatrics were legendary.

All weekend he had thought about his own children, ages six and two, and how he, too, had snapped a photo of one of them hanging from a bar at seven months old, the same sort of photo the defense was using to show parental cruelty.

Sunday night and Leslie Abramson had her hands full with her infant son, born during the trial, and her obsession with getting her closing right. She'd rehearsed it in her head in the shower and in her Jaguar while driving the circuit between her home, the courthouse, and jail.

"I don't want compromise," she told her newspaper editor husband. "He doesn't deserve that. I don't want any bargains made when the jury thinks they're doing us a favor. Second-degree is no favor at all. I don't want them to do that to bring in a verdict. I think there are maybe some jurors who will hold out for first and others who may vote not guilty or manslaughter. I'd rather try it again than get a compromise verdict."

The phone rang. It was Erik Menendez. He had questions. What about . . . ? And what about . . . ? He wanted to know.

It was 9:30 AM, December 13, 1993, a sparkling clear day, no smog in sight, and exceptionally cold for Los Angeles, temperatures in the low forties. The judge was on the bench: "In the trial, the blue jury is in court …"

Lester Kuriyama posted seven bloody crime scene pictures and then began his argument. He promised to be brief, and he was.

He touched on Erik's relationship with his parents, the killings themselves, the brothers' version of events of that fateful final week, summing up the evidence in a straightforward, abbreviated, and slightly terse manner. Reading from pages in a three-ring binder and making little eye contact, Kuriyama said the prosecution proved that Erik's version of the week before the murders was mostly lies. Faced with the threat of being disowned, "Erik feared, all right. He feared that he would have to get off his butt and work, just like all the rest of us, and his father was going to cut him off."

The decision to kill both parents, Kuriyama said, was a "choice that the defendants made, and they're going to be held, they should be held, responsible for making that choice."

Five feet of frizzy blonde hair and outrage, Leslie Abramson was at the podium, feigning surprise. "Oh, it's the *blue* jury. I could have sworn I was just listening to a final argument to the *gold* jury, for Lyle Menendez." She just knew, she told the jurors conspiratorially, that Mr. Kuriyama would try to blur the lines between what each brother did.

As Kuriyama began taking down the color autopsy and crime scene photographs, Abramson spun around and asked him to leave them up.

"These photographs are here right now through Mr. Kuriyama's entire argument for no other reason but to upset you and inflame your passions because they are ugly." It is, she declared, "a cheap prosecutorial trick to put up these dreadful photographs in the hopes it would so inflame you against the defendant that you'll forget to ask the important question, which is: Why did this happen?"

She warned jurors she'd be talking a long time. The defense had called fifty-eight witnesses.

She asked them to give Erik—always overshadowed by Lyle, always second-rate, second-best—his due and to not ignore the years of constant cruelty and molestation to which he was subjected. Although, she noted, both brothers were "equally screwed-up."

"Where is the picture of Jose Menendez bending Erik over the footboard of his bed when he's twelve years old so that his father can now go all the way in spite of the child's screams? Well, there *is* such a picture but, unfortunately, it only lives in Erik's mind now."

In an angry, dramatic display, she pinned up a nude photograph of Erik at age six and began jabbing tacks into it. "I cannot show you the crime that Jose Menendez committed on him, but you heard about some of the things that he liked to do to his little boy. And one of them was to stick tacks like this in his thighs and his butt and to run needles across his penis." Furiously, she jabbed more tacks *here*, and *here*, and *here*.

"Now, that's this man. And I don't recall if there are autopsy photographs of this man where you can see his penis, the one that he stuck in this body that Mr. Kuriyama tells you is all made up. The proof that it isn't all made up is who Erik wound up being."

And so it continued for two and a half days, as Abramson worked the courtroom like a nightclub. It was a tour de force laced with humor, profanity, and personal stories. She rolled her eyes, gestured wildly, and with a flourish noisily crossed off each point on her outline in a big black binder. She free-associated. Never condescending, she roped in each stray listener, speaking of *we* and *us*; the prosecutors were *they*.

What she was, the television reporters agreed in stand-up after stand-up, was "riveting."

She pointed out that the prosecution "refused" to cross-examine Erik about the molestation. That its "whole case" rested on Dr. Oziel, and "we were able to show what sort of person *he* was." The molestation evidence was completely uncontroverted; the defense brought in experts only to help interpret the brothers' imminent decision-making.

Erik doesn't want pity for what he has been through, she insisted. The evidence of his childhood was used to show how he was put on a "collision course with violence . . . We want your understanding, and we want you to apply the law."

She explained, in simple language, the difference between perfect self-defense, often called justifiable homicide, and imperfect self-defense. She said what differentiates murder from manslaughter is the presence or absence of "malice," which she defined as killing "without a damn good reason." And she told them that homicides committed after provocation, in the heat of passion, are also manslaughter because either fear or passion can "erase" malice, so to speak. They could go down different paths and still arrive at the same verdict, she told them.

And she reminded jurors that when considering circumstantial evidence for which there were conflicting reasonable explanations, such as the guns purchase, they were required to go with the one that inured to Erik's benefit. "Erik didn't do anything bad . . . I mean, Mr. Kuriyama got up here and actually talked about these people as if they were Ozzie and Harriet versus the bad seeds, and that's not what this family was like, and you know that." In fact, the "greatest sin" that Erik appeared to have committed, "before he was driven over the edge," was to tell his father to "shut up," and that was so out of character for him that several witnesses recalled it.

She delighted in talking about Oziel: "I have never seen a witness as destroyed as Dr. Oziel . . . he pumps for details with which he can blackmail [Erik] for the rest of his life." In assessing his credibility against that of his former mistress, Judalon Smyth, she asked jurors to ask themselves, "Which one of them would you rather have a cup of coffee with? I mean, it boils down to that."

She had an explanation for everything. So Erik misstated the name of the gun store they went to? He had dysnomia, a learning disorder affecting memory. They bought guns? They were afraid and wanted to be able to defend themselves. They used false identification? Lyle's driver's license was suspended and Erik's was lost. Actions look like planning? You're just looking at panic. Those guns weren't fully loaded; they had no advance disposal plan for the weapons or bloody clothing. They left everything in the car, parked out front of the house when they called the police. They had no alibi.

Refreshed and apparently rewound the next morning, Abramson strutted into the courtroom.

The defense, she explained, was "not attempting to show you that Jose and Mary Louise Menendez were such bad people that they should have been shot . . . I'm not trying to blacken these people . . . Our point, and we have tried to make it both through the testimony of Erik Menendez and the testimony of Lyle Menendez, the testimony of expert witnesses and the testimony of the family members, is that this was a family environment that was run by fear . . . by power."

She was concerned that the jury not judge Erik by comparing him to Lyle, and that they not use things about Lyle against Erik.

"I don't want Erik to be taking the rap for Lyle. The evidence in this case does not prove that Erik killed *anybody* . . . Lyle testified that he is the person who administered the fatal wound to Jose Menendez . . . [and] that he administered the contact wound to the head of Mary Louise Menendez, and that was an instantly fatal wound." The other shots were only "potentially fatal," she said. "I just want to make it clear that there's no evidence in this case that Erik killed anybody."

Abramson said that when she read about the case two days after the shootings, "I looked at it, and knowing what I know and what I'm willing to understand, I said, 'The boys did it.'"

With her indignation increasing, she aimed her attack at her opponent.

"Was Mr. Kuriyama on a tennis court at five o'clock in the morning when he was ten years old, drilled and grilled for three hours, and then went to school and then taken around for more tennis courts for more hours of drilling and grilling, and then went back home to have dinner, which was like *Jeopardy*, and more drilling and grilling, and then had to satisfy his father's perversion, and then had to do his homework until ten o'clock at night? And he wants to talk about this kid's not working. This kid worked every day of his life to please these people, every single day of his life. This is the hardest-working kid I've ever heard of."

Next, she put up poster-size charts listing adjectives used by those who knew the family to describe Jose, Kitty, and Erik: the power-tripping father, the alcoholic mother, the frightened, learning-disabled child. She warned jurors that Mr. Kuriyama in his closing remarks was going to advance a "revolting suggestion" that would add another adjective to Erik's list. Jurors looked puzzled.

"I can tell some of you are very resistant to what I'm saying," she told the panel, some of whom sat with arms folded across their bodies.

"I'm not blind, and I'm not stupid. But you owe us, as jurors, one thing only, that you must entertain the possibility that we're telling the truth . . . [and] you must try, however foreign to you it may be, to put yourself in Erik Menendez's shoes . . . in order to understand if he did what he did for the reasons we say he did."

They must go with him in Monsey, New York, as at age six he learned to ride his bike, and in Beverly Hills at age seventeen when he tried to say no to his father and was rewarded with a knife to his throat and a forced sex act. "If my client's name were Erica, would it make a difference? It shouldn't," she demanded.

Erik Menendez, she said gently, is a "good person who did a bad thing . . . If either [parent] had been a halfway decent parent, this dreadful thing wouldn't have happened . . . [and] if he had wound up . . . in the hands of anybody decent (instead of Dr. Oziel), he would have been saved. This wouldn't have happened."

Bad karma, she said. "Erik has had the worst karma of anyone I've ever known."

———

Wednesday morning, days over her estimate of how long she was going to take, Abramson drowned the jury in detail: Jose was standing when he was shot. The district attorney could only prove eight shots. Craig Cignarelli was troubled and ambitious. Jose was a power junkie. Kitty was angry at life. Oziel said Erik never threatened him. Erik was operating on a survival instinct. That was not intent to kill.

"I'm aware of the fact that besides wanting to comment on all of the evidence, I've given you a very long closing argument because I don't want to let go of him . . . For three and half years I have definitely felt . . . that we are responsible for Erik, and we have had him in our hands all this time, and now I have to give him up to you. And the minute I am finished, he is out of my hands. And whatever happens to him depends on what you do."

She asked the jury not to compromise.

"You have to stick to your position, even if it means there will not be a verdict. There will be a hung jury. That is preferable to compromising both sides' right to have the individual opinion of twelve separate jurors ... Either you accept what we have proven to you or you do not. But you do not compromise because you do neither side any good in doing that."

Her voice became wistful. "I have had a fantasy since the day I started representing Erik. If people were to ask me, after three and a half years of thinking about him in this case every single day, somehow or another, even on vacation, what is it I want out of this? My answer is not necessarily a legal one ... I want to see him walk down a street, not in chains and not in shackles and not with a deputy sheriff standing next to him. To fulfill my dream, my fantasy, you'd have to come in with a verdict of not guilty. And if you don't feel you can do that, based on the instructions that you're getting, I would ask that you come in with a verdict of involuntary manslaughter, because I believe that's what the evidence shows."

"You have been a remarkable jury ... and I thank you," she concluded, snapping her binder shut.

Erik smiled, broadly—not an expression seen often in this courtroom.

"I'd like to get back to the *murder* case that we started off with back in June and July of this year," Lester Kuriyama told jurors as he began the second half of his closing argument. He likened the defense strategy to Shakespeare's *Tragedy of Macbeth*. Like Macbeth after he stabbed King Duncan, Erik Menendez was visited by recurrent nightmares. "But the fact that somebody has nightmares, has a guilty conscience for what he did, does not change a murder into a manslaughter." Outside the penalty phase, remorse is irrelevant.

"Now, Mrs. Abramson indicated that lawyers play games, that she engaged in game-playing in this case. I can assure you that the People of the State of California don't consider this a game. We've been entrusted with a job to bring the murderers of Mr. and Mrs. Menendez to justice, and the People put on evidence, four weeks of evidence, to establish that the defendant and his brother premeditated and deliberated the murder. The defense, on the other hand, put on about three and a half months of a lot of witnesses that talked about things that happened years and years ago, put on a lot of irrelevant photographs. And what they've done, in playing a game, they've dressed up their defendants in sweaters, they've referred to them as 'kids,' as 'boys,' as 'children.'

"Homosexuality is a personal choice," he continued, "and gender preference issues are personal ones, and one can certainly understand the reluctance to come out. But because of the defense and because of what they've tendered in this case, I think it's relevant and I think that I have to address it."

Then, over defense objections, Kuriyama suggested that Erik was gay and that he used details from his homosexual lifestyle to fabricate his description of sexual abuse at the hands of his father.

"If Erik indeed engaged in consensual homosexual activities with other men, that would account for him being able to describe for you the accounts he described to you about sexual encounters with his father," he said.

He noted that Erik had expressed doubts about his sexuality, that he destroyed tapes of his telephone calls made by his mother, that she confronted him about being gay and gave him a six-month deadline to get a girlfriend, that his father called him a "faggot," and that he bought bumper pads for his bed—like the ones used to make sodomy more comfortable—*after* he killed his alleged molester. He said Erik was examined by a physician expert on child abuse, and that the exam revealed no physical symptoms of molestation.

The abuse claim did not surface until after he'd been in jail for six months, which was a year after the killings. Kuriyama said the brothers shifted defense plans:

Plan 1: We were at the movies.

Plan 2: Well, our parents abused us.

Plan 3: Get the jury to believe we thought we were about to be killed, maybe that will get us down to manslaughter.

He ticked off a long list of proven lies by Erik Menendez.

He sniped at Abramson.

The prosecution was not required to show motive, he noted, just that there was an intentional, premeditated killing. "However, we've shown you reasons why the defendants killed their parents, reasons being the relationship between the parents that preceded this, this killing, the burglaries that had occurred, and how the parents were disappointed in their sons, and they're going to disinherit them and disown them."

It was of no consequence that Erik's defense team claimed that it was Lyle who administered the coup de grâce, Kuriyama told jurors, because Erik was both a principal participant and an aider and abetter.

He quoted the jury instructions and then gave jurors the legal definition of aiding and abetting: Erik may not have been the actual killer but would be considered equally responsible and guilty, Kuriyama said, as he asked jurors to find Erik Menendez guilty as charged.

CHAPTER 54

MISTRIALS

A **ND NOW IT WAS THE JURIES' TURN.**
Judge Weisberg had given them four possible verdicts for each killing: first- or second-degree murder, or voluntary or involuntary manslaughter. Although the judge had ruled that the facts of the case did not warrant the option of outright acquittal, jurors could ignore the instruction and still vote Not Guilty.

Had the brothers acted out of real but unreasonable fear? Or was this a case of two cold-blooded, premeditated murders?

The following account of what jurors went through while trying to reach verdicts comes from interviews I did with them afterward as well as statements they made to the media.

When Lyle's jury began discussing the case, it was awkward. For the past six months, they'd been instructed not to talk about anything that went on in court. After several hours, the jurors decided to cast their first vote with a show of hands: Six for manslaughter. Six for murder. The jurors mostly aligned with the people they'd been eating lunch with during the trial.

The vote relieved Michelle, a twenty-five-year-old Cuban American, who worried that she might be the only one who believed this was a case of manslaughter. Based on the little she'd seen in the media before the trial, she expected there would be a murder conviction. "Someone isn't going to kill their mother and father just for the hell of it," she'd written on her prospective juror questionnaire.

Tom, the jury foreman, was a thirty-five-year-old postal worker, married without children. Before the trial began, also based on the little he'd seen in the media, he thought the case would likely end in a death penalty sentence. But after watching the testimony, he felt great empathy for the Menendez brothers.

Sharyn, a forty-two-year-old born-again Christian whose brother was a sheriff's deputy, supported the death penalty but thought the evidence for it was lacking in this case. She kept a handwritten journal that was more than four hundred pages by the time deliberations began. On the emotional first day of Lyle's testimony, she went home and wrote for six hours. On other nights she cried, happy that she hadn't been part of the Menendez family, and sad for what the brothers had endured. When the prosecution rested their case, she thought to herself, "Is that it?" In her journal she wrote: "With how far apart we are, it will be a miracle if we can all agree on a verdict."

On the fourth day of deliberations, Jude Nelson, an unemployed fifty-two-year-old Army veteran with three children, exploded into a shouting match with Jim, a sixty-six-year-old Navy veteran, a widower with two grown sons. Jude's face turned beet red as he pounded on the desk. He called Lyle a "bad seed." (Jude later appeared on several TV shows to talk about his experiences as a juror.)

Patty, a fifty-year-old married to an L.A. County deputy district attorney in the Family Violence Division, told Jude that he should be more reasonable and listen to other people's opinions. Patty had written in her questionnaire that she regretted having spanked her daughters when they were growing up.

Jude created a list of "twenty-five points of fact and law" that he felt showed the brothers had committed first-degree murder. His opponents wouldn't accept any of them. "They disliked me personally, or they just couldn't see what I saw, which were the facts," he told me after the trial.

On Thursday, December 16, as Lyle's jurors began their fifth day, Erik's panel started its first day of deliberations. There were six men and six women; nine were parents.

Within the first hour, they voted with a show of hands. Were the brothers guilty of first-degree murder in the case of Jose Menendez?

No, said the six women.

Yes, said the six men.

Each of the panel members explained their reasoning. Some of the men cited evidence from their notes. One man said, "I'll believe what I want to believe, and you can't make me believe anything different." The women argued that if Erik was guilty of anything, it was manslaughter.

The foreman, Paul, a fifty-nine-year-old chemist who was a dean at California State University, Northridge, suggested that the panel discuss the prosecution's contention that Erik had learned details for his testimony about molestation through his own homosexual experience. It became a recurring topic.

"Don't get me wrong," Paul said later. "I'm not homophobic, but I think this has something to do with the crime." The women, who didn't believe that Erik's sexuality had anything to do with the molestation or whether he planned to kill his parents, reminded the men that information from the closing arguments was not evidence.

Erik's jury asked for various exhibits, including Dr. Oziel's December 11 tape. Richard, a sixty-five-year-old Navy veteran who served in Vietnam, was the most vocal prosecution supporter. The fact that Jose sent Erik to a therapist, who would have an obligation to report sexual abuse to authorities, proved that Erik later invented his molestation story, he said.

"Jose was protecting himself all the way down the line because of his future plans. Jose's a much smarter man than that," said Richard.

But the women argued that Jose "owned Dr. Oziel." There was no way that Erik would've revealed the molestation. He had signed a waiver of the doctor-patient confidentiality. And keeping the family secrets had always been of paramount importance in the Menendez family.

Another of Lyle's jurors, Twinkles, had taken extensive trial notes. She was thirty-two years old, single, African American, and a part-time college student. Her animated conversation made her popular among her fellow jurors.

On Monday, December 20, Twinkles expressed her own ideas about what happened the night of August 20, 1989. The brothers had probably been molested but became fed up and decided to kill at some point.

Carl, one of the quieter jurors, a fifty-nine-year-old mechanic with two daughters, suggested buying shotguns was an indication that there had been no planning. Shotguns are extremely loud; it was a warm summer night, and many neighbors might have had their windows open.

Jude disagreed. Lyle was so sharp, he suggested, that he'd learned the routine of the Beverly Hills Police; they wouldn't have been patrolling Elm Drive at the time of the shootings. Other jurors immediately challenged that.

Jude at times described the brothers as a pair of "slick kids" who were "maniacal, evil, and liars." Some jurors thought he didn't like Lyle and Erik because they were "smarter and richer" than him. To Jude, the entire defense was a big fabricated conspiracy.

Tom thought the defense had volunteered many incriminating pieces of information. If they had invented all of this, wouldn't they have come up with a more convincing story? If this was their best, the brothers deserved a refund from their attorneys.

"If Lyle and Erik were lying during their testimony, why didn't they lie and say Jose and Kitty had directly threatened them before closing the doors?" asked Michelle.

At the end of the day, thirty-two hours into their deliberations, Lyle's jury took its second vote: 6–6 between murder versus manslaughter.

On December 21, Erik's jury had a spirited debate of the meaning of "malice aforethought." As they reread the jury instructions several times, they noted that juries had to give the benefit to the defense if the prosecution did not prove their case beyond a reasonable doubt. Two of the jurors, including Wendy, a fifty-one-year-old phone company administrator with two daughters, announced they'd now be changing their votes to manslaughter.

On December 22, Sharyn from Lyle's jury wrote, "Sometimes I feel we are just going in circles. I still think we will have a hung jury because of Jude."

Erik's jury was having similar problems. Exasperated, the men sometimes called the women "ignorant asses."

"They couldn't deal," wrote Hazel Thornton, who also kept a journal throughout the trial (she later wrote a well-regarded book, *Hung Jury: The Diary of a Menendez Juror*, published in 1995 by Temple University Press). "They were frustrated with us because we couldn't see it their way. Their way of dealing with it wasn't to go through their notes and try to convince and reason with us, but to throw their hands up in frustration, call us names, and pound the table.

"Somebody raised their voice every day. There never was a reasonable, calm discussion of the evidence. We discussed evidence, but it wasn't with everyone having an open mind."

Richard had his own problem with Hazel. "Hazel took charge of the women," he said. "A lot of times I had to shush her up because I'd ask Annie a question and Hazel would answer for her. That created a lot of tension. I'd say 'Hazel, please—you're not her mouthpiece. I'm talking to Annie.'"

Two days before Christmas, Erik's jury listened to the court reporter read back six hours of testimony, including that of Erik's cousin Andy Cano. Mark, a forty-five-year-old electrician, took issue with that. According to Hazel, he "thought there was no way a twelve-year-old boy is going to ask his ten-year-old cousin about sexual abuse. Mark said when he was twelve, he knew it was wrong. He wouldn't have to ask anybody."

On December 28, Lyle's jury returned to the December 11 tape.

"It wasn't necessarily exactly what the brothers said on the tape," said Jude. "It was how they said it—their attitude and matter-of-fact tone of voice. It was like they were discussing a tennis match—not the murder of their parents. It didn't sound to me like it was coerced, like the defense people said it was."

"When I first heard it, I thought it was not that big a deal," said Sharyn. "What about the other eight hours of that session? And why was the tape made?"

On Erik's panel, the men considered the tape the single most important piece of evidence. "That more or less put the icing on the cake," said Richard.

"Every single man felt there had been emotional abuse," said Hazel. "They disagreed if there had been sexual abuse."

Lyle's jury charted their major points of dispute four days after Christmas and debated whether each situation or action taken by the brothers had been reasonable or not. Most of the facts could be argued either way. Everyone agreed that the arguments from both sides were reasonable.

On Monday, January 3, 1994, Erik's jury took its first formal vote since deliberations began.

Jose Menendez: first-degree murder: three men; second-degree murder: three men; voluntary manslaughter: six women.

Kitty Menendez: first-degree murder: five men; second-degree murder: one man, one woman; voluntary manslaughter: five women.

When Lyle's jury returned from lunch a few days later, Jude and Twinkles had posted all the bloody crime scene pictures on a bulletin board. Jude was frustrated that no one was listening to his list of twenty-five points of fact. It was time to employ "shock value," he said.

"You need to take those down," said Tom, the jury foreman, as he walked into the room.

"You are gonna look at what they did throughout these deliberations!" shot back Jude. "You're gonna see the results of what they did, so things will be fair."

"That's not gonna happen. Take them down," insisted Tom.

"I need them up to refer to them," said Jude.

"No. We'll pass them around if you need to refer to anything. It's not right to put up certain parts of the evidence and not everything."

Twinkles was also upset as she removed the pictures, tack by tack.

On January 6, Erik's jury listened to testimony read back from both brothers about the day of the killings and the events just before they entered the family room and shot their parents.

"I had my doubts at times," said Richard. "The brothers were very, very believable . . . And I felt sorry for them. I really did. I couldn't help it. I know they had a tough life whether they were sexually molested or not. They had a tough life, but goddamn it so did I, and I didn't go and blow away anybody.

"If I had believed the sexual molestation, I would've been right there on the other side," he told me after the trial. "I just couldn't believe it. I thought it was a little too far out. And I really wanted to believe it. I made the statement one day that if these guys were molested like that, goddamn it, they're going to get my vote to walk. But they didn't prove it to me."

The women kept reminding the men that the prosecution hadn't proved that the brothers weren't sexually molested. One of the men suggested that "Jose and Kitty discovered that Lyle and Erik were having a homosexual affair, that's why they had to kill them."

"I must admit, my first thoughts were skeptical thoughts, because of the fact that initially there had been denial of involvement," said Paul. "But, as I did think more about that, I think that I could understand how such a scenario could develop."

Erik's jury asked for "all testimony about or allusions to Erik's homosexuality." They listened to a rereading of Erik saying that he was "real confused" about his sexual identity, that his father had called him a "faggot," and his mother gave him a deadline to find a girlfriend. As the court reporter slowly read back his testimony, Erik sat quietly, not showing emotion.

"Now we've done it," Hazel wrote in her journal. "The whole world now knows what an issue Erik's sexuality has become in our deliberations . . . It was Annie's idea. She wasn't expecting it would change anyone's mind, but she wanted to send a message to the judge that this was an issue. Erik was mortified. You could tell by looking at him.

"Greg's comment, immediately upon our return to the jury room, was 'See, I told you we could talk about faggots.' Annie had argued the jurors couldn't discuss homosexuality because it wasn't evidence. Greg insisted it was. Since the word 'faggot' was in the transcript that made it okay."

Annie was a thirty-six-year-old clerk for the phone company, single, and the youngest of eight. She owned a shotgun and a .22 rifle. Greg, a fifty-one-year-old African American, was a former law enforcement officer who had two sons and a daughter.

Hazel didn't give much value to Lester Kuriyama's suggestion in closing argument that the real Menendez family secret was Erik's homosexuality. "What I did think was they obviously couldn't prove any kind of motive. They went from greed to hatred to control, and they couldn't prove any of those things so they leapt to, 'Oh, he's gay.' The fact that they kept changing motives made me less likely to buy their theory."

"I saw the prosecution kind of crumbling at the end," said Richard. "All along I felt they were caught by surprise by this defense they were using. They thought they had an open-and-shut case going in. They hadn't planned on this sexual molestation as a defense and didn't plan for it. They were groping on a day-by-day basis. Lester's closing remarks were extremely weak."

Even before deliberations began there had been hints of a gender split. When the defense presented its expert witnesses, some of the men sent clear messages with their body language. They'd fold their arms, stare at the ceiling or into the audience, and display looks of disdain.

"The experts were hired guns. I admit I had a chip on my shoulder about those professional witnesses," said Richard. "I discounted all of Dr. Vicary after he admitted he didn't date his notes. He was manipulating the system so he couldn't be pinned down. They were doing what they'd been paid to do. Those women beat us to death with the fact that the prosecution didn't rebut the molestation."

Meanwhile, Lyle's panel had spent little time on the topic of Erik's sexuality. "It came up the first day but never again," said Michelle. "We decided that whether or not he was—which most of us didn't believe he was—it didn't matter."

Lyle's jury asked for all of Lyle's testimony about the day of the murder to be read back to them on January 10. Actually, they only wanted to hear about when he picked up the shotgun shells. But because they were concerned that the media might focus on that if it was the only section read, they listened to hour after hour of testimony.

On the way to the parking lot, two of the jurors agreed that their panel was deadlocked.

"You can't just insinuate Erik is gay," Hazel wrote in her journal. "If you think he's gay, you've got to prove it. And then you have to demonstrate a link between being gay and being molested. During the trial, if they even hinted that Erik was gay, some of the men would go, 'Yeah.'" She argued with the men that a young man, gay or not, could just as easily be a molestation victim as a young woman.

After taking its third vote, the foreman of Erik's jury sent a note, which Judge Weisberg read in court without the jury present: "The Erik Menendez jury is deadlocked. Our positions have essentially not changed after three weeks of discussion and debate. I see no hope for reaching an agreement on any of the counts."

Erik, sitting between Leslie Abramson and his second attorney, Marcia Morrissey, did not react. Pam Bozanich and Lester Kuriyama stared straight ahead. Abramson objected to the jury being given new guilty verdict forms that might lead to a decision on some of the charges.

When the jury entered, minutes later, the judge read the jury's note again before asking them to deliberate further. After the jurors filed out, Abramson ranted at the judge for not first telling the attorneys what he was going to do.

While the hearing was on, the wire service reporters had not been allowed to leave. When they could, they burst out of the courtroom and ran for the phones to file the urgent story of the deadlocked jury. Within half an hour, there was a full-scale media frenzy in the courtyard in front of the courthouse.

After debating whether the brothers were worried about fingerprints on the shotgun shells *before* the killings, Lyle's jury voted 7–5 for murder. It was their strongest pro-prosecution vote of the deliberations.

Michelle made a note to herself: "I think we're hung."

On January 12, Twinkles worried that Lyle and Erik might set an example for "how to get away with it. I understand, but it's not fair. They can't get away with this," she declared.

A voice vote was taken: 7–5 for manslaughter.

Three of the murder votes didn't believe the expert witnesses: Chuck, a forty-two-year-old divorced father, said that the panel wouldn't be doing its job if they didn't consider their testimony. Ruth, a sixty-year-old widow with two daughters, called them "just a sound bite."

"It was just the opinions of psychologists and psychiatrists who were paid to interview the brothers after they were incarcerated," said Jude. "I was looking for more corroboration of the molestation and it never came, except for hearsay from relatives that was unsubstantiated by facts."

Lyle's jury sent a letter to the judge on January 13 asking him to define the difference between "honest" and "unreasonable" danger. Tom had tried to explain it, but they'd gotten stuck over semantics. Twinkles and Jude said that if the judge agreed with the pro-defense definition, they'd change their votes to manslaughter.

After Judge Weisberg answered their question in open court, Twinkles, in tears, said she'd switch to voluntary manslaughter. But Jude refused to change. The panel's vote was 9–3 for manslaughter.

"The people who are for manslaughter did interpret it right," Sharyn wrote in her journal. "That a killing in the honest but unreasonable belief (even though you might harbor malice or there are acts of malice), it negates the malice part and makes it manslaughter, not murder."

The holdouts for murder were now Ruth, Chuck, and Jude, who'd each agreed to come down to second degree on Jose. Chuck felt that the imminent danger had to be in the seconds just before the killings. Otherwise, he thought, there was no fear. He also argued that the brothers were ages eighteen and twenty-one and could've left home.

"I can't believe some of my people have moved to the other side," declared Jude.

Ruth continued to see the case as a first-degree murder. To her, Lyle Menendez was a cold-blooded killer. Her biggest problem with the defense was Lyle's arrogance and apparent lack of remorse. How could he have gone on the spending spree with his parents' money?

Erik's jury took a fourth vote. It would be its last:

Jose Menendez: first-degree murder: five men; second-degree murder: one man; voluntary manslaughter: six women.
Kitty Menendez: first-degree murder: five men; second-degree murder: one man, two women; voluntary manslaughter: four women.

They sent another note to the judge: "We remain deadlocked. Since our last report to you, we have been unable to move closer to agreement on any of the counts. If anything, we have become more entrenched in our positions. A poll taken this morning shows the jury believes there is no reasonable probability of our reaching a verdict or verdicts without violence to our individual judgments."

Erik bit his nails and ground his teeth. The attorneys had already told him what happened.

Judge Weisberg took the bench and had the jury enter before reading their final note: "We are unable to reach unanimous verdicts in counts 1, 2, and 3 and have thus been unable to fill out any forms."

The judge polled each juror to whether further deliberations might resolve the deadlock. Everybody said no. A few blinked back tears. Judge Weisberg accepted that Erik's jury was hung and declared a mistrial.

In front of the courthouse, Leslie Abramson faced a half circle of two dozen cameras and more than a hundred reporters.

"This is not a victory," she said. "A victory would be if my client was free. This is unfortunately now a very expensive learning experience."

She refused to say anything about Erik's reaction. If the prosecution didn't seek the death penalty again, there would be a possibility of applying for bail. But there was no family money left. "I hope to be Erik's lawyer, but I can't go bankrupt," Abramson told reporters. Further, "I do not believe any jury will ever find Erik Menendez guilty of first-degree murder."

When Lyle's jury asked to leave early, just after 4 PM, a bailiff told them they'd have to "wait a little bit, there were things going on." Looking out the window onto Delano Street behind the courthouse, they saw why: TV crews and reporters were swarming. When the bailiff returned, he asked them to remove their juror badges and follow him to the basement. There, they were put on a bus used to move prisoners and driven across the street to the garage where their cars were parked.

The TV crews weren't fooled. As the bus pulled out of the courthouse's underground driveway, the crews rushed toward the vehicle. Bailiffs drove around for a bit, but when they eventually got to the garage's back entrance, the crews and reporters reappeared from the shadows and chased jurors to their cars. That evening, one of Lyle's jurors saw a TV news headline announcing Erik's mistrial.

Later that night, in a three-way phone call facilitated by one of the brothers' friends acting as ad hoc switchboard operator, Lyle tried to cheer up Erik. Both brothers had fantasized about being able to apply for bail. If jurors had acquitted Erik of first-degree murder but deadlocked on lesser charges, prosecutors would have been foreclosed from seeking a first-degree conviction at a second trial. But freedom remained an elusive dream.

"I'm surprised at how down I am," Erik told his brother.

On Friday, January 14, when Lyle's jury returned, they were relocated into the room where Erik's panel had been deliberating. All of the other jury's coffee pots and personal items that had been there for months were gone. It wasn't too hard to figure out that Erik's jury was finished.

One by one, panel members were brought into the court and asked if they knew anything about what had taken place the day before. Judge Weisberg had agreed to hold the announcement of the verdict if one jury returned sooner than the other. Nobody had considered what to do for a hung jury.

———————————

At 4:30 AM on January 17, 1994, Southern California had a 6.7 magnitude earthquake that killed sixty people and caused billions of dollars in damage, collapsing freeways and apartment buildings. It was centered in Northridge in the San Fernando Valley, where many of the jurors lived. Aftershocks during the next week kept the entire city awake.

Lyle was knocked from his bed to the floor and injured his arm. Both brothers were locked in their cells for three days without showers because of jail staff shortages. The Van Nuys courthouse had structural damage and broken glass. Jury deliberations were shut down since many of the panel members had significant damage to their homes.

When they resumed a week later, yellow crime scene tape sealed off the courthouse entrance. The court would now convene in a wide-body trailer behind the courthouse.

That day, the jury spent just ninety minutes deliberating. They took another vote: Now it was 7–5 for manslaughter over murder.

On January 25, four of the five voting for murder agreed to drop down from first- to second-degree. The last holdout for first-degree was Jude. Earlier, he'd been willing to move to second if the manslaughter voters would come up to meet him. Twinkles suggested a compromise of manslaughter for Jose and second-degree for Kitty, but jurors sympathetic to the defense didn't see how they could separate the level of killing.

Later they sent a note to the judge saying they were deadlocked. In open court, Judge Weisberg polled each juror before ordering them to deliberate further. Two hours later, jurors returned to the courtroom and announced that "nothing will allow us to come to a unanimous decision."

Judge Weisberg issued new verdict forms and asked the jurors to return in two days to consider whether any decisions could be reached.

On the morning of Friday, January 28, jury foreman Tom spoke to the panel with passion: "Everyone has put so much into this. There's no twelve people in the world that will ever be able to hear the evidence in the way that we did because so many people have followed this trial and been tainted by the media. We owe it to the court to see if we can come to a decision on any of the counts."

"Bull fucking shit!" blustered Jude at Tom's idea of finding Lyle not guilty of first-degree murder of Jose. "I'm not gonna let you do that!"

Ruth now said there was no possibility she'd ever change her vote from first-degree. Twinkles agreed with her.

"Others saw my passion and jumped back on," said Jude. "Had I not been there, Lyle wouldn't be facing first-degree murder again."

Chuck, Patty, and Wendy, a twenty-two-year-old administrative assistant at a medical center who had gone back and forth between second-degree and manslaughter, voted for second-degree murder, not believing that the brothers had been in fear for their lives. Patty said she didn't want to "tie the hands" of the next jury. Everyone else voted for voluntary manslaughter except Sharyn, who decided that Kitty's killing had been involuntary manslaughter.

At 12:09 PM, a 3.8 aftershock rumbled through Southern California. Six minutes later, the jurors sent a note to Judge Weisberg: "We deeply regret to inform the court that we are still unable to reach unanimous decisions on any of the three counts or lesser charges."

Inside the courtroom, as the public was allowed inside, Lyle seemed relaxed. He already knew the outcome. At 12:25 PM, six months and eight days after opening statements, Judge Stanley M. Weisberg announced that the jury was hopelessly deadlocked and declared a second mistrial.

PART TEN

AFTERMATH

CHAPTER 55
ERIK, LYLE, AND O.J.

N THE WEEKS THAT FOLLOWED THE TRIAL, LESLIE ABRAMSON was everywhere. The *New York Times* called her the "queen of miracles." The *Washington Post* described her as a "fire-eating, mud-slinging, nuclear-strength pain in the legal butt." *Marie Claire* declared her one of America's foremost "ball-busters."

"People are poking fun at us," D.A. Gil Garcetti admitted during a meeting with his deputies. "We're a laughingstock," veteran prosecutor Sterling Norris told the *Los Angeles Times*. Like others in the office, Norris, who ran against Garcetti for district attorney in 1992, was upset about the recent outcome of the tension-wrought Rodney King and Reginald Denny beating trials as well as Menendez. "It's not often the D.A. can burn down half the city, alienate half the city, and then turn around and lose a major murder case," Norris said.

In the fickle world of the media, there was soon a new crime saga that would eclipse all others. "We're going to find O.J. Simpson and bring him to justice!" Gil Garcetti declared at a late-afternoon news conference five months after the Menendez trial. Charged in the slayings of his ex-wife, Nicole Brown Simpson, and her friend Ron Goldman, the once beloved NFL athlete known as "The Juice" had vanished after failing to surrender to law officials a few hours earlier. "Don't blame anyone," said Garcetti. "How many members of the media have been surrounding Mr. Simpson's house, and he was able to get away somehow."

"How exotic: a top criminal justice official accusing the media of letting a fugitive slip through their fingers," wrote *Los Angeles Times* TV critic Howard Rosenberg.

A few hours later, on June 17, 1994, the capper of all heretofore grand tabloid stories climaxed with the bizarre "chase" through Southern California's freeways after O.J. Simpson by a phalanx of police cars as spectators cheered. At 10:20 that Friday evening, Simpson arrived at the L.A. County Men's Central Jail. Within a few hours after being booked, O.J. Simpson, prisoner #4013970, met his new neighbor, prisoner #1878449.

Erik Menendez knew something was up. On Friday afternoon, sheriff's deputies ordered him to scrub the floors and walls of the entire seven-cell pod. Erik had been preoccupied for weeks writing a science-fiction novel. As he scoured the floor on his hands and knees, he watched the O.J. Simpson Bronco chase on TV. "It was very depressing, very sad," said Erik. "I almost cried when his suicide letter was read on TV." Just before 10:30 PM, a group of deputies escorted the former football hero to the empty cell next to Erik Menendez.

The first night was rough. "I didn't see him cry, but I believe he was," Erik told me from jail. "I could hear him moaning."

Shortly after his arrival, Erik overheard Simpson talking about his case with one of the deputies. A deputy and a sergeant were stationed on suicide watch on chairs directly outside O.J.'s cell. A few minutes later, Simpson called out to his neighbor.

"Hey, Erik, it's O.J.!"

"Okay, O.J., let me explain a few things about jail to you," Erik whispered back.

"I told him not to talk to the deputies or inmates about his case. I told him not to worry—just calm down and relax. After that long chase, you can imagine what shape he was in."

By Saturday morning, the impact of his ex-wife's death was consuming the despondent Simpson. "He wasn't happy to be in jail like anyone else," said Erik. "He wasn't any worse than I was or Lyle was. He was real delusional, thinking that he was going to get out in three weeks." Erik still occasionally heard moaning. Simpson spent hours making calls on a portable phone that was brought to his cell.

At one point, Erik told O.J. that he and Lyle had met the football star when their father was a Hertz executive in the late 1970s. Later that day, the two neighbors spoke again through the flaps in their doors. O.J. told Erik he was worried about the loss of his prestige.

"I guess I won't be working for NBC anymore," said Simpson.

"He said it in a very sad way," said Erik. "He was worried about his reputation and that he's being slandered. I just told him that you're going to have to deal with the media." Throughout the day, Simpson and Menendez peered out through the flaps in their doors and watched the continuing TV news coverage. O.J. groaned every time he heard something new.

By Sunday morning, the two neighbors saw their cases linked together by Gil Garcetti. The D.A. was on a weekend media blitz. "Well, it's not going to shock me if we see O.J. Simpson say, 'Okay, I did it, but I'm not responsible.' We've seen it in Menendez." Robert Shapiro, who had represented Erik early on, called the D.A.'s public relations offensive "unconscionable," something that "undermined the presumption of innocence."

Erik was angry that Garcetti compared the two cases. "He kept bringing it up as if my name is becoming—my defense is becoming synonymous with some sort of thinking—here's another 'I did it but don't blame me kind of thing' or 'Here's the reason why,'" said Erik. "It was really aggravating." Simpson was devastated—worried that people would stare at him the rest of his life.

Erik Menendez wanted to help. It was difficult to have a conversation with the jail guards right outside their cells, so Erik wrote a lengthy letter to O.J. that he left in a shower stall down the hall. "I told him a lot of things. 'This is his life,' I said. 'When you cry—remember those tears. Hold them because you're crying for your children, you're crying for everything you're losing.' I said remember who's doing it to you and fight—continue to fight. I told him you've got to start worrying about your life, not your reputation."

Simpson thanked him. The letter had helped.

On Father's Day, Erik heard O.J. speaking "baby talk" to his young children on the phone. The football star was improving but still morose after little sleep. Old football injuries made it difficult to relax without an orthopedic pillow.

That afternoon, Erik and O.J. had a conversation about lawyers. Menendez was unhappy about his own surrender, which Shapiro arranged in March 1990. After he voluntarily surrendered in Los Angeles, Erik discovered that he should have turned himself in while he was in London. Britain has no capital punishment—the death penalty would have been ruled out as a condition of his extradition. He blamed Shapiro for the mistake.

Deputies constantly stopped by to ask for the football star's autograph. "I had to continually tell him, don't talk about your case," said Erik. "The sergeant actually had to tell him, too." O.J. repeatedly proclaimed his innocence. "He kept talking about how the spousal abuse wasn't true," said Erik. "He said he never really hit [Nicole] except for that one time. He said that she was actually very abusive toward him. She would throw things at him and hit him."

Although they'd been talking for five days, the only time Erik actually saw O.J. was on the way to the shower. "It was sad to see O.J. Simpson on the other side of that wall. I told him to be courageous. Every time he walked by my cell, he smiled and gave me a wink."

A week after Simpson's arrest, Erik was moved. He didn't know why.

"They were giving him good food—the officer's food (roast beef, pork chops, burritos), and they were letting him use the phone all day. They kept his cell open all the time," said Erik. "They were treating him like royalty. Everyone was in awe of him. Everyone wanted to talk to him."

O.J. Simpson wasn't the only one with devoted fans. At the height of their popularity as pop culture icons, Erik and Lyle began receiving a thousand letters a week. The majority were from abuse survivors who said nobody ever believed them as children when they tried to tell relatives they were being sexually molested. Some were from young women—groupies—who included naked pictures and tried to show up unannounced to visit the brothers in jail.

One of Lyle's most devoted supporters was Norma Novelli. The native of England and mother of four rarely missed three years of court hearings. Novelli's first contact with Lyle was in June 1990 when he wrote a letter commenting on an article critical of Pope John Paul II that ran in *Mind's Eye*, a newspaper she circulated in prisons. After a series of phone calls and letters, Novelli became a switchboard operator of sorts, connecting Lyle to friends, family, and pen pals via three-way phone calls. Lyle complained about the preppie outfits with pastel sweaters the attorneys made him wear. He asked Norma to give the defense team copies of *GQ* magazine to show the style he preferred.

Shortly before the trial, Novelli, who frequently wore short skirts and go-go boots, became angry when the defense team asked her to stop coming to court. They worried people would think the fifty-four-year-old woman had a relationship with twenty-five-year-old Lyle. "I have something to do with Lyle and I'm not going to disappear," she angrily told me. "I want it to look like they have supporters. I'm in control of my tongue." The Menendez family believed Novelli had a "romantic fixation" on Lyle and called her behavior "disgusting."

Besides nightly phone calls, Novelli visited Lyle three times a week at the L.A. County Jail. "When you're in jail, you find out who your friends are," Novelli told me one day. Lyle Menendez discovered the true meaning of Norma's friendship when she published a book in 1995 that contained transcripts of Lyle's calls that Novelli had been surreptitiously recording for four years. *The Private Diary of Lyle Menendez* was released by Dove Books, the same company that published a book by Faye Resnick, a close friend of O.J.'s ex-wife, Nicole Brown Simpson. Dove founder Michael Viner told *Newsweek* in 1995 the tapes "would put Lyle away for good." Novelli voluntarily turned over boxes of tapes of the illegally recorded phone calls. There was nothing of significance on them and none were ever admitted as evidence into court.

Lyle Menendez met O.J. Simpson in the L.A. County Jail's attorney room. Inmates would meet with their lawyers and material witnesses at long Formica tables separated by dividers. O.J. and Lyle began talking frequently while they were waiting for their lawyers. They had more than one hundred conversations. In the early days after his arrest, Lyle advised Simpson to consider a plea bargain.

At one point, Lyle wrote O.J. a long letter. "I told him I thought the public would understand," Lyle told me. "I expressed my concern that Robert Shapiro wouldn't let him tell the truth. I said I knew it obviously wasn't planned, and that he had snapped in the heat of passion." Lyle thought the case was a manslaughter.

The pair discussed the difference between manslaughter and murder. "I told him you don't have to expose the painful part of his life," said Lyle. But O.J. was preoccupied and "worried that his reputation would not survive" if he admitted he was responsible for the deaths of his ex-wife and Ron Goldman.

I asked Lyle if Simpson gave him the impression he was responsible for the murders. "Absolutely," he told me. "He knew Erik and I and trusted us."

In September 1994 the D.A.'s office announced they would not seek the death penalty against O.J. Within an hour, Leslie Abramson held a news conference to express her outrage at a decision she said was "politically motivated." She praised Garcetti for deciding not to seek the death penalty against the football star but called him hypocritical for wanting to execute the Menendez brothers since both were domestic violence cases.

"What kind of moral or legal decision would merit the death penalty for eighteen- and twenty-one-year-olds who killed their abusers but not for a wealthy, independent adult who they believe killed the person he was abusing?" she asked. "The only answer is if you are perceived to have the support of an important voting component of the community—in this case the African American population—then you are going to be given considerations and privileges the average citizen does not get."

CHAPTER 56

THE SECOND TRIAL

PROSECUTORS TRADITIONALLY HAVE AN ADVANTAGE IN A RETRIAL since the defense has already revealed their strategy. Still, Erik and Lyle Menendez were hopeful after the two hung juries in the first trial. Since the Menendez estate was officially broke, Superior Court Judge Cecil Mills appointed Leslie Abramson to be paid $125,000 a year. Mills decided Abramson was a better deal for taxpayers than the expense of somebody starting from scratch. "It isn't very much," Abramson quipped. "I'm the cheapest famous lawyer in the world at the moment." Barry Levin, a former LAPD officer, joined Abramson as second chair. Jill Lansing resigned because she wanted to spend more time with her young daughter. Charles Gessler, a respected veteran public defender, replaced Lansing. Terri Towery, who worked with Gessler in the public defender's office, became second chair for Lyle.

David Conn, the acting head of the D.A.'s special trial unit, was named the new Menendez lead prosecutor. The New York native started in the D.A.'s office in 1978. Carol Najera was appointed second chair. Judge Stanley Weisberg ruled there would be only one jury for both brothers in the retrial. In early August 1995, Leslie Abramson argued the jury should be the ones to decide if the brothers honestly believed they were in danger. "Imminent danger was not present in this case," countered Conn. "It can't be used as an excuse for the killings. They should have driven away. There was no necessity for them to kill their parents."

Weisberg said it was a close call but announced "the court is inclined to analyze and rule there was sufficient evidence" to give an imperfect self-defense instruction. Abramson and Towery exchanged looks of relief. The judge would allow the testimony of therapy experts. But there would be limits since the prosecution was raising an objection, unlike in the first trial. "Most of the [family] history is irrelevant," said the judge.

Evidence would be allowed in only if it could be connected to the brothers' "sense of fear." Weisberg ominously warned he wasn't going to allow "minutia" to be repeated in the retrial. "The focus of the evidence should be on the mental state at the time of the killings," he ruled. "The abuse is irrelevant unless it corroborates their mental state at the time of the crime."

––––––––––––––––

On September 28, 1995, a jury of seven men and five women was seated. Leslie Abramson had a bad feeling about the panel. During a recess from a hearing on October 2, a bailiff said the O.J. Simpson jury had reached a verdict that was going to be announced the next day. Moments later, a voice came out of the deputy's two-way radio shouting, "Not guilty! Not guilty!" The next morning, October 3, Southern California was baking in a heat wave. A gauntlet of LAPD officers surrounded the Criminal Court Building twenty miles away from Van Nuys in downtown Los Angeles. Large crowds surrounding the high-rise court erupted in cheers when Simpson was formally declared "not guilty."

"The investigation was incomplete and incredibly sloppy. That's what got them in trouble in the Simpson case and it will get them in trouble in this case," declared Leslie Abramson. "Persisting in a theory they can't prove." She accused prosecutors of being desperate to "win one for the Gil." Stanley Weisberg ruled there would be no TV camera for the Menendez brothers' retrial. There was no mention of the Simpson case, but the backlash was evident. "No TV?" said Abramson to Weisberg. "Why couldn't you do it the first time?"

––––––––––––––––

One year and nine months after two juries deadlocked, a panel of twelve people gathered on an unseasonably cool, foggy morning to decide if Erik and Lyle Menendez murdered their parents or killed in self-defense. The pastel sweaters were gone—this time around both brothers wore shirts and ties. Lyle looked relaxed, but Erik fidgeted while anxiously scanning the packed courtroom.

When David Conn stood up just before 11 AM, he reminded jurors the prosecution did not have to provide a motive for why the brothers killed their parents. "We will prove they were ambushed by a storm of gunfire," declared Conn. "There was no place to hide, there was no place to run."

The prosecutor displayed large-scale photographs of the bloody crime scene, the gaping hole in Jose Menendez's head, and a disturbing close-up of Kitty Menendez's pellet-shattered face. Erik and Lyle "turned on tears," declared Conn, to "disarm and persuade the police."

The new jury would hear the voices of Erik and Lyle tell Dr. Jerome Oziel they'd considered killing their parents for days before doing it. Prosecution witnesses would testify that the brothers tried to fabricate evidence and solicit perjury. There was an angry objection when Conn said the "defendants want to put their parents on trial."

During lunch, Leslie Abramson stood off to the side puffing on a cigarette as David Conn insisted to reporters that "abuse had nothing to do with murder . . . even if they were abused, they could premeditate murder." When it was her turn, Abramson declared there was "only one truth about what happened in this family." She said the jury would see beyond the prosecution's "soap opera theory."

Back in court, Leslie Abramson's delivery was low-key compared to her passionate closing at the first trial. "Not all homicides are crimes," she said. The brothers had acted in "mind-numbing, adrenaline-pumping panic and fear of death" on the night of August 20, 1989. Erik developed "post-traumatic stress syndrome" and "low self-esteem—like you see on *Oprah*."

His sexual abuse began as seduction followed by repeated acts of oral copulation, rape, and sadism. "You can fool a six-year-old easily," she said. By age thirteen, Erik Menendez understood he was a "worthless sex slave who only existed to do whatever his father wanted."

A substantial portion of Abramson's opening focused on Kitty Menendez—her killing was the mystery most people couldn't understand. Kitty was a "hostile perpetrator," a "knowing accomplice," and a "deficient mother." She told relatives "she hated her sons."

"Some parents cannot and do not love their children," proclaimed Abramson.

Erik Menendez was a "child who knows he made a bad mistake." He had killed from "fear, not hatred." He "had no choice." Erik wanted to kill himself but "he's not asking you to feel sorry for him," Abramson said. "Our witnesses will not tell you the abuse is an excuse."

Outside court, the diminutive attorney said she was tired after almost three hours of speaking "but the truth is complicated and takes a while." As jurors were driving home, John Kobylt, the cohost of KFI radio's top-rated *John and Ken* talk show, called Abramson "evil" and said "those Menendez brothers gall me even more than O.J."

––––––––––

There were three simple themes to the prosecution's case: hammer home the brutality of the murders, show the brothers' extensive planning and repeated deception, and suggest they'd killed to inherit money. David Conn had a major advantage over the first trial's prosecutors—he'd been able to study the defense and analyze what many considered a major flaw in the original prosecution: the failure to challenge the brothers' claims of abuse.

Conn wasted little time getting to the carnage of August 20. Detective Les Zoeller provided play-by-play narration as the crime scene video was shown on a huge TV monitor. There was the messy foyer with clothes strewn about. A walk down the hallway to the double doors of the family room. A hush fell over the courtroom when the camera suddenly turned to reveal Jose Menendez's dead body, his head, swollen like a ripe pumpkin, slumped awkwardly on his shoulder. The jury appeared transfixed.

The next morning, jurors heard taped interviews with the brothers recorded in New Jersey a month after the murders. Leslie Abramson became upset when she realized prosecutors were playing an edited version that left out passages sympathetic to Erik. As the courtroom emptied for a recess, tempers flared. Abramson and Carol Najera began trading insults. As their shouting grew louder, Najera glared at Abramson and bellowed, "Do your job, lady!" As David Conn pulled Najera away, a bailiff positioned herself to block Abramson, who was quickly moving across the courtroom toward her.

During Zoeller's cross, Abramson skillfully began weaving the defense story into a series of sharp questions. She made sure jurors were aware of the seventy-eight-year-old woman with gray hair sitting in the audience by inquiring several times about Maria Menendez. Defense attorneys kept her away from much of the first trial because they knew she'd be upset with the negative portrayal of Jose. In the retrial, the brothers asked her to be there. Maria sat stoically day after day as the large-scale bloody crime scene pictures were displayed.

On redirect, the detective introduced the December 11 Oziel tape, one of the prosecution's most powerful pieces of evidence. Jurors followed on transcripts as Lyle explained how killing his parents "took courage beyond belief" and said "there was no way I was going to kill my parents without Erik's consent." But this time there was no defense spin to soften the impact. On cross, the defense insisted Lyle had displayed "genuine emotion" when he made the 911 call.

As the trial continued, prosecutors brought in a parade of familiar faces from Menendez One. Carlos Baralt said Jose Menendez told him he'd removed Erik and Lyle from his will because he was "disappointed" and "frustrated" with his sons. Perry Berman testified Lyle suggested the killings were related to his father's business. Howard Witkin repeated his account of erasing the family computer's hard drive for Lyle. "I called police and said someone named Lyle tried to destroy evidence," he volunteered. "Great. Objection!" shouted Leslie Abramson.

The brief appearance of Donovan Goodreau brought forth little of the drama from the first trial. In a dozen interviews between 1990 and 1993, Goodreau told me Lyle confessed to him months before the murders that he and Erik had been sexually abused. In Menendez One, this information disrupted the trial. Now, the element of surprise was gone. Prosecutors had successfully challenged the admission of this evidence. The story could not be brought in unless Lyle Menendez testified.

Neither side liked Amir "Brian" Eslaminia. In a 1991 letter, Lyle asked Eslaminia to testify that the brothers had asked him to loan them a handgun—such a loan never happened. Brian Eslaminia met Erik at Beverly Hills High, but he hadn't met Lyle until after the brothers were arrested. He was shocked by the murders. Within minutes, it was obvious Eslaminia would be a reluctant witness for the prosecution.

"Do you have problems with your memory?" asked David Conn.

"I do . . . I don't. For three years, you wanted me to remember a certain thing."

"What was that?"

"I don't remember." The audience laughed.

Eslaminia had visited both brothers a half-dozen times in jail.

"Were you willing to provide false testimony?" Eslaminia glanced at Lyle before quietly answering "yes." But Eslaminia said Lyle phoned him months after sending the letter to say he was abandoning the plan since "truth was the route he was taking."

"Aren't you trying to help Erik Menendez?"

"No, sir. He killed his parents. To me, friendship is based on trust. Erik violated all those things."

Eslaminia told Conn he "never actually agreed" to the letter scenario. He said he advised Lyle to get some "spiritual guidance." During cross, Eslaminia said he offered to arrange for a helicopter to break Erik out of the L.A. County Jail. "I was just a teenager," he said. "They were too," Abramson added quickly.

Ex-roommate Glenn Stevens's direct closely mirrored his first trial testimony. During Charles Gessler's three-hour cross, Stevens admitted Lyle was one of his two best friends. When he tried to dodge questions, Gessler read back his answers from the first trial. Stevens denied he'd "been spying" for the police. Gessler stood directly behind Lyle, forcing Glenn to look at his former roommate. Stevens had briefly worked as the manager at Lyle's restaurant. He admitted to taking money from the cash register and said he didn't like working for somebody who was "condescending."

In the first trial, Lyle's former fiancé Jamie Pisarcik testified she'd brought Lyle copies of cases she looked up of "kids who got off after killing their parents." Now, she claimed she'd given the nonexistent cases (acquittals are not written up; only appeals are) to Jill Lansing. Kitty's brother Brian Andersen had seen the Menendez family argue about the brothers' exorbitant spending. He said he didn't believe his nephews had killed their parents in 1989.

Marzi Eisenberg, the woman who described herself as Jose Menendez's "office wife," repeated her first trial testimony about riding in a limousine with Lyle after the Hollywood memorial service. After flexing his foot back and forth, she claimed he said, "Hey, Marzi, who said I couldn't fill my father's shoes?" before admitting he was wearing Jose Menendez's shoes. Once again, she described the shoes as "black or dark-colored tassel loafers." On cross, Eisenberg said she'd been "extremely uncomfortable" with the "bizarre" shoe conversation. The defense played a TV news video that showed Lyle walking out of the memorial wearing a pair of green cowboy boots.

A showdown over the reconstruction of the grisly crime scene on North Elm Drive was billed as the conflict that would decide the brothers' fate. Combining 800 police photographs with state-of-the-art computer imaging, Failure Analysis Associates, an engineering company, attempted to re-create the crime scene. It was the heart of the prosecution's new case. Over the next sixteen days, jurors spent hour after hour absorbing gory autopsy photos, mind-numbing debates on blood splatter, and legal maneuvering over technical minutia. It was too much from both sides.

FaAA, which changed its name to Exponent in 1998, was known for reconstructing accidents and catastrophes, including the notorious 1989 *Exxon Valdez* oil spill in Alaskan waters and the tragic explosion of the NASA space shuttle *Challenger* in 1986. The defense argued that FaAA had no expertise in crime scene evaluation and forensic medicine. "We think Roger McCarthy is a fraud," said Leslie Abramson. "He's a scandal in every case he shows up in." McCarthy, the head of FaAA, had never appeared in a criminal trial as an expert witness.

Dr. McCarthy testified that both Jose and Kitty Menendez were seated (not standing as the brothers said) when the shooting began. The first shot, a wound to Kitty's left breast and Jose's right arm, took McCarthy forty minutes to explain. An image of the wound to the back of Jose Menendez's head showed a shaved skull with a large black hole outlined by jagged red lines. "He's dead when this happens," said McCarthy.

On cross, Charles Gessler pointed out that McCarthy had never surveyed a crime scene, attended an autopsy, or personally seen real gunshot wounds. Leslie Abramson attacked him for lacking the background necessary to analyze a crime scene. She read an FaAA internal memo from another trial: "This example will be used to confuse juries."

On November 20, the prosecution rested its case. Thirty witnesses had testified in the seven-week-old trial.

CHAPTER 57

DEFENSE ON
THE ROPES

THE TRANSITION TO THE DEFENSE WAS BARELY NOTICEABLE, AS a counterattack of FaAA's crime scene reconstruction was launched full force. In the first trial, prosecutors lost control of their case with the soap opera of Jerry Oziel's personal life. This time, it was a horror show with the defense on the ropes, forced to explain what Abramson called "grim on grim."

The first witness was Dr. Martin Fackler, a wound ballistics expert who served as a combat surgeon in Vietnam.

"If I asked you to reconstruct the Menendez case, would you?" asked Abramson.

"I don't believe it can be done because of the tremendous variables," said Fackler.

"Is Dr. McCarthy's a scientific reconstruction?"

"As best he could . . . but it contains many errors."

"What we're showing is that the district attorney's office has done something really sleazy, really wrong," bellowed Leslie Abramson outside of court.

"We're basically fine-tuning how an ambush took place," said David Conn. "Day after day, we're hearing testimony about how the parents were attacked, unarmed and defenseless. When is the defense going to start the defense?"

The focus of the trial shifted from blood spatter to the defense theory of what led up to the night of August 20. Twenty-five-year-old Erik Menendez walked slowly to the witness stand before describing how he killed his parents two months after graduating from Beverly Hills High.

The powerful bond between the brothers was obvious. As he testified, Erik frequently looked over at Lyle, who leaned forward, straining to hear every word. Erik's anxiety increased noticeably as he told jurors of growing up with a father who sexually abused him and a mother who piled on humiliation in a dysfunctional family spinning wildly out of control. Erik insisted he loved his parents. But he believed his father would carry through on his threat to kill him to avoid a family scandal.

"My father was afraid I was going to reveal things," he said. "I wanted to please Dad, but I didn't want to do it. I felt icky and dirty before vomiting. He was kind. He was gentle. He was patient. And he loved me."

"Did you kill your parents because you hated them?" asked Levin.

"Certainly not," said Erik.

"Did you kill your parents because you wanted their money?"

"No."

After the jury left, Levin echoed Abramson's earlier comment that Erik was suffering from post-traumatic stress syndrome. David Conn countered that the only issue that mattered was why he killed his parents. The judge had the last word: "This is not a PTSD trial."

The first mention in the retrial of Dr. Jerome Oziel came on Erik's last day of direct. Erik explained the therapist wanted to record a therapy session to "make himself feel more comfortable that the brothers trusted him." Lyle and Erik decided before the December 11 recording they weren't going to reveal the Menendez family secrets.

The opening minutes of cross set the tone for the next eight days as Conn unloaded a condescending and relentless attack, accusing Erik Menendez of fabricating his defense. The prosecutor insisted there was no evidence to corroborate the brothers' allegations of molestation.

At times, Conn's cross of Erik felt like a tennis match between two highly skilled players.

"You don't want to talk about the molestation?"

"No."

"But you'll do it if it gets you your goal of manslaughter. Do you use tears to manipulate people?"

"No. I just want people to understand why I did this," said Erik. "I don't completely understand myself."

"You weren't helpless?"

"No."

"Rather than becoming suicidal you became homicidal?"

"No," Erik said quietly. "He absolutely did molest me for twelve years."

"Did you lie about your involvement?"

"Yes."

"Did you conspire with your brother to lie to law enforcement?"

"Yes."

Erik admitted he'd spent a lot of money and "didn't want to go to jail."

"Did you have compassion for your mother when you shot her to death?"

"I was afraid," said Erik with a deep sigh. "I've been in jail for six years, and I'll be punished for the rest of my life."

In the days before the murders, Erik said he'd even called Dr. Jerome Oziel because he was "searching for help," but he never went in for an appointment.

———————

Dr. John Wilson, a psychology professor from Cleveland State University, testified after Erik and said he suffered from chronic PTSD and battered person's syndrome. The evidence? His recurring nightmares and disassociation. Without the jury present, David Conn accused Abramson of "playing three-card monte" and "serving up a trauma stew."

During one of the frequent disputes over the admission of evidence, Charles Gessler revealed some cracks in the joint defense. He accused Leslie Abramson of "rolling the dice with my money—it's my client's life that is at stake."

"I've had the sense this ship is out of control for years now," Abramson replied.

On January 12, 1996, two days after Lyle turned twenty-eight, Gessler signaled that his client would not be taking the stand. Lyle told me he didn't want to testify without Jill Lansing. In a hearing without the jury present, Gessler stated that Lyle had killed "in the heat of passion" and that he would be asking for "reasonable self-defense."

"Heat of passion has no bearing on this case," said David Conn.

The brothers' unified position in the first trial was imperfect self-defense—that they did not react to danger the way a normal person would because they had suffered years of abuse. Lyle's defense was now dealing with new evidence that he'd asked friends to fabricate stories—the letter to Brian Eslaminia and a letter to a former girlfriend—that could be used to impeach him if he testified. The fallout meant Lyle would be unable to call his own therapy experts. The second trial jurors would never see the powerful testimony Lyle gave in 1993.

"This is not a trial to determine if Erik or Lyle was an abused person," said Judge Stanley Weisberg as he continued to limit the appearance of many key defense witnesses from the first trial. "The only evidence of Lyle's mental state is from Erik." Without Lyle's testimony, jurors would not be allowed to hear from many of the family, friends, and coaches who'd been the heart of the original defense.

Allan Andersen, the son of Kitty's brother Brian, did testify about two summers he spent with the Menendezes. He described four-year-old Erik as being "outgoing with happy eyes." Two years later, Erik had become "introverted, nervous, and afraid to talk with him." The brothers would "cower" when their father was angry.

Diane VanderMolen, Kitty's niece, testified that she "adored" her aunt and "tried to please her" during several summers she lived with the family. She described the Menendezes as "the royalty of my family." But she became emotional when explaining how Jose and Kitty were abusive to her young cousins. VanderMolen talked about Kitty's treatment of her.

"Mr. Conn, she attacked everything about me during her rages," VanderMolen said. "I'm still trying to regain my self-esteem." In the hallway, defense attorneys hugged VanderMolen, celebrating one of the few moments in the retrial that matched the power of the original defense.

Andy Cano returned with his account of how twelve-year-old Erik shared his secret of being molested when Andy was ten. In an aggressive cross, David Conn suggested he'd do anything to help his cousin and demanded to know why Cano never went to his mother to report the abuse. Cano said he was "loyal to Erik" and "too embarrassed" to tell his parents.

On January 31, the defense quietly rested after presenting only twenty-five witnesses compared to the fifty-one in the first trial. "We were only allowed to put on a *Reader's Digest* version of the defense," said Leslie Abramson. "It hurt us because this jury doesn't have as much information as the first trial jury."

For rebuttal, the prosecution had Craig Cignarelli repeat his account of how Erik asked him a week after the killings, "Do you want to know what happened?" Craig claimed Erik had told him Lyle was standing by the closed doors to the TV room holding two shotguns when Lyle told Erik, "Let's do it." But when Cignarelli met with the BHPD ten days before wearing a wire, he qualified the confession by saying Erik had said "it could've happened." The jury gasped on cross when Cignarelli admitted he'd been paid $25,000 by the tabloid TV show *Hard Copy* for an interview. He testified he "deserved the money because of all the time he lost from school."

Some of the fiercest battles over evidence took place before the testimony of Dr. Park Dietz, the prosecution therapist Leslie Abramson called "Dragon Dietz." He recorded sixteen hours of video at the BHPD in a room with two-way glass so prosecutors could watch his evaluation of Erik. Dietz was a former Harvard Medical School professor with a PhD in sociology. He'd been an expert witness in several high-profile cases, including serial killer/sex offender Jeffrey Dahmer, terrorist Ted Kaczynski (a.k.a. the Unabomber), and would-be presidential assassin John Hinckley.

"What I did was try to determine Erik Menendez's mental state at the time of the homicides," Dietz testified on February 8. "Erik's mental functioning was very good. There were no hallucinations or delusions— no disruption in his ability to use logical thought."

Dietz said Erik's excessive anxiety caused him to frequently worry. The effects? Restlessness. Difficulty concentrating. Muscle tension. Sleep disorder. Irritability. Erik thought Lyle might "abandon him" and admitted his "theatricality" had angered his father.

On cross, Dietz agreed he was not a child abuse expert.

"Does it matter that his mother was a coconspirator?" asked Leslie Abramson.

"That would help explain things," said Dietz.

Leslie Abramson wasn't feeling well on Valentine's Day. Just before lunch, there was an intense debate over whether forensic psychiatrist Dr. William Vicary should be allowed to testify. Conn strongly objected on the basis that Dr. John Wilson had already testified for the defense.

"Dr. Vicary is going to testify to Erik's mental state five years and eight months ago when he first saw him," said Abramson. "Dr. Dietz suggested Erik was coached on his answers, so it's critical for Dr. Vicary to describe him. Erik was very, very, very sick in the summer of 1990."

Conn objected, but Abramson insisted: "Dr. Vicary disagrees with Dietz's diagnosis of anxiety disorder." Shortly after 3 PM, Abramson said she was worn out and too sick to continue. Court was recessed for the day.

The next morning, the fierce debate raged on.

"They want to confuse the jury even more. That was the goal in the first trial and here," said the prosecutor. "Enough is enough."

"We think the jury has been misled and want to clarify," countered Abramson. "We were prevented from calling scores of witnesses." Just after 10 AM, Weisberg ruled against the defense. Abramson looked grim.

"I want to put on the record I was utterly incompetent," said Abramson in an astonishing statement. "Dr. Vicary is an expert I should have called in my case in chief. I've been incompetent." During a break, David Conn boasted to reporters, "There's going to be a penalty phase, and our star witness will be Dr. Oziel."

After lunch, Dr. Vicary was allowed to take the stand, but his testimony was severely limited. Vicary was prohibited from saying he believed Erik was sexually molested or that he had killed out of fear, essentially the heart of the original defense. Erik Menendez "had gotten better" since he began treating him in June 1990. Abramson fought hard, but David Conn was relentless with objections.

During one argument without the jury present, Abramson said she was "trying to rely on the last mood swing of the court."

"What was that?" snapped Weisberg. "You mean your misinterpretation of the law."

With the jury back, Abramson asked, "Which is more likely to a victim of child abuse? General anxiety disorder or PTSD?"

"PTSD," said Vicary.

David Conn's cross blew by in five minutes.

As Maria Menendez played with a tiny crucifix, the street-fighting tone of arguing continued during a hearing about jury instructions.

Conn maintained that there was no imminent danger to the brothers.

"His state of mind was that at any moment, they were coming at him," countered Abramson. "Given the history of provocation in this family, there was a euphemism for rape: 'Go to your room.' Belligerently asserting your rights to have sex with your son is sufficient provocation."

"There was no provocation from Kitty," declared Conn.

"That Thursday night, Erik thought Kitty was the one who wanted him dead," said Abramson.

As he watched, Lyle Menendez displayed one of his nervous tics, tapping down the top of his toupee by slowly rotating two fingers around the crown of his head.

"The brothers had no reasonable belief that the parents were going to kill them," Conn told reporters outside. "The brothers did not have to kill their parents. It doesn't matter if the brothers were molested. It doesn't give them an excuse. There's more than sufficient evidence for a first-degree murder conviction."

After lunch, Judge Weisberg dropped the hammer by further limiting the jury instructions. There was "no evidence for heat of passion for Jose and defendant Erik Menendez" and "insufficient evidence of provocation for Kitty and Lyle."

"The court is redefining imperfect self-defense?" asked Abramson.

Abramson shook her head as the judge declared there was "no evidence to justify involuntary manslaughter for Lyle in the death of Jose."

The defense refused to give up: "The mother is a conspirator," Abramson argued. "It's improper for the court to take this from the jury." The judge said he'd "given Mary Louise Menendez a lot of thought" and declared "both defendants are not in the same boat."

Abramson accused the judge of making a judgment call: "It's for twelve jurors to decide based on their life experience."

"My decisions here are based on the law," said Weisberg.

Back outside, Abramson told reporters, "He has made himself the thirteenth juror . . . I'm surprised he doesn't just take out a rifle in the courtroom and shoot them."

Then, it was David Conn's turn. "An acquittal is not an appropriate argument. It's nothing less than second-degree murder," he said, facing a half circle of TV news cameras. "The testimony of Erik Menendez did not describe imminent danger." Conn called the court's rulings "well supported." Leslie Abramson calling the judge the thirteenth juror was "an unfair characterization." A beaming David Conn was taking a premature victory lap with the media. Defense attorneys were clearly shaken.

Four days later, it was pouring rain in Van Nuys. Judge Weisberg let the defense argue about the law for almost two hours. How had Kitty Menendez provoked Lyle? he asked. "Fear and anger were described by Erik's testimony," said Terri Towery. The judge said there was "little on the record about Lyle's state of mind." He repeated his belief that the "danger to Erik was not imminent," the "evidence for Lyle was even less substantial," and there was "no legal basis for a heat of passion instruction on Kitty."

"If the court is right, the California Supreme Court has eviscerated imperfect self-defense for domestic violence victims," argued Leslie Abramson. She asked for a stay so the defense could get a writ to delay closing arguments. The judge denied it.

"The abuse is a total fabrication," said David Conn as he began four days of closing argument. "The strategy in this case is to get you to hate the victims." He called the brothers' story a "script" and the "silliest story ever told in a courtroom." Jose Menendez had loved his sons, Conn maintained, and accused the brothers' family members of being coached to manufacture false evidence. The December 11 tape was a "smoking gun." Conn demanded that Erik and Lyle Menendez be "held responsible for their actions." He described the case as a "perfect example of the abuse excuse" and said second-degree murder would be a "travesty of justice."

"I don't need to go as long," said Leslie Abramson in the first of her three-day closing. "My case is strong enough." She admitted that some jurors might believe Erik was lying. "You're going to be very bored," she said. "I'm talking to those of you on the fence."

She accused the prosecution of blending evidence to invent a new person: "Lyle-Rik," somebody, she said, who does not exist. Kitty Menendez had done nothing to help Erik and Lyle. "You don't have incest without enabling by one parent," Abramson told jurors. "Is Kitty Menendez a bad person? She and God have worked that out by now." As for Jose, she asked, "What kind of success is a man killed by his own children?"

"We don't have to prove innocence," she reminded the jury. "It is better to hang than compromise."

As Abramson finished, she told the panel, "I could sob for an hour. If I only had a time machine, I could go back and grab them."

CHAPTER 58

THE VERDICTS— LIFE OR DEATH?

O N MARCH 21, 1996, THE JURY RETURNED WITH A VERDICT AFTER four days of deliberation. Just before noon, the court clerk read their decision: Erik and Lyle Menendez were both guilty of first-degree murder as well as conspiracy to commit murder. Jurors had also voted for two special circumstances: lying in wait and multiple murders. That meant there would be only two options in the penalty phase: life without parole or death. Both brothers were stunned by the verdict. Erik stayed in bed, staring at the ceiling of his cell for several days. In the D.A.'s office, they proudly dubbed the trial "Menendez II: The Wrath of Conn."

Six days after the verdict, the penalty phase began with Jose's sister, Terry Baralt, the first of seventeen defense witnesses.

"There have to be powerful reasons for what happened," she said.

"Did you love your brother? asked Terri Towery.

"Very much," she replied.

On cross, David Conn complained that Baralt wouldn't meet with Les Zoeller to discuss the case. "Mr. Conn, you want to kill my nephews . . . the family members do not want any more blood. This is my family, not yours," she snapped.

Both Jose and Kitty were "cruel and insensitive" to her nephews, said Marta Cano. Her brother constantly mocked the brothers, and Kitty never stopped him. The family was "devastated" by the convictions. "I wish I would've done something before," Cano said.

Father Ken Deasy began visiting both brothers shortly after they were arrested in 1990. Deasy had met the entire family in 1988. Jose had thought it would help in juvenile court if Erik was counseled by a priest after his arrest for the Calabasas burglaries. Deasy regularly spent time with the brothers, including every year on Christmas Day.

Erik had asked the priest, "Does God still love me? Does he hold it against me?" Erik wanted to know if his parents forgave him. The priest told him, "Don't limit God's forgiveness to our inability to forgive one another . . . God gives unconditional love."

Under cross, David Conn asked Father Deasy about when Erik admitted he'd killed his parents. "It was because he was being hurt, molested, abused by his parents, emotionally, physically—not greed," Deasy said.

"You believe him, don't you?" Leslie Abramson asked on redirect.

"Very much so," replied Deasy.

During the second week of testimony, Conn asked Dr. Vicary about his evaluation of Erik. It became apparent at one point that Conn was working off a different set of Vicary's therapy notes than the ones in front of the witness. Under aggressive questioning, Dr. Vicary admitted he'd deleted a half-dozen sections of his notes at the request of Leslie Abramson. Vicary said he'd removed information Abramson told him was "prejudicial" and "out of bounds." Several law professors told the *Los Angeles Times* it appeared that Abramson and Vicary had violated legal ethics.

The next day, both Abramson and Vicary came to court lawyered up. In a hearing without the jury, Abramson asserted her Fifth Amendment privilege twice—to protect herself from self-incrimination—when questioned by Judge Weisberg. Vicary testified that Abramson had ordered him to remove twenty-four pages from his original notes. Vicary rewrote another ten pages. The deletions included Erik's statements that a week before the killings he hated his parents and "couldn't wait—I wanted to kill them."

The other three defense attorneys immediately asked for a mistrial. They worried the jury would think there'd been misconduct by the defense. They accused the prosecution of proceeding with a "witch hunt" against Abramson. Barry Levin argued that Erik's due process rights had been violated and suggested that an independent attorney should be appointed for him.

Now there was a potential conflict between Levin and Abramson. "You know where the blame is to be found," the judge said. "There's nothing improper about what the prosecution did. The blame lies somewhere else." During the lunch break, Abramson stood by herself smoking as a car stereo blared the Marvin Gaye song, "What's Going On."

Defense attorneys Barry Levin and Charles Gessler passionately argued there should be a mistrial, but the judge denied their motion. "I now view this penalty phase as a death march," Levin said. He advised Erik to remove Abramson from the case. But at the end of the day, Judge Weisberg decided there had been no impact on the jury and said the penalty phase would continue. He said Levin could represent Erik since he was "untainted" and "conflict free."

The next morning, the *Los Angeles Times* featured a front-page picture of a frustrated Abramson looking over her shoulder in the courtroom. The media exploded with stories that defined why L.A. law was so different than the legal system anywhere else. "What I would really like to do," Abramson later told a reporter, "is become completely invisible for the rest of my life because I don't find celebrity very much fun."

On April 9, Levin and Gessler made a motion to remove Abramson. Gessler claimed it had been impossible for the jury to avoid the intense media coverage. He worried the jury's verdict on life or death could become a referendum on Abramson.

Then, Abramson told the judge she'd made a "hasty decision" and withdrew her assertion of the Fifth Amendment. Her request to go in camera (that is, in private) was denied. Later, in chambers, Erik Menendez begged the judge to let Abramson stay. Judge Weisberg ruled Abramson would remain as cocounsel with Levin. As she left the courthouse, Abramson smiled for the TV cameras. Privately, she expressed her anger toward Vicary: "That weasel—he accepts fifty percent of the blame and lets Erik take one hundred percent of the impact."

As testimony resumed, Dr. Vicary said Erik was so sick when they met that it was "almost time to take him upstairs and put him in a rubber room." Kitty Menendez's brothers, Brian and Milton, testified for the prosecution but were not allowed to plead for the death penalty. "Sometimes I wake up at night screaming at the vision of her and the way she was murdered, knowing she was alive for part of that time," an emotional Brian Andersen told the jury. "I wish I'd been there to help protect her."

———————————

Erik and Lyle Menendez deserved to die, said David Conn as he began his closing argument for the penalty phase. "If not this case, what case?" Conn said it shouldn't matter if a defendant came from Compton, East L.A., or Beverly Hills. He pounced on Dr. Vicary, calling his note-changing the "corruption of the criminal justice system" and an attempt to trick the jury. He mocked the defense as "fraudulent" and "desperate." "You should not accept this 'country club abuse excuse' defense," he demanded.

In an arrogant tone, Conn told jurors they had to weigh the "horror of the crime versus too much tennis and not enough hugs." The prosecutor described the brothers as out-of-control sons who had grown up with silver spoons, and then premeditated murder.

"They chose death on Friday when they went shopping for shotguns," Conn said. "They chose death on Saturday when they reloaded their shotguns with more lethal ammunition. They chose death on Sunday when they shot their parents to death. And now they want you to choose life for them?"

"This is not a little child here," said Conn, pointing at Lyle. "It was a cold-blooded killer." He sneered at Lyle, and declared, "Look into his eyes. You see black eyes, dead eyes. And they should be dead for the horror he committed."

———————————

After six years, Leslie Abramson, the public face of the defense, would remain silent. Just after 3:30 PM, Barry Levin began in a quiet manner by admitting he was terrified and scared. He told jurors this was the most important decision they would make for the rest of their lives. He reminded the panel that David Conn was from the same D.A.'s office that said O.J. Simpson shouldn't get the death penalty.

"We're talking about him looking at you with a straight face and telling you that of all the people who commit a crime, Erik Menendez must die. What about O.J.? He wasn't even eligible for consideration. O.J. was the abuser," Levin said. "That's so much worse."

As he warmed up, Levin channeled the passion and electricity of Abramson, urging jurors not to sentence Erik to death based on the slick words of a prosecutor. "You can't be mad at Erik and give him death out of spite or revenge," Levin said. "You can be strong, merciful, independent, and understanding."

Levin argued that the death penalty should be reserved for the most vicious and heinous criminals who had a history of violence and no remorse. He accused Conn of victim bashing in reverse: If you liked Jose Menendez, you must kill Erik. Wasn't it possible to love all four family members? Levin asked.

"The family has closure. The prosecution has its conviction. Enough is enough," he preached in an emotional crescendo. "You shouldn't kill Erik Menendez because you don't have to. You'll be protecting no one. You'll be appeasing no one . . . If you feel any compassion, this is the time to use it. If you feel any mercy, this is the time to use it."

Outside the courtroom, Maria Menendez hugged Levin and thanked him.

The next day, Terri Towery pleaded for Lyle's life. "I'm not saying that Jose and Kitty Menendez deserved to die. Of course they didn't," said a soft-spoken Towery. "But you must consider whether the parents' treatment of their son, Lyle Menendez, played a role in what happened." If both sons had killed their parents, she said, "doesn't it make you ask why?" As she finished, Towery asked the panel to choose compassion, mercy, and understanding for Lyle Menendez. After court, the defense team congratulated each other.

Just before 2 PM on April 17, it was announced that the jury of eight men and four women (two female jurors had been replaced during deliberations for health reasons) had reached a verdict after three days of deliberation. Erik and Lyle appeared somber when they entered the packed courtroom surrounded by nine bailiffs. Erik's head slumped as the first verdict was read: life without parole. Lyle hugged Charles Gessler as he heard his identical sentence. Sitting in the audience, Maria Menendez rubbed her eyes.

Three jurors and two alternates took questions from reporters in the courtroom. They said there had never been any disagreement in reaching the first-degree murder conviction or deciding on the punishment. Andrew Wolfberg, a twenty-five-year-old recent law school graduate, believed life without parole was the right decision based on the law. "It's eerie to be in the position of deciding someone's life or death," he said. "It was almost like the defendants when they made their decision to kill."

Thirty-four-year-old Bruce Seitz, a postal worker, said jurors were surprised they didn't hear Lyle Menendez testify. Thirty-six-year-old Leslie Hillings, also a postal worker, said the panel was unanimous in the belief that the brothers had been psychologically abused. "Sexual abuse? I don't think we'll ever know if that's true or not," she said. The abuse had never been part of the jury's deliberations. None of the five who spoke believed the brothers had been in fear for their lives the night of the murders.

Two floors below the courtroom, D.A. Gil Garcetti provided instant analysis by saying that most people around the country now believed that justice had been served. Garcetti was glad his office had not settled the case with a plea bargain. Both David Conn and the D.A. believed the convictions would hold up on appeal.

Outside, Leslie Abramson was the focus of the media. "On the good side, I would say that they're such considerable human beings that they're going to find a way to be productive," she said. "And in fact, some of the jurors were saying that, too."

Several of the jurors told me later they would not have voted for murder if they'd heard more of the family history during the guilt phase of the trial.

CHAPTER 59

LWOP AND A WEDDING

This is a tragedy that destroyed a family . . . all four of them had remarkable strengths as well as terrible weaknesses and it did not have to be. If at any time over the course of the lives of the four Menendez family members some effective person could have intervened, everyone would still be alive and well and healing. All four of them needed help. And there never was any help for this family.

—LESLIE ABRAMSON, the day before sentencing,
July 1, 1996

TWENTY-FOUR HOURS BEFORE ABC's *20/20* AIRED AN interview with the brothers in June 1996, an L.A. TV station reported that Lyle Menendez was trying to get married. "I have someone I love very much," Lyle told TV reporter Barbara Walters. "She is a saint to put up with all of this." Her name was Anna Eriksson. The media called her "Rapunzel" because of her long blonde hair. Anna and Lyle's secret plan to wed was hatched when Leslie Abramson's friend, Superior Court Judge Nancy Brown, agreed to marry the couple in her courtroom on Monday, July 1, the day before sentencing. Brown swore her staff to secrecy.

But the secret leaked, and all seven Los Angeles TV stations (plus CNN and the tabloid TV shows) had cameras waiting at the Criminal

Courts building. Shortly before 11 AM, the dark hallway was filled with blinding TV lights as Anna Eriksson walked off an elevator flanked by Abramson and Father Ken Deasy.

She was clearly dressed to be wed in a calf-length white linen short-sleeved suit with pearl earrings and matching white pumps. Her hip-length blonde hair was pinned up with a barrette. Eriksson appeared anxious and uncomfortable as reporters shouted questions at her.

Inside Department 126, Judge Brown was conducting routine criminal case hearings. The judge had signed transport papers to bring Lyle from jail so she could marry the couple during her lunch hour. But the order was revoked at the last minute by Supervising Judge John Reid, who said taxpayers shouldn't have to pay for driving the Menendez brothers the one mile between the jail and the court.

In sweltering 95-degree heat outside the courthouse, Leslie Abramson went on the attack. "This poor guy can't even get married," she said. "He loves this woman and she loves him, but they aren't allowed to have any romance." She couldn't "tolerate any more cruelty" to the brothers.

Southern California's unusually humid heat wave continued Tuesday morning. The courtroom buzzed as many of the regulars gathered for one last appearance in Department N in Van Nuys. There was an overflow crowd of reporters for the fifteen media seats. Many of them approached Anna Eriksson. She wasn't talking.

Jill Lansing sat in the front row with her seven-year-old daughter. Ally Lansing would say hi to Lyle during his frequent calls from jail to her mother. Also on hand were five jurors from the first trial. The courtroom became silent when the brothers walked in at 9:25 AM. Judge Weisberg quickly dismissed the defense motion for a new trial. "The rulings were the subject of extensive litigation, and the court is satisfied each ruling was correct," he declared. "There are no grounds for a new trial."

At four minutes past ten, Erik and Lyle Menendez were sentenced to life without the possibility of parole (LWOP), as the jury had recommended. "It is quite clear the defendants considered killing each parent separately," said the judge. "This was a decision made over several days. They considered killing one parent, or both, and decided on both and followed that decision." Weisberg called each murder a "separate act of violence." Because of that, he said, the prison terms would be consecutive. He added on twenty-five years to life for the conspiracy conviction.

Both brothers received credit for the 2,306 days they'd already been in jail. Neither displayed any reaction. Both Father Ken and Anna had their hands clasped in prayer. The consecutive sentences meant there would be little chance Erik and Lyle Menendez would ever step foot outside of prison.

In a firm, clear voice, each brother said they understood their right to appeal. At 10:13 AM, they were remanded to custody of the state Department of Corrections. Barry Levin touched Erik's arm gently. Lyle huddled briefly with Charles Gessler and Terri Towery. As he stood to return to the lock-up, Lyle smiled and waved at Anna Eriksson, whose eyes were filled with tears.

Terry Baralt, wearing a bright cranberry blazer, sobbed heavily as she left the courtroom. Les Zoeller approached her with words of comfort. Nearby, four jurors from the second trial made small talk. "I don't really feel badly for them," said juror Andrew Wolfberg. "I'm confident we did the right thing, and I can live with it."

Outside the courthouse, David Conn and Carol Najera approached an eager throng of media. Conn called the sentence "appropriate," since the brothers had committed a "heinous" offense. Was the outcome a personal victory? "It's very gratifying to see to it that justice was done in this case," said Conn. "Judge Weisberg did his job by keeping out trivial accusations."

"Child abuse is trivial?" asked a reporter.

"Child abuse was not kept out. They were permitted to present all the allegations concerning their parents," said Conn. "They kept out trivial accusations like how many times they had to swim laps in the pool."

Then, Les Zoeller approached the microphones and said he'd recommended the brothers be placed in separate prisons "because they conspired" to murder their parents. "I was concerned about them conspiring to commit crimes within the facility they're housed in."

"It's so outrageous," declared Leslie Abramson as she took center stage. "It never ends. The probation report indicates they are not a danger or threat to anyone." She accused the prosecution of being "exceedingly cruel" by making a "last-ditch attempt to inflict even greater punishment" on the brothers. "I don't hear them making statements like that about serial killers. About baby rapists. But because these are highly notorious defendants—thanks to you all—they think it's a free-for-all for inhumanity, and I've had enough of it."

The defense appeal would be based on thirty different issues. Abramson would not be formally involved but planned to spend substantial time helping the court-appointed appeal lawyers. The abuse evidence David Conn described as "trivial" had resulted in two hung juries in the first trial, she reminded everyone. Judge Weisberg had "eviscerated the defense" the second time around.

How did she feel now that the case was over? asked KTLA-TV's Warren Wilson.

"It will never be over for me because I will never sever my ties to Erik Menendez or Lyle Menendez or their family. We are a large extended family now. The legal part is over, but the human part continues." As she walked away, the diminutive attorney turned and waved like a homecoming queen: "That's it, guys. Bye-bye. Farewell."

As she sat in court at the sentencing, Abramson said she felt a "mist lift from my brain." Why not a proxy marriage? Both Anna and Lyle had already signed the license. They didn't even need a ceremony. But she knew Lyle wanted one. So she came up with a new secret plan to marry the couple that evening.

Just before 7:30 PM, Anna left her apartment wearing a T-shirt and sweatpants, with her hair tucked up under a baseball cap. The tabloid reporters camped outside her apartment didn't follow. Terry Baralt and I met in Abramson's office with Judge Brown. First Lyle and then Erik called in from their separate jail cells.

Fighting a cold, Judge Brown hoarsely whispered, "Lyle, are you ready?"

"I'm ready," came his voice from the speaker phone.

"Erik, you're there?"

"I'm here," replied the best man.

As she said the words "with this ring I thee wed," Judge Brown quickly improvised. "Now since you are not here in person in Leslie's office right now, I'm going to say that at some future date you are going to place the wedding band on Anna's ring finger, and you, Anna, will place the band on the ring finger of Lyle." Acting as proxy, Abramson placed a ring on Anna's hand. Then the couple addressed each other.

"Okay. I'm very nervous, but I gave it a lot of thought," said Lyle. "I think people who know us see us as so much happier since we came into each other's lives . . . I adore you."

"Lyle, I want you to know that you are my guardian angel," replied an emotional Anna. "I'll never leave your side, and I love you." After pronouncing the couple husband and wife, Judge Brown instructed them to "embrace each other in your mind's eye." Then the newlyweds made lip-smacking sounds into the speaker phone.

Terry Baralt leaned toward the phone and asked, "Hi, sweetie. How are you?"

"It's the best day of my life," declared Lyle.

Shortly before five o'clock the next morning, the brothers were placed on a bus and driven to North Kern State Prison, a classification center about fifty miles north of Bakersfield, California. For the first time in six years and four months, Erik and Lyle Menendez spent a night away from the Los Angeles County Men's Central Jail. Two months later, in September 1996, Erik and Lyle were woken up in the middle of the night and brought outside together. They were not allowed to say good-bye before they were placed in separate vans. Lyle still hoped they were going to the same prison. But when the vans reached a stoplight, they turned in different directions. It would be more than two decades before Erik and Lyle Menendez saw each other again.

CHAPTER 60

ERIK AND ANDY CANO — THE LETTER

And so the question has become: venal rich kids or tormented victims? Which are the Menendez brothers? Few seem to consider a third possibility: maybe both . . . The ultimate either-or decision belongs to the jurors in the Menendez case. But perhaps they will consider things that we overlook when we are turning public tragedy into social mythology: sometimes bad things happen to bad people, that it is possible to be both victim and victimizer.

—New York Times *columnist* ANNA QUINDLEN,
November 1993

ANDRES L. "ANDY" CANO WAS BORN ON JULY 14, 1973, IN New York City. He grew up in Puerto Rico and Princeton where he lived near his cousins, the Menendezes and the Baralts. The deaths of his aunt and uncle in August 1989 followed by the arrests of Erik and Lyle became an ongoing traumatic experience for this sensitive young man. He was under tremendous pressure to provide information for the defense team while being supportive of Erik. In the years following the trials, Andy saw a therapist to cope with his sadness. He blamed himself for not having gone to his parents to reveal the secrets confided to him by Erik. He was prescribed medication to help him sleep after he began to experience recurring nightmares over what happened.

In January 2003, Andy was visiting his father in Puerto Rico. On January 17, he flew to Costa Rica to visit friends. He had forgotten his sleeping medication, so he went to a pharmacy to replace it (there, most meds are sold over the counter). The pharmacist warned him to take no more than two of the pills in a single dose. But Andy hadn't slept in three days, so he took four. The next morning, January 18, 2003, his friends couldn't wake him up. At the age of twenty-nine, Andy Cano had passed away in his sleep. In my opinion, he was—along with Maria, Jose, Kitty, Lyle, and Erik—the sixth victim of the Menendez family's legacy of tragedy.

After Andy's death, more details of the emotional burden the young man had carried came to light. When Erik surrendered days after Lyle's arrest in March 1990, as related earlier in this text, he flew to Miami to meet his Aunt Marta and cousin Andy. The trio then boarded a plane to Los Angeles. During the five-hour flight, Erik and Andy went to the back of the plane. It has never been revealed before, but Erik confessed the murders to Andy during the several hours they were talking on the way to Los Angeles. Andy never told his mother about Erik's confession to him until many years later. (The brothers confessed to the rest of the family in the fall of 1990, six months after their arrests.)

"I imagined things, but I didn't want to know any specifics," Marta told me only very recently, recalling that fateful plane ride. She said that after talking with Andy for nearly three hours in the back of the empty coach cabin, Erik had come forward to sit by her. He leaned his head on her shoulder and cried softly—like a young boy with an emotional age between eight and ten years, as defense therapy experts described him at trial.

He said repeatedly that he "needed to tell [his aunt] something important."

"Whatever it is, I don't want to know," Marta told Erik.

She felt certain he wanted to confess some type of involvement in the deaths of his parents.

"I could not hear it then," she told me. "I did not want to have to lie later."

In December 2016, I was working as a consultant for Wolf Films, providing source material for the eight-hour limited series *Law & Order True Crime: The Menendez Murders* that aired on NBC in the fall of 2017. I spent several days with Marta Cano at her home in Florida, so I could fact check information for the TV series and this book. During my visit, Marta mentioned that she might have some letters Erik had written to Andy when they were teenagers. She thought they were in boxes of her son's possessions in her attic. She invited me to return at a later date to look for the letters.

In March 2018, I finally made a trip back from my home in California to visit Marta Cano in Florida. My peripatetic quest for the truth behind the killings of Jose and Kitty Menendez seemed to end exactly where it began. Nearly three decades earlier, I had met Lyle and Erik's Aunt Marta for the first time in her comfortable living room, surrounded by lush green tropical foliage. Now I sat in the identical spot at one end of her faded white leather couch with Mrs. Cano seated next to me on a matching love seat. The second time we'd met, in September 1989, two weeks after her brother's death, she took me to an evening mass at a charismatic church in the outskirts of West Palm Beach. The service had included a five-piece band and people speaking in tongues as they twirled around the church. The room in which I now sat with Marta had become a full-blown shrine, filled with lifelike statues of Catholic saints and various religious artifacts. Each one had a detailed story Marta enjoyed sharing with visitors.

We began to go though her son Andy's possessions. Within an hour, we found a handwritten letter from Erik to Andy from December 1988— eight months before the killings of Jose and Kitty. The letter began with Erik expressing his frustration that he hadn't been able to visit Andy and "some high school buddies" at Thanksgiving a few weeks earlier.

Erik wrote a routine account of a Christmas party the Menendezes had hosted for Jose's staff at LIVE Entertainment shortly after the family had moved into the mansion on Elm Drive. Erik said his mother had exchanged a giant Christmas tree three times until she found one she liked. The tree was professionally decorated. "Where's the Christmas spirit in that!!" he wrote.

Then, the letter abruptly changed in tone to a different, more serious subject. Erik's words are transcribed here unedited:

Mom isn't doing too good. It's like she's here physically but mentally, she's just like gone, if you know what I mean. She freaks out over nothing. I feel bad for her. I don't know why she puts up with dad's shit. At times, I wish I could talk to her about things, you now? Some day . . . Especially dad and I but the way she worships him and tells him everything, I so afraid she'll tell him whatever I say. I just can't risk it.

A subsequent paragraph contained this:

I've been trying to avoid dad. It's still happening Andy but its worse for me now. I can't explain it. He so overweight that I cant stand to see him. I never know when its going to happen and its driving me crazy. Every night I stay up thinking he might come in. I need to put it out of my mind. I know what you said before but I'm afraid. You just don't know dad like I do. He's crazy! hes warned me a hundred times about telling anyone. Especially Lyle. Am I a serious whimpus? I don't know I'll make it through this. I can handle it, Andy. I need to stop thinking about it.

As I read that paragraph aloud to Marta Cano, she became emotional. But just as suddenly, the letter took another abrupt turn to routine topics as Erik asked Andy, "How's your new girlfriend, Allison?" and said he heard Andy was "playing a lot of soccer." In closing, Erik wrote, "I think if I really do well in tennis, mom and dad will ease [off] some just in time for me to start college at Brown or Berekley [sic]. Anyway I'm playing great and we really like our new coach Mark [Heffernan—the first person the brothers would later call after returning home to encounter their parents' bodies on August 20]."

At the bottom of the page were simple drawings of a Christmas tree with the caption "for the Christmas's to be" and a snowman with the caption "for the Christmas's to come." "I miss you Love E," wrote Erik.

As we discussed the letter, Marta recalled her nephew's excitement at the prospect of attending Brown University. She had visited Beverly Hills in November 1988, shortly after the Menendezes moved into their elegant home on North Elm Drive. Erik was more upbeat and excited than Marta had seen him in years. He told her that he'd been accepted on a full tennis scholarship to Brown University in Providence, Rhode Island. It was only after the killings, Marta told me, that she accidentally discovered that Erik's joyous moment of finally being able to leave home never would have happened. While going through her brothers' files, Marta discovered Erik's application to Brown in a drawer in Jose's office. The paperwork was completely filled out but had never been mailed. Jose had no intention of letting Erik leave home.

Marta had returned to Beverly Hills in June 1989 to attend Erik's high school graduation. Her nephew's mood was 180 degrees opposite from that of the previous November. He was morose and cried frequently during his aunt's visit. He would not explain what was going on. Marta asked her brother why a cloud of gloom had descended on the family. Jose and Kitty exchanged an uncomfortable look before Jose replied, "I'd rather not talk about it right now."

A few days later, Marta went with Kitty to pick up Erik's graduation present—a shiny new white scooter. Kitty told her Erik would be using it to commute to nearby UCLA. Marta was surprised. Jose explained that he had arranged for Erik to enroll at the school a few miles away in Westwood. He told his sister that Erik was having "psychological problems," and that due to his dyslexia, Erik's homework needed to be supervised by Jose.

Jose bragged to Marta that he had made a large under-the-table cash donation to UCLA to get Erik accepted last-minute. Freshmen were required to live on campus, but Jose made a second donation and paid for the dorm room he was never going to allow his son to live in. "I need to be with him," Jose curtly told Marta.

Jose had waited until a few days before the high school year ended to tell Erik that he would not be allowed to leave home for Brown. Marta tried to comfort her emotional godson, who begged her to help him, still not saying why. "Aunt Marta, please!" he said through tears, "I really need to leave! Please help me."

When she returned to West Palm Beach, Marta told her son about her troubling visit with Erik. Andy immediately expressed deep concern about his cousin continuing to live at home. "That's not good for Erik," he told his mother. "He needs to be free." Like Erik, Andy did not reveal the underlying reason for his worry. "Erik needs to go away, leave the house and grow up," said Andy. But that never happened.

After discovering Erik's long-ago letter to his cousin, Marta and I called Cliff Gardner, the Berkeley attorney who handled the brothers' appeals. I had told him a few months earlier about the possibility of new evidence in the form of letters between Erik and Andy. Gardner checked with Leslie Abramson and Jill Lansing, who told him they had never heard of any letters like the one described above. It never came up during the trials or any evidence hearings. Gardner was extremely surprised to hear the details when I read him the letter over the phone. The letter—and the possibility of other letters between Erik and Andy, which the family is now searching for—might be able to qualify as new evidence that could lead to the filing of a new appeal and a new trial for Erik and Lyle Menendez.

EPILOGUE

In a final note, I want to express my personal thoughts about the Menendez family and the criminal case. There were dozens, if not hundreds, of family, friends, teachers, coaches, and others who were eyewitnesses to Jose and Kitty Menendez physically, verbally, and emotionally abusing their sons. The public and the media were hung up on answering one question: Had the brothers been sexually molested? The answer was never my sole criterion for evaluating the criminal case. I believe physical, verbal, and emotional abuse can be just as damaging to a small child as sexual molestation.

Prosecutors, defense attorneys, and the media have turned high-profile criminal cases into sporting events, with characters reduced to black hats and white hats. The reality is that real life is gray. Erik and Lyle Menendez were neither all bad nor all good. They grew up in an environment of spoiled rich kids in Princeton and Beverly Hills. The façade of the family living in the mansion in Beverly Hills was perfect on the outside. But behind the gates, a highly dysfunctional set of parents raised two troubled children. The real story of the Menendez brothers was never about two greedy rich kids killing Ozzie and Harriet in a hurry to inherit their parents' money.

The heart of the defense case in the first trial—the testimony of family, friends, and others who knew the Menendezes well—was not allowed into the second trial (or it was severely limited). That family history testimony was presented in the second trial's penalty phase. Several jurors told me after the penalty phase verdict they would not have voted for murder if they had heard the detailed family background during the guilt phase.

In the brothers' appeal in front of the Ninth Circuit Court of Appeals in 2005, Justice Alex Kozinski suggested there had been "collusion between the L.A. County District Attorney's office and Judge Stanley Weisberg" to convict the brothers in the second trial. The D.A.'s office was desperate for a conviction after the humiliating losses in the Rodney King and O.J. Simpson trials. Still, Justice Kozinski voted to turn down the Menendez appeal.

None of the jurors who voted for manslaughter were trying to set the brothers free in the first trial. Everybody agreed a crime had been committed; the question the juries couldn't agree on was the level of guilt. If Erik and Lyle had been convicted of manslaughter in the first trial, they might have received a sentence of twenty-two years—eleven years for each count.

As we approach the thirtieth anniversary of the killing of Jose and Kitty Menendez, it is time to reconsider the future of the brothers. The streets of California are not safer tonight because Erik and Lyle are locked up for life without parole.

In April 2018, the Menendez brothers were at last reunited in the same California prison. If the Menendez trial were held today in the social media world of 2018, it is likely there would have been a much different ending. We live in a modern era where there is much greater understanding of abuse and family violence than there was in 1993. Nothing should ever give you a free pass to kill your parents. But if there are mitigating circumstances—as there clearly were in this case—the resolution should be manslaughter and not murder. Because we live in a more enlightened, more compassionate society, the time has come to seriously consider releasing Erik and Lyle Menendez from prison.

—ROBERT RAND

EPILOGUE 2024

NEW EVIDENCE—
MENENDEZ + MENUDO +
THE HABEAS PETITION

Dear Lyle,

As you know, to me, family is the most important thing in my life and I hope it will be in yours. I can't tell you how much I miss being able to talk to my father. I miss him a lot. I have total trust in both you and Erik and I have no concerns about your future role in your country. Both you and Erik can make a difference. I believe you will!

Love, Dad

> —Excerpt of July 1987 letter from
> Jose Menendez to his son Lyle

BEVERLY HILLS—SEPTEMBER 1989

One month after the deaths of Jose and Kitty Menendez, Erik and Lyle's aunt, Marta Cano, was having trouble sleeping at the mansion on North Elm Drive in Beverly Hills. She was staying there with the brothers. A close friend in the church told Cano, a devout Catholic, that the spirits of her brother and sister-in-law were trapped inside the house. The solution? An exorcism type of ceremony, a healing mass, that was led by a priest from Washington, DC.

Erik, Aunt Marta, and cousin Henry Llanio gathered in the family room where the killings had taken place. Lyle was out of town on the East Coast. Before the mass started, Cano was instructed to open all the windows in the house a few inches.

"The priest raised his hands toward the ceiling before rapidly lowering them. As he did, the room was plunged into darkness—even though the morning sun was shining brightly outside," Marta Cano told me decades later. "Moments later, the priest raised his hands and sunlight poured [back] into the room."

Here's how Erik Menendez described the ceremony to Craig Cignarelli, his best friend who Beverly Hills Police had wear a wire during a dinner at Gladstone's in Malibu in November 1989:

> He [the priest] heals the soul, heals you, makes you feel better . . . This fucking healing man starts doing this thing in Latin . . . fuckin' A . . . I could not open my eyes, and I went through a trance for at least nine, ten minutes. I go, "What the hell happened?" But I went, I saw the swirling circle like this . . . and I'm going through this black hole with this . . . around me. I'm going through the center of it. Then, all of the sudden, I saw my parents. I saw the souls being lifted up to heaven. I saw my parents in heaven . . . they were standing, I was praying in front of them on my knees.

After the healing mass, Marta Cano never had any problems falling asleep again.

BEVERLY HILLS—OCTOBER 1989

On Sunday, October 22, 1989, I spent three and a half hours talking alone with Erik Menendez in the pale green living room at the Menendez mansion in Beverly Hills. It was two months after the killing of his parents and five months before he and his brother were arrested. Erik and Lyle were not publicly suspects at this point, and I had no reason to be suspicious of them. Erik and I sat at a card table across from a baby grand piano that held the sheet music for Don McLean's "American Pie," a song that had become a number one hit in 1972.

Erik spoke about his father with great reverence. When we were together with his brother two days earlier, Lyle had done most of the talking. Now, Erik was very chatty. He told me that Jose Menendez was "a stand-out athlete who excelled at swimming and football." At twelve, while playing with a cousin, Jose Enrique, as his family called him, accidentally burned down half the country club the Menendezes belonged to in Havana. Erik described the incident as Jose just being "mischievous" and said, "I think of all the things that I've done now, and they can't be as bad as what he did."

Erik told me that his parents met and fell in love at Southern Illinois University in the early 1960s. His grandparents were opposed to Jose marrying at nineteen, but Jose wrote a long letter to Maria and Pepin explaining he'd been on his own in a foreign country for three years so he was entitled to make adult decisions. In 1963, the newlyweds moved to New York City where Jose went to Queens College while working at the famous 21 Club in Manhattan. Jose sold encyclopedias door to door while Kitty worked on her master's degree with a goal of teaching. Her ambition of becoming a broadcaster had ended with the birth of Lyle in 1968. During this time, the couple was so poor they slept near the open stove to stay warm and bought a salty ham each week for five dollars that they'd stretch to last all week.

Erik said he didn't know how his parents' marriage was going when Jose was considering a new job offer in California in 1986. "I think they had a little rough spot right there, so it was a real big thing. My dad said, 'You can stay here [in Princeton] with Lyle and I'm going to take Erik and we'll go to Los Angeles.' And mom said, 'You're not taking Erik. No.' And she finally agreed to move out. The debate took place over two weeks between Jose and Kitty. He asked for a ridiculous amount of money [from LIVE Entertainment], and they accepted immediately. Jose thought he should've asked for more. My dad simply used logic on my mom and she agreed. My dad was sad a lot. And my mom was pretty depressed."

After arriving in California, Kitty told an old friend from New Jersey, "If I wanted to have a marriage at all, if I wanted to save my marriage, I had to make the move and give it all I had."

At one point when discussing his father's time at RCA Records, Erik mentioned the Latin boy band Menudo and the fast and loose culture in the record business. "There were all kinds of bribes as well. I remember this one man offered him a Ferrari. Help these people out and I'll give you a Ferrari. He asked Lyle and I, 'What should I do?' We didn't understand. It was Menudo. The person who was running Menudo wanted to buy my dad a Ferrari because things were going so well. They were making so much money, he wanted to express his gratitude for trusting them and giving them a chance.

"Lyle and I were like, 'why not?' We didn't understand why he shouldn't [take the Ferrari]. It wasn't like a bribe. My dad said, 'No, I can't do it. I don't want to take a chance on my reputation, even on a legitimate deal.' And this guy [Edgardo Díaz] wanted to take him to Italy to pick out cars. He had a Ferrari himself and my dad drove it. This guy wanted to do that for my dad, but my dad said no."

After our formal interview was over, Erik was energized from our conversation and offered to take me out to Calabasas to give me a tour of what he called his parents' "dream house," a large home on fourteen acres of land that Kitty and Jose were remodeling at the time of their deaths. Maria (the brothers' paternal grandmother), Erik, and I drove out to the San Fernando Valley from Beverly Hills, a forty-minute trip, in Erik's new tan Jeep. We spent another three hours together walking through the enormous country house. Nine days later, Erik made an appointment to see his therapist, Dr. Jerome Oziel, and confessed that he and Lyle had killed their parents.

LOS ANGELES—JULY 1992

I heard a rumor in the summer of 1992, a year before Erik and Lyle's first trial, that there was some sort of mysterious connection between Menudo and Jose Menendez when he was a top executive with RCA Records in the mid-1980s. Major acts were signed to RCA during the Menendez era, including the Eurythmics, Barry Manilow, and Grim

Reaper. Former RCA A&R executive Alan Grunblatt said, "Jose was initially hated at RCA. He didn't know the music business. He was a fish out of water. He was a business guy, not a music guy. The music business was still counterculture and Menendez was a straight arrow."

But Jose Menendez had a vision to expand RCA's Latin music roster by opening an office in Miami. Menendez wanted to cross Menudo over to the American market. Edgardo Díaz, a young Puerto Rican businessman, came up with a concept for a music group in 1977 that would remain eternally youthful, boys from twelve to fifteen years old who would each be retired at sixteen and replaced with a new twelve-year-old. Thus, Menudo was born. Six years later, Menendez signed the group, a pop act that was mostly lip-syncing their songs in live concerts, to a $30 million contract in November 1983, an astronomical sum for a band that had never recorded a single song in English.

NEW YORK CITY — JUNE 1993

In 1993, I began conducting phone interviews with John Peduto, an elderly man living in New York City who'd been Jose Menendez's personal assistant at Hertz and RCA. The boss and his secretary were extremely close over the years they worked together. Peduto told me he spent more time with Menendez than Jose did with his family.

Peduto never called his boss Jose. "It was always Mr. Menendez," he said, although he told me that shortly after Jose hired him, Menendez confided to him that after graduating from college he'd seriously considered changing his name because he didn't think that anybody with a Spanish surname would ever reach the top of the corporate ladder. Peduto answered all of Menendez's calls at the office. There was even a code name for Jose's New York mistress, Louise: Lou Miller. Kitty Menendez called the office several times a day to check in and go over Erik and Lyle's schedule.

I had a half dozen phone calls with John Peduto that began in June 1993 and continued for the next eighteen months. Each time we talked, Peduto would bring up that Jose Menendez was "obsessed with Menudo and the singer Ricky Martin." The first few calls, I didn't even note it. When he was still talking about Jose's focus on Menudo over all other RCA acts in our subsequent conversations, I began to pay more attention.

NEW YORK CITY—APRIL 1994

I met photojournalist Bolivar Arellano, a staff photographer at the *New York Post*, three months after the two mistrials were declared in January 1994 following the first Menendez trial. Arellano was a warm, friendly man in his early forties with a bushy moustache. He'd traveled with Menudo on tour for ten years, shooting thousands of photos. Arellano documented their rise from the barrios of Puerto Rico to sold-out concerts in São Paulo, Caracas, Manila, and Tokyo. At the height of the group's popularity in the 1980s, Bolivar and his wife, Bruni, opened Menuditis, a Menudo souvenir store in Manhattan. In addition to selling Menudo merchandise—posters, buttons, jeans, and watches—current and former members of the group made personal appearances at Menuditis to meet their passionate fans, mostly young girls.

The public unraveling of Menudo's squeaky-clean image began with a pot bust at Miami International Airport in November 1990 when a drug-sniffing beagle alerted customs officers to small amounts of marijuana that two members of the band had brought with them from Mexico City. The pot bust made front-page headlines in the *Miami Herald* and was heavily covered by Spanish language media everywhere. Not long after, an even bigger PR bomb was on track to explode when Arellano found out that the rumors he'd heard of Menudo members being sexually abused were true. Bolivar spoke privately with several boys in the group and asked them to point at photos of individual band members who'd been molested.

On May 22, 1991, the *New York Daily News* ran the front-page headline "Menudo Sex Shocker: Teen rock idols abused by their promoter, photog charges." *Daily News* columnist Juan González wrote, "Menudo, the Latino predecessor of New Kids on the Block, has been rocked by allegations of sex, drug, and financial scandal. The accusations include charges that several of the boys, under 16 at the time, were sexually abused and regularly plied with alcohol and drugs by the three men who made millions off them."

The *Daily News* article marked a significant turning point in public interest in the Menudo story. A few weeks before the *Daily News* column came out, Bolivar Arellano had held a news conference in New York City to announce that nine of the twenty-seven members of Menudo had been sexually molested. But only five journalists showed up. No TV news cameras. No mainstream reporters. Arellano was crushed. So he went to Puerto Rico where he appeared on May 9 on *Controversial*, a highly rated live TV talk show hosted by investigative reporter Carmen Jovet, a woman who González described as "a combination of Bob Woodward and Phil Donahue." Arellano repeated his accusations of sexual abuse. But this time, relatives and friends of former Menudo members backed him up.

"They had signed sworn, notarized statements," González wrote. "They said they saw [Edgardo] Díaz in bed on three occasions with members of Menudo." One of the eyewitnesses was twenty-year-old Raúl Reyes, the brother of Ray Reyes, a popular former Menudo singer. He said he'd seen Díaz sleeping in bed naked with a Menudo member in Orlando. Another friend of the group members said he'd been threatened before appearing on the TV show. He said he'd participated in drug and sex parties with several men who managed the band, including Edgardo Díaz.

Orlando Lopez, a Menudo attorney, showed up at Jovet's studio with three police officers to arrest Arellano for "defamation of character," but he was not taken into custody. However, after a second Jovet show on the scandal a week later, fifteen police officers arrived at the studio and arrested Bolivar Arellano. The TV station bailed him out. Now, it was Arellano's word against three powerful and politically connected businessmen: Edgardo Díaz, Orlando Lopez, and Jose Antonio Jimenenz, the president of Padosa, Menudo's Panama-based holding company. They'd all refused to appear on Jovet's program.

But the day after Jovet's second show, Edgardo Díaz appeared on a different station in San Juan and denied he'd ever been involved in any inappropriate behavior with any Menudo members. "These are kids who had serious emotional problems," Díaz said. "All the problems that are found in our society were also found in Menudo."

When I met Bolivar Arellano in 1994, he was eager to share his story of what happened when he tried to expose his investigation of Menudo three years earlier. He recommended that I travel to Puerto Rico to continue my reporting.

SAN JUAN—JANUARY 1995

I wanted to dig deeper into Jose Menendez's relationship with Menudo, but none of the former members of the band would speak to me on the record. One of the first people who would talk was investigative reporter Carmen Jovet. Jovet told me she'd done ten shows about Menudo for Channel 7 in San Juan in 1991, including the programs where Bolivar Arellano appeared. Jovet's interest in Menudo began when she received a phone call from a former Menudo member.

"Menudo was like a sect or cult. They all lived in a mansion where Edgardo Díaz would take care of them. Many of the boys were from troubled homes," Jovet told me. "Edgardo wouldn't force the kids to have sex. He'd beg them by getting emotional if they turned him down. If they freaked out, he'd beg their forgiveness. If they balked, he'd move on to the next one."

During one of her show's episodes about Menudo, a young man in his early twenties appeared behind a screen to protect his identity and said that he'd "been taken to a party with record company executives to have sex with them." The man said there was wild partying—including orgies—during a Menudo tour in Brazil in the 1980s. "The boys didn't consider themselves to be victims at the time because they voluntarily went along with everything," Jovet said.

In July 1991, a popular Miami-based, Spanish-language TV talk show hosted by Cristina Saralegui on the Univision network broadcast two programs about the Menudo scandal. *El Show de Cristina* aired on six hundred stations in fifteen countries. In the two months since Bolivar Arellano made his accusations in the *New York Daily News* and appeared on Carmen Jovet's program in Puerto Rico, the Menudo story was gaining momentum.

The panel on *El Show de Cristina* included Edgardo Díaz; former Menudo member Ralphy Rodríguez and his father; Ramon Acevedo, the father of former Menudo member Ray Acevedo Jr.; Orlando Lopez, Menudo's lawyer; and Soraya Zambrano, the director of *TV y Novelas*, a popular Mexican magazine that had published several investigative stories about the Menudo scandal. Five new members of Menudo—including Ash Ruiz—were introduced in the audience.

The most dramatic moment of the show came in a confrontation between Ralphy Rodríguez and Edgardo Díaz:

> RALPHY RODRÍGUEZ: When we were in Argentina on a farm, I didn't have a room because all the rooms were taken. I had a bed next to Edgardo's bedroom. It was a second-floor room and you had to go up the stairs and it was a balcony and a room only. When it was time to go to sleep, we had all gotten ready to go to bed. I was in my bed ready to go to sleep. And he [Edgardo Díaz] went upstairs with one of the boys to his room.
>
> EDGARDO DÍAZ: What boy?
>
> RALPHY: I'm not going to say his name.
>
> EDGARDO: Well . . .
>
> RALPHY: (the audio is bleeped out as Ralphy says the name of a Menudo member)
>
> EDGARDO: Look, all the names you are saying here are going to be bleeped out. They're not going to go on air because they are all underaged.
>
> RALPHY: Correct.
>
> EDGARDO: Look . . . look, you know what?
>
> RALPHY: No, let me finish.
>
> EDGARDO: He just mentioned a famous name.
>
> RALPHY: Are you going to let me finish?
>
> CRISTINA: Of course he's going to finish. Let him finish.
>
> RALPHY: I was laying down in my bed like this. The door here was on my left. He came up with the boy. It was time to sleep. What did he have to do in Edgardo's room? He

entered with Edgardo, close[d] the door, and turn[ed] on the radio.

EDGARDO: My room didn't have a radio.

RALPHY: I was like this laying down and couldn't sleep because of the radio. When I opened the door to say, "Hey Edgardo, lower your radio a little," I saw that he was with the boy.

CRISTINA: [Where?] was he?

RALPHY: The boy was behind him.

People watching the TV show at home never learned the boy's name because it was bleeped out when the episode aired. But the audience in the studio did hear the name of the underage Menudo member who Ralphy Rodríguez identified.

In June 1993, six weeks before the first Menendez trial started, Sgt. Tom Edmonds of the Beverly Hills Police Department called Darrin McGillis, a promoter who worked with Menudo in San Juan. According to McGillis, Edmonds was trying to find Edgardo Díaz or former members of the group. McGillis said Edmonds told him the Menendez brothers were going to testify that they were molested by their father. Edmonds was looking for people who could say something positive about Jose Menendez.

MEXICO CITY—DECEMBER 1993

In the fall of 1993, I was extremely busy covering the first Menendez trial. But I began to hear more rumors about a connection between Jose Menendez and Menudo, including many focused on Ricky Martin. It would be six years before Martin became an international superstar with the release of the song "Livin' la Vida Loca" in 1999. A Latin music artist unknown in the United States, Ricky Martin was twenty-one and hoping to cross over to the American market with a small part on the TV soap opera *General Hospital*. When I contacted Martin's music manager, Ricardo Cordero, in Puerto Rico, I had nothing concrete—just a hunch—but I was able to convince Cordero into letting me interview

Martin by saying I was about to publish a story in the *Miami Herald* about Jose Menendez and Ricky Martin when he was a member of Menudo. After weeks of negotiating, Cordero agreed to let me meet Martin in Mexico.

By the time I flew to Mexico City, it was early December 1993, the closing days of the first Menendez brothers' trial. I had one of the twelve reserved seats in the tiny courtroom in Van Nuys, about twenty miles northwest of downtown Los Angeles. Two hundred other media members were watching the Court TV video feed of the trial in a building a block away. I was twenty feet away when Lyle and Erik Menendez gave their dramatic, emotional testimony about how they had killed their life-long abusers, their parents.

After Martin had made and canceled several appointments with me, we finally met up on my third day in Mexico City. Just after two in the afternoon, Ricky walked in with a posse of half a dozen friends, including Jose Luis Vega, the choreographer and stylist for Menudo, who was known by his nickname "Joselo." Over the next two and a half hours, Martin told me about his time performing in Menudo and several encounters he had with Jose Menendez in California. Near the end of the interview, Ricky declared that everything he'd just told me was "off the record." Normally, when somebody speaks with a reporter, ground rules are set in advance, which sometimes includes topics that will not be discussed.

For twenty minutes, I tried to change his mind, but Martin refused. He said if the Menendez attorneys attempted to force him to come to Los Angeles, he would deny he knew anything about Jose Menendez. Six years later in 1999, an American tabloid published a cover story with the headline "Ricky Martin Sex Attack Shocker—Link to Menendez killers probed by cops." The inside story headline shouted, "Was Ricky Martin victim of sex attack by Menendez father?" I was not the source or involved with that story in any way. The narrative had little relation to anything Ricky Martin told me in 1993. Martin later denied to *Page Six* at the *New York Post* that he had ever met Jose Menendez; that was untrue based on photos that later surfaced of Jose Menendez with Martin, other members of Menudo, and Edgardo Díaz. Martin has never publicly said anything negative about his time in Menudo. In more than thirty years, I've never revealed what Ricky told me that afternoon in Mexico City. It's his personal decision if he ever wants to publicly talk about our interview.

In 2004, Martin created the Ricky Martin Foundation, a charity that fights against the sex trafficking of minors and supports adults who were molested as children. In late February 2024, Ricky Martin was interviewed for an in-depth story that appeared in *GQ* magazine:

> A recent documentary explored the dark side of Menudo, with some members accusing the band's adult creator of inappropriate behavior, including sexual abuse, though Martin says that was not his experience. "I feel horrible. I don't know what they went through. It's not my case," he says. He says he drew strength from the challenges of those years. "Every phase gave me something that lifted me and didn't break me."

In 1985, Papo Gely was a talented musician in his thirties with long, curly hair who was hired to transform Menudo into a legitimate performing group from what had previously been a band that lip-synced along to prerecorded audio during their concerts. I spoke to Gely in 1995 and in the years since about his time with the band, and he confirmed that rumors were swirling about Menudo and Díaz for many years. We met in 1995 in San Juan but are still in contact today.

Jose Menendez went on tour with Menudo for three weeks in Brazil in the fall of 1985. A photo in this book shows Menendez on stage at Estádio do Morumbi in São Paulo, Brazil, at a sold-out concert with 100,000 fans on September 15, 1985. Insiders in the music industry have told me that the head of a major record label never goes on the road with one act for three weeks. According to several people who were working on that tour, some of the boys in Menudo were dressed in women's clothes and makeup and given drugs and alcohol at afterparties following the concerts. One man who worked on the tour told me that Jose Menendez was "like everyone else—partying their ass off. Brazil is a very sexual place."

SAN JUAN—APRIL 1995

Once he began touring with Menudo, Papo Gely witnessed a number of strange things about the band. In theory, four kids were to be divided into two rooms. The fifth boy—usually the youngest—was assigned to stay in a room with Jose Luis Vega, Menudo's choreographer. In reality, Vega would be by himself, and Edgardo Díaz would have the newest member of the band stay in his room.

"Edgardo would always have a kid rooming with him," Gely said. "There were many times they'd all be hanging out together in Edgardo's room and it wasn't strange for them to be not naked, but not fully dressed—in their underwear. I didn't see anything sexual, but it didn't look normal."

Gely told me Edgardo Díaz always had the kids very close to him. "He would be very physical in ways that I could see a relative being that close, but it was kind of shocking—like having kids sit on his lap all the time. You could see a father doing this with his son, but it would look very strange," Gely said. "Caresses in their hair or putting his arm across their shoulder, holding them in an embrace position. It looked strange to me—out of the normal. I would never behave like that with somebody else's kids."

Gely was told by an insider that the fringe benefits of working with Menudo were the Menudo fans, mostly underage girls around twelve or thirteen. "He was bragging about it," Gely said. "He told me he liked young girls, and the Menudo thing was the perfect set up for picking up little girls. He offered them an opportunity to go backstage to meet the boys in Menudo. But then he'd make sexual advances on them." The insider carried around a briefcase allegedly containing Polaroid photos he'd shot of his conquests undressed or naked. The insider tried to show the photos to Gely, but Gely refused to look at them.

Gely noticed that Edgardo would frequently bring his personal friends, mostly adult men, to meet with the boys in Menudo backstage or at the band's hotel. "It wouldn't be uncommon that these friends would take the kids out. The kids were permitted to go out—either one by one or a couple of them together," Gely said. "We'd be at the hotel and some of Edgardo's friends would come by to pick up one kid or another and take them out for dinner. I saw that happen. I didn't want to think about what might be going on."

Papo Gely thought the FBI or law enforcement in Puerto Rico would investigate the molestation accusations. "I thought the public would realize there was something very wrong going on that was worth investigating. But nothing happened and Edgardo Díaz went on as usual," Gely told me in 1995. In spite of the rumors that circulated among journalists I spoke to, Menudo was the pride of Puerto Rico. The band's success helped promote the island's tourism business. Nobody in the Puerto Rican government wanted to investigate the group or Edgardo Díaz, who made large contributions to political parties. Most of the media had no interest in running negative Menudo stories because they'd be cut off from access to the band.

LOS ANGELES—2020 TO 2023

In October 2020, Amazon Prime Video released a fifteen-episode scripted series titled *Súbete a Mi Moto*, about the history of Menudo, on their Spanish-language channel. Edgardo Díaz is not listed on the show's official credits on IMDb, but the story is told from his point of view through one of the lead characters portrayed by an actor. Within days after its premiere, several former members of Menudo started appearing in interviews on Spanish-language media in the United States and around the world to criticize the series as not being an honest depiction of Menudo's story. I saw a new opportunity to reopen my Menudo reporting and the connection of the boy band to Jose Menendez. I called Nery Ynclan, a Pulitzer Prize–winning journalist and former colleague I had worked with at WPLG-TV in Miami. Not only is Nery an outstanding reporter with many years of network news producing experience, but she is also fluent in Spanish, which I am not. That phone call was the start of the development of *Menendez + Menudo: Boys Betrayed*, a three-episode documentary that premiered on Peacock, NBC's streaming service, in May 2023.

From late 2020 to 2022, Nery and I went down many rabbit holes as we reached out to more than one hundred people who were in Menudo, worked closely with the band, or were an integral part of the Menendez brothers' case. Starting with my original reporting and sources from the 1990s, we expanded to others who knew inside information. Among the people Nery met was former Menudo member Roy Rosselló, who told her he'd been molested by Edgardo Díaz throughout his time in Menudo.

They'd been talking for over a year when Roy dropped a bombshell.

"You know I know that guy from RCA Records who was killed by his sons," Roy said one afternoon.

"What guy?" Nery asked.

"Jose Menendez," replied Roy.

At first the details came out slowly, similar to how Erik Menendez first started confiding over many months to Dr. Bill Vicary about the molestation by his father in the Menendez case. Vicary, an experienced forensic psychiatrist, told me you can tell who's faking a story because the people making it up start telling you details on the first day you talk to them. With Erik Menendez, Vicary said it was "like pulling teeth" to get Erik to reveal even the tiniest bit of information. Nery had a similar experience with Roy. Little by little, he began to reveal what had happened to him.

One day in New York City in the fall of 1983, Edgardo Díaz told Roy he needed to do "something great for Menudo. That I was going to do a favor for him and Menudo as well." Even though they had never recorded anything in English, RCA Records signed Menudo to a $30 million contract for twelve albums. (The boys in the band and their families were told it was a $5 million deal.) Díaz excitedly told Rosselló they were going to have dinner at Jose Menendez's house in New Jersey. The first time Roy met the record executive was in the back seat of a limousine in Manhattan with Díaz. Roy remembers Menendez "gave [me] a look like he wanted to devour me."

An hour later, the trio arrived at the Menendez home in Princeton, New Jersey. Roy remembers seeing young Erik and Lyle just after he walked in. The brothers appeared to be "sad and quiet." There was something off about the Menendez family. Jose Menendez poured thirteen-year-old Roy a full glass of wine and urged him to "drink all of it because it's very expensive wine." Within minutes, Roy began to feel "tired and heavy and couldn't move anymore." Roy has a memory of being dragged upstairs to a bedroom. The next thing he remembered was waking up in Edgardo Díaz's room at Menudo's hotel in New York City. Roy was in pain for a week. The pain was unbearable. Díaz told him to "relax—it will heal soon."

"I understand the Menendez brothers' rage and hatred because I was in the same situation," Roy said. "I wanted to kill Edgardo Díaz."

In May 2021, Nery Ynclan and I had gone along with Bolivar Arellano and a camera crew to San Juan for the funeral of former Menudo star Ray Reyes. Reyes had died unexpectedly at the age of fifty-one from a heart attack. There were rumors that Edgardo Díaz had molested Reyes when he was in Menudo. The memorial was a giant Menudo reunion with former members from different generations of the band along with fans and reporters. Draco Rosa, Ricky Melendez, René Farrait, and Johnny Lozada were some of the former Menudo members who came to mourn Reyes's passing.

Out of the corner of my eye, I thought I spotted Edgardo Díaz, but I wasn't sure since everybody was wearing masks because of the COVID-19 pandemic. Also, this man looked younger than I would've expected of Díaz, a man in his mid-seventies. But it was Edgardo Díaz. Nery quickly swung into action and began peppering Díaz with questions. Fortunately for us, Díaz was parked several blocks away and the camera crew recorded everything as we walked. On the other side of Díaz across from Nery was an entertainment reporter from Miami. Díaz ignored all of Nery's questions but quickly answered when the other reporter asked, "Edgardo—you've done so much for the children of Puerto Rico. Tell us about that?"

Our documentary was focused on Roy Rosselló's search for justice as he traveled around the country meeting with friends and colleagues from his past. In New York City, Roy saw Bolivar Arellano for the first time in thirty years. Arellano had been on a mission for more than three decades to expose the nefarious secrets of Menudo. Papo Gely later told

Roy he knew the youngest band member was always staying in Edgardo Díaz's room and they would come downstairs for breakfast together in the morning.

The most heartbreaking moment of the docuseries was when Roy met with Raúl Reyes, the brother of Ray Reyes. Raúl was a backup singer and sometimes toured with Menudo in the 1980s. He was hoping to become a member of the group, but his brother discouraged him. One morning, Raúl saw Rosselló and Díaz asleep, naked in bed together, at the Menudo mansion in Orlando. The Menudo members were too young to understand that a fourteen-year-old boy could not be having a consensual relationship with a man in his thirties. In a poignant scene, Raúl Reyes brought out a small vase with his brother's ashes and apologized to Roy as the two men hugged.

"We misjudged you," Reyes said to Roy. "We didn't know how to properly interpret the situation. We feared what our family and the fans would think. We didn't know if they would believe us. We were kids. I know that you were a victim."

Ray had told his younger brother, "this is why I don't want you to be a part of Menudo."

Ray Reyes recorded an audiotape shortly before he died. "Edgardo was a very sick pedophile and his [own] mother knew it. Imagine you're all alone because you don't have your family around. If my dad had ever found out, he would've killed him," said Ray on the tape. "There are so many stories, but it's not about me, it's about them. But my stories are there, too."

Raúl Reyes told us he could feel something was happening with his brother. "These past few years, it was tearing him apart. He needed to tell the truth about what happened in Menudo," Reyes said. "That desperation may have led to his death."

When we filmed in Los Angeles, Roy Rosselló told me, "That's the rapist. That's the pedophile," as he pointed to a photo of Jose Menendez with Edgardo Díaz and Menudo holding gold records. I told Roy I knew there was somebody out there for thirty years who knew the secrets I was trying to uncover. As I put my arm around his shoulder, I said I now knew that person's name.

Later, I interviewed both Erik and Lyle Menendez over the phone for the documentary. (Cameras are not allowed in California prisons.) Erik said he remembered meeting Roy in the 1980s. Both brothers had gone to parties after Menudo concerts in New York. Also, the band came to the Menendez home in New Jersey for barbecues. "I specifically remember my dad saying he wanted to go off with one of the boys and talk to him alone. And they went off into the house upstairs," Erik told me. "My dad was one of the guys choosing and selecting the new members of the group because the group members would cycle out. He'd get very excited about selecting new boys that would come in to the band."

To audition for Menudo, the prospective new members' parents would drop off their young sons at the Puerto Rican Menudo estate on a Thursday afternoon and pick them up Monday night. The Menudo mansion in San Juan was like Michael Jackson's Neverland Ranch, with games, animals, and a swimming pool.

When I told Erik about Roy, he said, "I feel horrible. It's sad to know that there was another victim of my father. No one should have been forced to endure rape or molestation at the hands of my father. I don't know how many more victims there are. I suspect that there are more. I always hoped that one day the truth about my dad, what he did, the rape, the molestation, would come out. And that I would be believed. And for so long, people just refused to believe it. But I never wished for it to come out like this. The result of trauma that another child has suffered. And it makes me very sad."

Nery Ynclan and I remain hopeful that other former members of Menudo will come forward and reveal what happened when they were in the group.

———————

Twenty-four hours after the documentary was released in May 2023, appellate lawyers Cliff Gardner and Mark Geragos filed a writ of habeas corpus to vacate the Menendez brothers' 1996 murder convictions. The court filing was based on new evidence that was not part of the trials in the 1990s. It included Roy Rosselló's account of being raped by Jose Menendez as well as a separate sexual assault by Menendez at a

Menudo concert at Radio City Music Hall in the 1980s. The habeas petition also featured the 1988 letter Erik Menendez wrote to cousin Andy Cano complaining about the ongoing abuse by his father that was first reported on when this book was originally published in 2018.

As of April 2024, the Los Angeles County District Attorney's office is reviewing the Menendez habeas petition. A Superior Court judge assigned to the case could hold evidence hearings with witnesses. The judge has asked the D.A.'s office whether the new evidence could have been discovered during the trials in the 1990s and if prosecutors believe the letter Erik wrote to Andy Cano would've been admissible.

"If the state painted a false picture of Jose Menendez, if in fact Roy is credible when he maintains that Jose raped him, then the sexual abuse allegations made by Erik and Lyle look very different," appellate attorney Cliff Gardner told us in the documentary. "There's now a credible witness supporting them." Cliff Gardner doesn't want the Menendez brothers to have any contact with Roy since he might become a witness in their case.

"Life without parole is a death sentence. It shouldn't have happened, and if the trial had been an honest trial, it would not have been," Joan VanderMolen, Kitty Menendez's ninety-two-year-old sister, told us. "It hurts me. They shouldn't be where they are. They should be out in the world enjoying life. And they didn't get a chance to do that. I would love to see that happen for them."

As the promos for Dick Wolf's 2017 NBC series *Law & Order True Crime: The Menendez Murders* asked, the question was always, "Why?"

Edgardo Díaz had never been investigated or charged with breaking any laws connected to Menudo until the LAPD opened a criminal investigation after Roy Rosselló made a criminal complaint against him on November 8, 2022. Díaz has always denied all allegations that have been made against him over the years since he created Menudo in 1977.

R.J. DONOVAN CORRECTIONAL FACILITY, OTAY MESA, CA—MAY 2023

Lyle and Erik Menendez have been incarcerated for more than thirty-four years since I met them at the Menendez mansion in Beverly Hills. They are very different people than the college-aged young men I met in October 1989. Both brothers have a positive, upbeat attitude that is a constant presence throughout all of our visits and phone calls, even when our discussions turn serious. Both Erik and Lyle have repeatedly expressed their remorse in media interviews about the family tragedy that consumed their family. The Menendez brothers have spent more than half of their lives in custody since their arrest in March 1990.

They've chosen to be of service to those around them, helping other incarcerated men who are processing their own childhoods. Lyle is head of the Donovan inmate government as he was at his previous facility, Mule Creek, for fifteen years. Erik created a hospice program for inmates and teaches four classes a week, including a victim impact course. Both brothers are enrolled in college classes. Erik is the lead painter of an enormous mural to beautify Donovan, a program created by both brothers that includes landscaping the prison yard.

Lyle Menendez has told me that the brothers have accepted that this is their life, that they will never be released from prison. "We've seen too many friends get their hopes up with appeal filings and commutation requests. They've marked the days off on calendars," he said. "In the end, they are turned down and sadly sink into a deep depression."

Lyle was overwhelmed when he learned that Roy Rosselló had come forward. "We heard rumors that something might have happened with Menudo through the years," he said. "It's a remarkable thing that it's happening so many decades later. I don't know what brought him to this point in his life where he felt a need to talk about it. But a lot of victims eventually get there. And it's usually later in life." Roy Rosselló's testimony could have made a huge difference for the Menendez brothers if he had appeared at their trials in the 1990s.

Erik Menendez believes the truth about the case will come out in the end. "That's my hope," he has told me. "I want healing for my family as well as the other boys who were in Menudo."

"It's very validating for me on a personal level," Lyle said. "What it means on a legal level, I don't know. I'm pretty discouraged by the system at this point. I live my life working with other victims of abuse of which there are a huge number in here. So I try to find purpose in what happened to me and the suffering of what I went through and my brother went through. But I don't look too far beyond the prison walls with it."

In the end, a decision on the Menendez habeas petition will be decided by a judge.

"Hopefully Roy's testimony will make a difference," said Lyle. "You would think in a fair world that it would. Whether we live in that fair world really, I guess we'll find out."

———————

On February 22, 2024, I traveled from Los Angeles to Donovan prison with Esther Reyes, the showrunner and director of our docuseries *Menendez + Menudo: Boys Betrayed*. Our purpose was to meet Lieutenant Adam Garvey, the press information officer at RJD with whom I'd been talking for several months. Garvey had invited us to see a large mural that he'd sent me several photos of before. The mural project and a garden area that was going to be built in the center of Echo Yard had been underway for three years. Two of the leaders of the beautification project are Lyle and Erik Menendez. Erik, who is a talented artist, is one of the lead painters. A dozen other inmates have been working alongside the Menendez brothers. Prison officials have considered making a documentary about the creation of the enormous mural, which circles the previously gray concrete walls of Echo Yard with various colorful scenes from throughout California. All of the paint and materials have been donated to the prison from private sources.

The photos had given us no idea of how large the mural really was. It was spectacular. Lt. Garvey, along with Captain Sherman Rutledge from RJD, told us how the mural had a positive impact on the moods of both the prisoners and the staff at Donovan. After we saw the mural, Garvey and Rutledge showed us some of the experimental enrichment programs that are underway at the facility. In one large area, classes were taking place for inmates who are working on college degrees through UC Irvine. In another room, we saw dogs that were being trained at Donovan in what's called the POOCH Program (which is made possible with Guide Dogs of America/Tender Loving Canines, in partnership with RJD). The program trains prisoners to provide a safe, clean, and humane environment for the care, custody, training, and control of dogs. The trained dogs help people with PTSD and autism, in addition to being part of the participants' rehabilitation.

At one point, Lt. Garvey excused himself as we talked with an inmate in the dog training room. Several minutes later, Garvey opened the door and walked in with Erik and Lyle Menendez. I've visited Lyle at Mule Creek and Donovan, but it was the first time any journalist had seen the two brothers together in the twenty-eight years since they were sentenced to life without parole in July 1996. Both brothers had big smiles on their faces. We were all emotional as we hugged each other and laughed during our twenty-minute visit together.

Erik Menendez thanked Esther, my reporting partner Nery Ynclan, and me for the new evidence we revealed in our documentary that is the foundation of their May 2023 habeas petition to vacate their 1996 convictions. Lyle showed us charts and talked about what needs to be done to complete the mural and green space project. Erik and Lyle both work out daily, which was obvious seeing them in person.

The brothers have spent more than thirty-four years incarcerated since their arrest in March 1990—more than half their lives. The young college-aged guys I met when they were eighteen and twenty-one in October 1989 were now middle-aged men of fifty-three and fifty-six. If they do get out, I believe they will both devote their lives to helping other people as they are already doing in their inmate community.

ACKNOWLEDGMENTS

On Monday morning, August 21, 1989, I received a call from my long-time friend Steven Apple, the editor of *Video Insider* magazine, telling me that Jose and Kitty Menendez had been killed in their home in Beverly Hills, California. Steve and I had just been together at the Video Software Dealers Association annual trade show, where I had been reporting a story about the home video business for *Inside Story*, a local Miami TV magazine show. The reason you are holding this book in your hands is because of that phone call from Steve Apple.

Ten days later, I learned that Jose Menendez had a sister, Marta Menendez Cano, who lived in Palm Beach County, Florida. I had been doing freelance writing for two years at *Tropic*, the Sunday magazine of the *Miami Herald*. I called Mrs. Cano and she immediately invited me to her home—about ninety minutes north of Miami. We spent four hours together that day as she shared the fascinating story of the Menendez family's immigrant saga from Spain to Cuba and then to the States. The next morning, I met with Tom Shroder, the editor of *Tropic*, at the *Herald* newsroom overlooking Biscayne Bay. I told Tom we didn't know much about the murder investigation but suggested Jose Menendez's rags-to-riches story ending in a terrible tragedy would make an interesting biography to pursue.

I owe my writing career to Tom Shroder and Gene Weingarten, the two editors at *Tropic* who took a chance on me—a never-before-published wannabe writer who had worked in TV news but never in print. The *Herald* paid for me to travel to L.A. in the fall of 1989 to interview people who worked with Jose Menendez, as well as Erik and Lyle Menendez themselves—the grieving sons of the murdered couple who were not suspects publicly. On Christmas Eve 1989, almost four months to the day after Jose and Kitty Menendez were killed, the *Miami Herald* published the first speculation that the Menendez brothers were being considered as possible suspects. It was two months and two weeks before Erik and Lyle were arrested.

Nearly a year later, I was introduced to Stephen Randall, the L.A.-based articles editor for *Playboy* magazine. Randall had read my book proposal that was about to be shopped to major publishers. Hugh M. Hefner had a personal interest in the story—the magazine had assigned three of their regular journalists to write Menendez stories but Hef didn't like any of them, because they had no inside information as I did. Good news and bad news soon followed—*Playboy* wanted me to write a 7,000-word story about the case, but they wanted to rush it into their next issue, March 1991, on a deadline of only twelve days. I was only halfway through the list of what they wanted to include when I realized my word count was 5,000 words over the assignment. They told me to just keep writing and they would edit later. My first draft was 22,000 words—roughly 20 percent of the length of this book. The final article ran 14,000 words. I was told it was the longest article *Playboy* had ever run. Hef was really into the story.

Book agent David Vigliano repped me in my original deal for a contract with Simon and Schuster. Arthur Jay Harris helped me from the first week after the arrests with reporting, research, and the incredibly smart idea to begin selling articles to magazines all over the world.

I am grateful to Erik and Lyle Menendez; their aunts Marta Cano, Terry Baralt, and Joan VanderMolen; as well as many members of the Menendez and Andersen families—including cousins Henry Llanio and Diane VanderMolen, who spent unlimited time to fill me in on the history and dynamics of their families. Defense team members Jill Lansing, Michael Burt, Leslie Abramson, and Marcia Morrissey were invaluable in letting me backstage as the defense was preparing for the first trial in July 1993. Defense attorneys Charles Gessler, Terri Towery, and Barry Levin continued helping me in the second trial. Defense therapist Dr. William Vicary and I became personal friends when we went on the TV talk show circuit after the first trial in the spring of 1994. Dr. Stuart

Hart was one of the defense therapy experts who helped me understand the reality of this case—a completely different story than the false "greedy rich kids" narrative being told by the mainstream media.

Dominick Dunne, the iconic writer for *Vanity Fair*, and I agreed on NOTHING about the case, but we became personal friends who sat next to each other every day for six months in the first trial. Court TV reporter Terry Moran invited Dunne and me to debate the case regularly during Court TV's extraordinary gavel-to-gavel coverage of the first trial. Moran—along with the AP's legendary trial reporter Linda Deutsch—was the most professional and fairest of all the journalists covering the trial.

This book was put on hold for a number of years when I began taking care of my elderly mother, Irene Betty Rand Zurier, for the last fifteen years of her life. Then, in July 2016, I was hired by Wolf Films as a consultant on their eight-hour limited series *Law & Order True Crime: The Menendez Murders*. Thank you Dick Wolf, Peter Jankowski, Arthur Forney, series creator Rene Balcer, and the entire *LOTC* cast, including Edie Falco and my personal friend Harry Hamlin, who went to prep school with me at The Hill School near Philadelphia. Special thanks to Melissa Azizi, the film producer who networked me to Wolf Films.

Emmy Award–winning screenwriter Alison Cross has been one of my closest friends going back to our TV news days at KGO-TV in San Francisco. Alison helped me edit and write a five-page summary of the story that was part of my pitch to Wolf Films when they were considering hiring me as a consultant. Her husband, attorney Peter Grossman, represented me in my negotiations with NBC.

I returned to book agents David Vigliano and Tom Flannery, who sold this book a second time to BenBella Books in Texas. Thank you, Glenn Yeffeth, Adrienne Lang, Sarah Avinger, Alicia Kania, Jennifer Canzoneri, Aida Herrera, Leah Wilson, Vy Tran, Jessika Rieck, Yara Abuata, Lloyd Jassin, and Elizabeth Degenhard.

Special thanks to Arthur Jay Harris, Paul Skolnick, and Molly Pinero, who all pitched in on the editing and research of the book. Matt Carlini played a key role in cutting a 250,000-word manuscript down to 98,000 words. Laurel Leigh came on board as my editor in the fall of 2017 when I was exhausted from my work on the TV series, which ended in November 2017. Laurel never gave up on me and managed to take a fair manuscript and make it great. I will forever be grateful for her contributions that led to the book you are holding in your hands. Her persistence and inspiration were critical to the final completion of the work.

Finally, thank you to all of the supporters of Erik and Lyle Menendez—many of them adults who are survivors of childhood abuse. I am one of you. As you came forward one by one, I was inspired by your bravery. My family—including my children's mothers, Patricia and Carol, and my sister Nancy—survived many bumps in the road but we finally made it! And my children, Rhiannon and Justin, showed me how important a loving family can be for truly appreciating the beauty of life.

ABOUT THE AUTHOR

ROBERT RAND is an Emmy Award–winning journalist who works in TV, print, and digital media. He began covering the Menendez brothers case for the *Miami Herald* the day after the killings on August 21, 1989. He was in court daily for both trials and provided analysis for Court TV, ABC, and CBS News.

In March 1991, *Playboy* published Rand's article "The Killing of Jose Menendez." The 14,000-word story was the longest article ever published by *Playboy*. Rand's print work includes stories contributed to *People*, *The Guardian*, *Stern*, *Grazia*, and *Tropic*, the Sunday magazine of the *Miami Herald*. He covered the William Kennedy Smith rape trial for *Paris Match*.

In July 2016, Rand was hired by Wolf Films as a consultant working on the development of the NBC eight-hour limited series *Law & Order True Crime: The Menendez Murders*, which aired in the fall of 2017. Rand's unpublished manuscript of *The Menendez Murders* provided the primary source material for the series.

Rand has appeared as the primary interview in dozens of documentaries about the Menendez case, including ABC *20/20*'s "Truth and Lies: The Menendez Brothers" and *Dateline NBC*'s "Unthinkable: The Menendez Murders," which both aired in 2017.

Rand was awarded a Los Angeles Emmy Award for two years of stories at KCOP-TV in L.A. about an illegal immigrant who was wrongly convicted. The stories resulted in the overturning of a ten-year-old conviction and the release of the man from jail. He was a member of the Special Assignment investigative reporting group at CBS 2 in L.A. and the I-Team at KYW TV (Philadelphia) that won a Columbia-DuPont Silver Baton Award for a year-long series about wealthy property tax dodgers.